Sir Walter Ralegh,

AN ANNOTATED BIBLIOGRAPHY

Sir Walter Ralegh,

AN ANNOTATED BIBLIOGRAPHY

COMPILED BY CHRISTOPHER M. ARMITAGE

Published for

America's Four Hundredth Anniversary Committee

by The University of North Carolina Press

Chapel Hill and London

© 1987 The University of North Carolina Press

All rights reserved

Manufactured in the United States of America

Library of Congress Cataloging-in-Publication Data

Armitage, Christopher M.

  Sir Walter Ralegh, an annotated bibliography.

  Includes index.

    1. Raleigh, Walter, Sir, 1552?–1618—Bibliography.

I. Title.

Z8731.A75 1987 [PR2335]   016.94205'5'0924   87-40134

ISBN 0-8078-1757-0

The paper in this book meets the guidelines for

permanence and durability of the Committee on

Production Guidelines for Book Longevity of the

Council on Library Resources.

91 90 89 88 87   5 4 3 2 1

To my parents, Charles and Edith Armitage

CONTENTS

ACKNOWLEDGMENTS

This project has been substantially supported by America's Four Hundredth Anniversary Committee, the North Carolina Department of Cultural Resources. The late Professor Herbert R. Paschal, Jr., a member of that committee's publications committee, left extensive notes from which I have benefited. I wish also to thank the committee's executive director, Dr. John D. Neville, and William S. Powell, professor emeritus of history at the University of North Carolina at Chapel Hill, for their support, and especially for making possible the hiring of a graduate student assistant. In that capacity George Loveland assisted in my earliest searches for material and Karen Fatula throughout the major stages of the project: her energy and efficiency were invaluable. My colleague Professor Jerry Leath Mills generously provided a pre-publication copy of his *Sir Walter Ralegh: A Reference Guide* to the writings about him 1901–1984.

Information was sought at or from many libraries in the Americas, England, and other countries. Particularly helpful were Dr. H. G. Jones and his staff of the North Carolina Collection at the University of North Carolina at Chapel Hill, who accommodated me amid the refurbishing of the Louis Round Wilson Library, where an outstanding collection of Raleghana is housed. A. J. Flavell, assistant librarian in the Department of Printed Books, Bodleian Library, Oxford, sought out and sent information I had been prevented from obtaining because parts of the Bodleian had been closed while air conditioning was installed. Dr. W. Walter Jaffe, vice-president of K. G. Saur, Inc., provided material in advance of its publication in that company's very useful *British Biographical Archive*. David Perry of the University of North Carolina Press has been a congenial and expert editor. The responsibility for errors and omissions rests with me.

INTRODUCTION

John Milton, who arranged for the publication of *The Cabinet Council* because he believed it to be "the work of so eminent an Author" as Ralegh, declared in his essay *Of Education* that the properly educated man would be fit to perform all the offices both private and public of peace and war. Ralegh comes as near to satisfying that definition as can be readily imagined. He was, to name some of his roles, soldier, courtier, sailor, essayist, politician, explorer, colonial entrepreneur, poet, long-term prisoner, scientific experimenter, and historian. His actions, his reported sayings, his formal writings, and his letters reveal a man moved by the gamut of human emotions and motivations. He aroused reactions varying from admiration and devotion to mockery and hatred. He has occasioned comment and analysis for more than four hundred years and shows no sign of ceasing to do so.

A need has long existed for a bibliography covering Ralegh's life and works and the constantly expanding body of writing about him from his time to the present. In 1886 Wilberforce Eames in New York and Thomas Nadauld Brushfield, a physician in Devon, coincidentally published bibliographies of around thirty-five pages (expanded five-fold by Brushfield in 1908), focused mainly on Ralegh's own writings. In 1971 Humphrey Tonkin's classified list of 869 items connected with Ralegh appeared, items that had been published between 1900 and 1968. In 1986 Jerry Leath Mills produced a reference guide to over four hundred writings about Ralegh published between 1901 and 1984; he provides detailed annotations, especially on items concerning Ralegh's literary and intellectual activities. For a number of years Herbert R. Paschal, Jr., professor of history at East Carolina University, carried out extensive research for a bibliography of Ralegh. At his death in 1982 he left a large number of notes, particularly about the historical and colonizing aspects of Ralegh's career. At the request of America's Four Hundredth Anniversary Committee, of whose publications committee he was a member, I took over the project.

This bibliography notes nearly two thousand items published between 1576 and 1986. They have been divided into sections. Writings by Ralegh or attributed to him, and translations thereof, comprise the first section. The second concerns biographies of him, in several languages, varying in length from hundreds of pages to single-column entries in encyclopedias. The third section deals with particular aspects of his life or career that are connected with England, Ireland, or elsewhere in Europe. The fourth covers those connected with transatlantic matters that involved him personally or indirectly. The fifth focuses on literary history and criticism of his work, an area that has grown rapidly in the twentieth century. Grouped together in the sixth section are treatments of Ralegh in painting, music, poetry, fiction, and books written for children. The concluding section notes other bibliographies of him. Further, to assist the user, the index includes topic headings through which related items, necessarily separated by alphabetization, may be located.

The divisions are not intended to be rigidly exclusive. In the second section, for instance, the longer biographies normally cover or at least touch on all or most of Ralegh's activities on both sides of the Atlantic and also discuss his writings. Inevitably, some items are hard to classify. For instance, C. W. Baird's "Relic of a Regicide Judge" reports that one of the English judges who condemned King Charles I gave a copy of Ralegh's *History of the World* to a friend in New Haven, Connecticut. This item might be classified as English, or American, or even as a kind of literary judgment.

The usual alphabetical order is followed in all sections except the first, "Published Works Written by or Attributed to Ralegh," in which items are arranged under headings such as "Poems," "Naval Writings," etc., and, within those sub-sections, by date of publication.

Various kinds of material are intentionally omitted: Ralegh's manuscripts, 842 of which are documented in Peter Beal's *Index of English Literary Manuscripts* (1980); bibliographic descriptions of the binding and states of books published before 1700; the addresses of booksellers which appear on the title-pages of books; items occasionally—and usually unreliably—attributed to Ralegh, especially if they are found exclusively or mainly in manuscript; brief selections from his prose and poetry in anthologies and school and college text-books; passing references to him in the endless stream of general accounts of the Renaissance, of the reigns of Elizabeth and James I, and of exploration and colonization in that period; reviews of books about Ralegh, unless they are reprinted in collections of essays; news-paper items, except those in *The Times Literary Supplement*; and mentions of the appearance of items in relatively inaccessible places if the items were also published more accessibly (for example, William Carlos Williams's prose-poem "Sir Walter Raleigh" first appeared in the short-lived periodical *Broom*, then was reprinted in his book *In the American Grain*; only the latter appearance is recorded in this bibliography).

The annotations are descriptive rather than evaluative. If a title adequately communicates what an item is about, annotation may have been dispensed with. In the biographical section very few annotations are provided because all the items purport to cover Ralegh's life, and the degree of detail may be inferred from their length. In "The Function of Criticism" T. S. Eliot observed that a "note in *Notes & Queries* which produces a fact even of the lowest order about a work of art is a better piece of work than nine-tenths of the most pretentious critical journalism." Accordingly, annotations are provided for many brief items, especially if they were printed in publications that may be hard to obtain, such as *Mariner's Mirror* or *The Journal of the Royal Society of Antiquities of Ireland*.

The spelling of Ralegh's name has occasioned much debate, as numerous items in the third section and portions of many of the biographies attest. From about 1584 and the time he was knighted, Ralegh usually spelled his name thus, a practice followed by most modern scholars. Naturally, however, where a title employs some other spelling, I have reproduced it, while invariably using Ralegh in my comments. The same principle has been applied to other names of varied spelling, such as Harington, Hariot, and Stukeley.

Publications about Ralegh are continually appearing. A recent stimulus has been the four hundredth anniversary of his expeditions to North America in 1584–87. It occasioned several books and an international conference in the University of North Carolina at Chapel Hill in March 1987, the proceedings from which, edited by H. G. Jones, are forthcoming under the title *Raleigh and Quinn: The Explorer and His Boswell*.

Sir Walter Ralegh,

AN ANNOTATED BIBLIOGRAPHY

Chapter 1.

PUBLISHED WORKS WRITTEN BY

OR ATTRIBUTED TO RALEGH

Because all the works in this section were written by or attributed to Ralegh, it is not arranged alphabetically by author, but chronologically under these headings: The Last Fight of the "Revenge"; The Discovery of Guiana; The History of the World; Second Voyage to Guiana; Instructions to His Son; Military Writings; Naval Writings; Political Writings; Poems; Letters; Collected Works; Doubtful Works. Peter Beal, *Index of English Literary Manuscripts*, vol. 1, *1450–1625*, part 2, 356–445, 632–33 (London: Mansell and New York: Bowker, 1980), catalogs 842 manuscripts by or connected with Ralegh.

THE LAST FIGHT OF THE "REVENGE"

1. *A Report of the Truth of the Fight about the Iles of Acores, this last Sommer. Betwixt the Reuenge, one of her Maiesties Shippes, And an Armada of the King of Spaine.* London[:] Printed for William Ponsonbie, 1591. [26] pp.

2. "A report of the trueth of the fight about the Isles of Açores, the last of August 1591, betwixt [as in original title], Penned by the Honourable Sir Walter Ralegh Knight." In Richard Hakluyt, *The Principal Navigations . . .*, 2:169–76. London, 1598–1600. Under the revised calendar, the date became September 10–11. Hakluyt's work has been reprinted many times.

3. "A Report of the Fight about the Isles of Azores, between the Revenge commanded by Sir Richard Granvill, Vice Admiral, and the Armada of the King of Spain . . . ." In Henry Birkhead, ed. *Verses by the University of Oxford on the Death of . . . Sir Bevill Grenvill . . .*, 29–46. Oxford, 1643, reprinted London, 1684. 48 pp. Includes Ralegh's *Report* after the poems praising

Sir Richard's descendant, Sir Bevil Grenvill, who was killed in 1643 fighting for King Charles I.

4. "The Fight between the Revenge Man of War, commanded by Sir Richard Greenville, and fifteen Armadas of the King of Spain, in 1591. Written by Sir Walter Ralegh, Knight." In Thomas Astley [John Green], *New General Collection of Voyages and Travels* . . . . 4 vols. 1:216–21. London, 1745–47. Facsimile reprint. London: Frank Cass, 1968.

5. *Das Gefecht zwischen dem Kriegesschiffe, die Rache, welches R. Greenville geführet, und fünfzehn Armadas des Konigs in Spanien, 1591.* In Johann Joachim Schwabe, *Allgemeine Historie der Reisen zu Wasser und Lande.* 21 vols. 1:371–80. Leipzig, 1747–74.

6. [Title as in Hakluyt]. In Baron Somers, *A Third Collection of Scarce and Valuable Tracts.* 13 vols. 1:373–82. London, 1751. [Title as in Hakluyt]. In Somers' *Collection of Scarce and Valuable Tracts*, edited by Walter Scott, 1:465–73. London, 1809. 2d ed.

7. *Old English Valour: Being An Account of a Remarkable Sea-engagement, Anno 1591. Written by Sir Walter Raleigh, Knt., being proper to be read by Sea Officers and British Sailors.* London, Printed for R. Baldwin, 1757. 28 pp.

8. [Title as in Hakluyt]. In John Pinkerton, *A General Collection of the Best and Most Interesting Voyages and Travels* . . . . 6 vols. 1:824–32. London and Philadelphia, 1808–14.

9. [Title as in Hakluyt.] In Robert Kerr, *A General History and Collection of Voyages and Travels.* 18 vols. 7:402. Edinburgh and London, 1811–24.

10. *The last fight of The Revenge at sea; under the command of Vice-Admiral Sir Richard Grenville, on the 10–11th of September 1591. Described by Sir Walter Raleigh, November 1591, Gervase Markham, 1595, and Jan Huygen van Linschoten, in Dutch, 1596; English, 1598; and Latin, 1599*, edited by Edward Arber. Birmingham and London, 1871. 96 pp. Reprint. London: Constable, 1901. Contains Ralegh's *Report*, Gervase Markham's poem, *The Most Honorable Tragedie of Sir Richard Grinuile, Knight*, and *The Fight and Cyclone at the Azores* by Jan Huygen van Linschoten.

11. *The Last Fight of the Revenge. And The Death of Sir Richard Grenville (A.D. 1591). Related by Sir Walter Raleigh, Sir*

Richard Hawkins, Jan Huygen van Linschoten, Lord Bacon, and Sir W. Monson. *Together with the Most Honorable Tragedie of Sir Richard Grinuile, Knight, by Gervase Markham (1595). To which is added Sir R. Grenville's Farewell (circa 1543).* In Edmund Goldsmid, *Bibliotheca Curiosa.* 32 vols. 21:41–66, 1884–87. Also issued separately under same title. 2 vols. 1886.

12. [Title as in Hakluyt]. In Hakluyt's *Principal Navigations*, edited by Edmund Goldsmid. 16 vols. 7:93–105. Edinburgh: Goldsmid, 1885–90.

13. "The Revenge." In *In Danger's Hour; or, Stout Hearts and Stirring Deeds*, 160. London: Cassell, 1899. 244 pp.

14. *A Report of the truth concerning the last sea-fight of the Revenge. By Sir Walter Ralegh, Knight.* Cambridge, Mass.: Riverside Press, 1902. 20 pp.

15. *The Last Fight of the Revenge by Sr. Walter Raleigh with an introduction by Henry Newbolt and illustrations by Frank Brangwyn.* London: Gibbings, 1908. 130 pp.

16. [Title as in Hakluyt]. In *Sir Walter Ralegh: "The Shepherd of the Ocean." Selections from his poetry and prose*, edited by Frank Cheney Hersey, 41–59. New York: Macmillan, 1916. 109 pp.

17. [Title as in original ed.]. In *Sir Walter Raleigh: Selections from his Historie of the World, his letters, etc. Edited with introduction and notes by G. E. Hadow.* Oxford: Clarendon, 1917. 212 pp. Reprint. Folcroft, Pa.: Folcroft Library Editions, 1978. 212 pp.

18. [Title as in Hakluyt]. In *The Book of the Sea: Being a Collection of Writings about the Sea in All Its Aspects*, edited by A. C. Spectorsky, 408–18. New York: Appleton-Century Crofts, 1954. 488 pp.

19. *A Report of the Truth of the Fight about the Iles of the Açores (The last Fight of the Revenge) 1591. The Discoverie of the Large, Rich, and Bewtiful Empyre of Guiana 1596.* Menston, Yorkshire: Scolar Press, 1967. n.p., 112 pp. Facsimiles of the original editions.

THE DISCOVERY OF GUIANA

20. *The Discoverie of the Large, Rich and Bewtiful Empire of Guiana, with a relation of the Great and Golden City of*

Manoa (which the spaniards call El Dorado) And the provinces of Emeria, Arromaia, Amapaia and other Countries, with their rivers, adjoyning. Performed in the yeare 1595. By Sir W. Ralegh, Knight, Captaine of her Majesties Guard, Lo. Warden of the Stanneries, and her Highnesse Lieutenant generall of the Countie of Cornewall. Imprinted at London by Robert Robinson, 1596. 112 pp. At least three eds. of this popular work appeared in 1596, and many subsequently, including those in Hakluyt's *Principal Voyages* and in De Bry's *Americae*, part 8, in Latin in 1599 and 1625 and in German in 1599 and 1624.

21. *Waerachtighe ende grondighe beschryvinge van het groot ende Goudt-rijck Coninckrijck van Guiana . . . .* Amsterdam: Cornelis Claez, 1598. 48 pp. Reprinted 1605. Reprinted Amsterdam: Michiel Colyn, 1617. Reprinted in *Oost-Indische ende West-Indische Voyagien.* Amsterdam: Isaac Commelin, 1644. In all these, Ralegh's account of Guiana is followed by Keymis's.

22. *Kurtze Wunderbare Beschreibung, Desz Goldreichen Konigreichs Guianae . . . .* In Levinus Hulsius, *Sammlung von Sechs und Zwanzig Schifffahrten,* part 5, Noribergae [Nuremberg], impensis Levini Hulsii, 1599. 2d ed., 1601. 3d ed., 1603. 4th ed., 1612. 5th ed., 1663. In the 3d and subsequent eds., the title begins *Die Funffte Kurtze . . . ,* and the city of publication changes to Frankfurt.

23. *Drie Scheeps-Togten Na het Goud-rijke Koningrijk Guiana . . . .* Leiden: Pieter vander Aa, 1706. 71 pp. Also found in his *Naukeurige Versameling der . . . Zee en Land Reysen, na Oost en West Indien,* vol. 21, 1706, and in the folio edition, *De Aanmerkenswaardigste . . . Zee en Landreizen . . . ,* vol. 8, 1727.

24. *Relation de la Guiane . . . .* In *Voyages de François Coreal aux Indes Occidentales . . . .* 3 vols. 2:151–260. Amsterdam: Frederic Bernard, 1722. Also published in Paris in 1722 and in Brussels in 1736. Reprinted with title *Recuiel des Voyages dans l'Amérique Meridionale,* Amsterdam, 1738.

25. *Reise auf der Guiana, 1595.* In Johann Joachim Schwabe, *Allgemeine Historie der Reisen zu Wasser und Lande . . . .* 21 vols. 16:314–40. Leipzig, 1747–74.

26. *The Discovery of Guiana.* In *Works of . . . Ralegh.* 2 vols. 2:137–245, 1751.
27. *The Discovery of Guiana.* In Arthur Cayley, *The Life of Sir Walter Ralegh, Knt.* 2 vols. 1:157–281. London, 1805.
28. *The Discovery of Guiana.* In Appendix to *The History of the World.* 6 vols. 6:3–310. London, 1820.
29. *The Discovery of Guiana.* In *Works of . . . Ralegh.* 8 vols. 8:377–476, 1829.
30. *Discovery of the Large, Rich and Beautiful Empire of Guiana, with a relation of the great and golden City of Manoa . . . [etc.], performed in the year 1595, by Sir W. Ralegh, knt . . . Reprinted from the edition of 1596, with some unpublished documents relative to that country. Edited with copious explanatory notes and a Biographical Memoir, by Sir Robert H. Schomburgk . . . .* London, Printed for the Hakluyt Society, 1848. 75, 240 pp. Facsimile: New York: Burt Franklin, [1970]. The Appendix includes: Of the Voyage for Guiana; List of Ralegh's vessels on March 15, 1616; Sir Walter Ralegh's Journal of his Second Voyage to Guiana.
31. *The Discovery of Guiana, and the Journal of the Second Voyage Thereto,* by Sir Walter Raleigh. Introduction by Henry Morley. London and New York: Cassell, 1887. 192 pp. Reissued: London: Cassell; New York: Mershon, 1893.
32. *The Discovery of Guiana,* edited by W. H. D. Rouse. London and Glasgow: Blackie, 1905. 111 pp. Reissued 1913.
33. *The Discovery of Guiana.* In *The Harvard Classics: Voyages and Travels, Ancient and Modern.* 50 vols. 33:309–94, edited by Charles W. Eliot. New York: Collier, 1910. Reprint. 1961.
34. *The Discoverie of the large and bewtiful Empire of Guiana . . . .* Edited from the original text, with introduction, notes and appendices of hitherto unpublished documents by V. T. Harlow. Editor: N. M. Penzer. London: Argonaut Press, 1928. 106, 182 pp. Facsimile: Amsterdam: N. Israel; New York: Da Capo, 1968.
35. *Otkrytie obshirnoi bogotoi i prekrasnoi imperii . . .* (The discovery of Guiana). Ed. A. D. Dridzo. Moscow, 1963. 172 pp.
36. *The Discoverie of Guiana, with Antonio Galvano's Discoveries of the World.* Introduction by A. L. Rowse. Cleveland: World

Publishing, 1966. 112, 97 pp. Facsimiles of the original editions.

37. *A Report of the Truth of the Fight about the . . . Açores. The Discoverie of . . . Guiana.* Menston, Yorkshire: Scolar Press, 1967. n.p., 112 pp. Facsimiles of the original editions.

THE HISTORY OF THE WORLD;
AND ABRIDGMENTS, CONTINUATIONS, AND
SUBSTANTIAL SELECTIONS FROM IT

38. *The History of the World.* At London Printed for Walter Bvrre. 1614. Colophon: London[:] Printed by William Stansby for Walter Burre. 1614. Preface [40], Contents [40], History 651, 776, Tables [62] pp. Licensed to Burre by the Stationers Company on 15 April 1611, the book was published anonymously in 1614. King James I moved to suppress it by an order signed by the Archbishop of Canterbury on 22 December 1614. An allegorical frontispiece and accompanying poem by Ben Jonson appear in all editions through the tenth in 1687.

39. *The History of the World* by Sir Walter Ralegh, Knight. Colophon: London[:] Printed by William Stansby for Walter Burre. 1617. Pagination as in preceding ed. According to John Racin, *Studies in Bibliography* 17:199–209, this edition differs from the first in the correction of a few errors and in the addition, following the engraved title-page, of a printed title-page which included the following:

> *The History of the World. In Five Bookes.*
> 1. Intreating of the Beginning and first Ages of the same from the Creation unto Abraham.
> 2. Of the Times from the birth of Abraham, to the destruction of the Temple of Salomon.
> 3. From the destruction of Ierusalem, to the time of Philip of Macedon.
> 4. From the Reigne of Philip of Macedon, to the establishing of that Kingdome, in the Race of Antigonus.
> 5. From the setled rule of Alexanders successors in the East, untill the Romans (preuailing over all) made conquest of Asia and Macedon.
> By Sir Walter Ralegh, Knight.

The lower half of this title-page contains the fine portrait of Ralegh engraved by "Sim.Pass."

40. *The History of the World.* Engraved and printed title-pages as in 1617 ed. Colophon: London[:] Printed by William Iaggard for Walter Burre. 1621. Preface [42], Contents [27], History 555, 669, Tables [54] pp. In some copies, the colophon reads 1617, which John Racin argues is an error for 1621.

41. *The History of the World.* Engraved and printed title-pages as in 1617 ed., with *Historie* spelt thus on latter. Colophon: London, Printed for H. Lownes, G. Lathum, and R. Young. Anno Domini 1628. Paginated as in 1621 ed.

42. *The History of the World.* Engraved and printed title-pages as in 1617 ed. Colophon: London, Printed for G. Lathum and R. Young, 1634. Paginated as in 1621 ed.

43. *The History of the World.* Engraved and printed title-pages as in 1617 ed., but on the engraved page "1614" has been replaced with "London: Printed for Sam. Cartwright, R. Best & J. Place. 1652." Paginated as in 1621 ed. No colophon appears in this or in later eds.

44. *The History of the World.* The engraved frontispiece bears the imprint "London: Printed for R. White I. Place and G. Dawes, 1665." The printed title-page bears the imprint "London: Printed for Robert White, John Place, and George Dawes, 1666" (some copies "are to be sold by Thomas Rookes, 1666"). Preface [32], Contents [25], History 1143 (in double columns), Tables [53] pp.

45. *The History of the World.* London: Printed for George Dawes, 1671. Pagination as in 1666 ed.

46. *The History of the World.* The engraved frontispiece bears the imprint: "London: Printed for R. White, Tho. Basset, Jo. Wright, Ric. Chiswell, Geo. Dawes, & Tho. Sawdribge [sic], 1676." The printed title-page reads *History* instead of *Historie* for the first time since 1621 ed., and *Solomon* instead of *Salomon,* and continues: *Whereunto is added in this Edition, the Life and Tryal of the Author.* London: Printed for Robert White, T. Basset, J. Wright, R. Chiswell, G. Dawes, and T. Sawbridge, 1677. Preface [21], Contents [21], Life 54, History 1–660 and 577–885 (in double columns), Tables [44] pp. *The Life* is thought to be by John Shirley.

47. *The History of the World.* London: Printed for Tho. Basset, Ric.

Chiswell, Benj. Tooke, Tho. Passenger, Geo. Dawes, Tho. Sawbridge, M. Wotton, and G. Conyers, 1687. Preface 32, Contents [24], Life 41, History 813, Tables [8] pp. *The Life* has its own title-page: *The Life of the Valiant and Learned Sir Walter Raleigh, Knight. With His Tryal at Winchester. The Third Edition.* London: Printed for George Dawes, and Richard Tonson, 1687.

48. *The History of the World, in Five Books. By Sir Walter Ralegh, Kt. The Eleventh Edition, printed from a Copy revis'd by Himself. To which is prefix'd the Life of the Author, newly compil'd, From Materials more ample and authentick than have yet been publish'd; by Mr. Oldys. Also his Trial, with some Additions: together with A new and more copious Index to the whole work. In Two Volumes. Volume I[II].* London: Printed for G. Conyers, J. J. and P. Knapton, D. Midwinter, A. Bettesworth and C. Hitch, B. Sprint, R. Robinson, B. Motte, J. Walthoe, A. Ward, J. Clarke, S. Birt, T. Wotton, T. Longman, H. Whitridge, H. Lintot, and J. and R. Tonson, 1736. Life 232, Trial 17, Authors cited [7], Preface 32, Contents [24], History 817 (in double columns), Tables [28], Index [19] pp. The allegorical frontispiece and Jonson's accompanying poem are no longer included. The new engraved portrait is subscribed "G. Vertue, 1735."

49. *A Notable and Memorable Story of the Cruel War between the Carthaginians and their own Mercenaries. Gathered out of Polybius and other Authors, by that famous Historian Sir Walter Ralegh.* London: Tho. Underhill, 1647. 18 pp. Reprinted from Book 5, Chapter 2, of Ralegh's *History of the World.* Ben Jonson claimed, according to his *Conversations with Drummond*, section 12, that he had written this piece for Ralegh, "which he altered and set in his book."

50. Ross, Alexander. *The Marrow of Historie, Or an Epitome of all Historical Passages from the Creation, to the end of the last Macedonian War. First set out at large by Sir Walter Rawleigh, And now Abreviated by A. R.* London, Printed by W. Du-gard, for John Stephenson, 1650. 574 pp. The Second Edition, London, printed for John Place and William Place, 1662. The dedicatory epistle is written by Alexander Ross, who claims to "have reduced a large Historie to a brief Epitome."

51. _____. *The History of the World: The Second Part, in six books: Being a Continuation of the famous History of Sir Walter Raleigh, Knight: Beginning where he left; Viz. at the End of the Macedonian Kingdom, and deduced to these Later-Times: That is, from the Year of the World 3806, or 160 Years before Christ, till the end of the year 1640 after Christ . . . .* London, Printed for John Saywell, 1652. 647 pp. (Some copies bear the imprint "Printed for John Clark, 1652.")

52. _____. *Som Animadversions and observations upon Sr Walter Raleigh's Historie of the World. Wherein his mistakes are noted and som doubtful passages cleered.* London, Printed by William Du-gard for Richard Royston, 1653. 72 pp. Also issued under the title *Leviathan drawn out with a Hook; or Animadversions upon Mr. Hobbs, his Leviathan. Together with some Observations upon Sr Walter Raleigh's History of the World.* London, Printed by Tho. Newcomb, for Richard Royston, 1653.

53. Echard, Laurence. *An Abridgment of Sir Walter Raleigh's History of the World. In Five Books . . . Wherein the particular Chapters and Paragraphs are succinctly Abridg'd according to his own method, in the larger volume. To which is Added His Premonition to Princes.* London, Printed for Mat. Gillyflower, and Sold by Andrew Bell, 1698. [39], 415 pp. Below portrait are these words: London, Printed for Mat. Gillyflower. 2d ed. [Title as in 1st ed., with the following additions:] With some Genuine Remains of that Learned Knight, Viz.:
i. Of the first Invention of Shipping.
ii. A Relation of the Action at Cadiz.
iii. A Dialogue between a Jesuite and a Recusant.
iv. An Apology for his unlucky Voyage to Guiana.
Publish'd by Phillip Raleigh, Esquire, the only Grandson to Sir Walter. London, Printed for M. Gillyflower, and are to be Sold by Ralph Smith, 1700. Premonition [26], History 363, Essays 91 pp. In spite of the appearance of Phillip Raleigh's name in this and the 3d ed., "The Publisher's Advertisement to the Reader" bears the subscription "Laurence Echard," who claims to have received the work from a friend, further shortened it, and corrected its "obsolete" style before publishing it. Third Edition: [Title as in 2d ed. with this addition:] *The Third*

Edition. *To which is added, An Account of the Author's Life, Tryal, and Death*. London: Printed by W. Onley, for Ralph Smith, 1702. Premonition [28], History 363, Essays 91, Life 30 pp.

54. *The General History of the World; Being an Abridgment of Sir Walter Raleigh. With a Continuation From the Best Historians to the Present Times. In Four Volumes*. London, Printed for A. Bell, R. Smith, and J. Round, 1708. The Abridgment of Ralegh's *History* occupies the first volume and the Continuation the last three volumes; it is not the same as that by Alexander Ross.

55. *The History of the World. In Five Books [their titles] . . . A new edition revised and corrected. To which is added Sir W. Ralegh's Voyages of Discovery to Guiana*. 6 vols. Edinburgh: Archibald Constable, 1820. The sixth volume includes "The Discovery of Guiana," "Considerations on the Voyage to Guiana," "Orders to the Commanders of the Fleet," and "Apology for the last Voyage to Guiana."

56. Preface to the *History of the World*, in *Prefaces and Prologues to Famous Books*, 69–121. New York: Collier, 1910. 462 pp. (*The Harvard Classics*, vol. 39). Reprint. 1961.

57. Hadow, Grace Eleanor. *Sir Walter Raleigh: Selections from his Historie of the World, His Letters, etc. Edited with Introduction and Notes*. Oxford: Clarendon Press, 1917. 212 pp. Reprint. Folcroft, Pa.: Folcroft Library Editions, 1978. 212 pp.

58. Patrides, C. A., ed. *Sir Walter Ralegh: The History of the World*. London: Macmillan, 1971. 418 pp.

SECOND VOYAGE TO GUIANA

59. *Orders to bee obserued by the Commanders of the Fleete, and Land Companies, vnder the charge and conduct of Sir Walter Rauleigh Knight, bound for the South parts of America or else-where. Given at Plymouth in Devon, the third of May,* 1617. Printed in *Newes of Sr. Walter Rauleigh*, 19–28, 1618. Reprinted in *Works of Ralegh*, 1751 (1:xcvii–civ); in *Works* 1829 (8:682–88); in Cayley, 1805 (2:403–9); in *History of the World*, 1820 (6:135–46); in P. Force, *Tracts*, Washington, 1844,

as a part of *Newes of Sir Walter Rauleigh* (tract no. 4, vol. 3,
13–18); in V. T. Harlow, *Ralegh's Last Voyage*, 1932, reprint
1971 (121–26).

60. *Sir Walter Rawleigh His Apologie For his Voyage To Guiana: by
Sir Walter Rawleigh Knight*. London, Printed by T. W. for
Hum[phrey] Moseley, 1650. 69 pp. Also published in *Judicious
and Select Essayes*, 1650; in the Appendix to the *Abridgment of
The History of The World*, 1700–1702 (71–91); in *Works*,
1751 (2:249–81); in *Works*, 1829 (8:479–507); in Cayley,
1805 (2:82–122, 160–61); in the Appendix to *The History of
the World*, 1820 (6:149–76); in V. T. Harlow, *Ralegh's Last
Voyage*, 1932, 1971 (316–34). Includes "A Letter of Sir Walter
Rawleigh to my Lord Carew touching Guiana" and "Sir Walter
Rawleigh his Answer to some things at his Death."

61. *Sir Walter Ralegh's Journal of his Second Voyage to Guiana.*
Printed in Schomburgk's edition of *The Discovery of Guiana*,
1848, reprint 1970 (177–208); in *The Life and Letters of Lord
Bacon*, by J. Spedding, 1872 (6:421–25); and in Morley's
edition of *The Discovery of Guiana*, 1887.

INSTRUCTIONS TO HIS SON

62. *Sir Walter Raleighs Instrvctions to his Sonne and to Posterity.
Whereunto is added A Religious and Dutifull Advice of a
Loving Sonne to his Aged Father*. London, Printed for
Beniamin Fisher, 1632. Preface and Contents [10], 96, 57 pp.
The first essay, sometimes found on its own, has half-title, *Sr
Walter Raleigh to his Sonne*. The second has a separate title-
page, *The Dutifull Advice of a loving Sonne to his aged Father*.
London: Printed for Beniamin Fisher. Authorship of the second
essay is uncertain. Between 1632 and 1636 Fisher published
four more editions, which bear on the title-page the number of
the edition and the phrase "Corrected and enlarged according
to the Authors own Coppy." Reprinted in all editions of
Ralegh's *Maxims* and *Remains*, in *Works* (1751) 1:cv–cxiii,
2:341–57, and in *Works* (1829) 8:557–70, 689–96.

63. *Sir Walter Raleigh's Instructions to his Son*, in *Instructions for
Youth, Gentlemen, and Noblemen*, (9–55), London, 1722; reissued with the title *Walsingham's Manual, or Prudential*

Maxims for Statesmen and Courtiers: With Instructions for youth, gentlemen, and noblemen by Sir W. R., Lord Burleigh, and Card. Sermonetta, London, 1728.

64. *Instructions of a Father to his Son . . . To which are added A loving Son's Advice to an aged Father, and Select letters on interesting Subjects, by Sir Walter Rawleigh.* Glasgow: Robert and Andrew Foulis, 1754. 90 pp.

65. *Practical Wisdom, or the Manual of Life: The Counsels of eminent men to their children. Comprising those of Sir Walter Raleigh . . . with lives of the authors* (3–34). [By Elizabeth Strutt]. London: Henry Colburn, 1824. 336 pp. Reprint. New York: Wessels, 1902. 217 pp. London: Arthur Humphreys, 1907. 310 pp.

66. *Sir W. Raleigh's Instructions to his Son and to Posterity*, edited by Charles Whibley. London: Peter Davies, 1927. 64 pp.

67. *Sir Walter Raleigh's Instructions to His Son and to Posterity.* Reprinted by the Roanoke Island Historical Association. Durham, N.C.: Seeman Printery, 1939. 64 pp. A reprint based on the 1927 one by Charles Whibley.

68. Wright, Louis Booker, ed. *Advice to a Son: Precepts of Lord Burghley, Sir Walter Raleigh, and Francis Osborne.* Ithaca: Published for the Folger Shakespeare Library by Cornell University Press, 1962. 114 pp.

MILITARY WRITINGS

69. "Determinations of the Council of War, held November 27, 1587, for putting the Forces of the Realm in the best posture of defence against the threatened invasion." In Cayley, 1805, 2:297–301. An abstract of "An Advice of suche Meanes, &c.," dated "March (?) 1588" in the *Calendar of State Papers Domestic Elizabeth*, 219, 49, and reprinted in *Western Antiquary*, 7(1888): 276–79. Tentatively attributed to Ralegh by William Oldys in his "Life of Ralegh" in *The History of the World*, 1736, 39.

70. *A Discovrse of the Originall and Fundamentall Cause of Naturall, Customary, Arbitrary, Voluntary and Necessary Warre. With the Mistery [sic] of Invasive Warre. That Ecclesiasticall Prelates, have alwayes beene subject to Temporall*

Princes, And that the Pope had never any lawfull power in England, either in Civill or Ecclesiasticall businesse, after such time, as Brittaine was won from the Roman Empire. By Sir Walter Rawleigh Knight. London, Printed by T. W. for Humphrey Moseley, 1650. [65] pp. Also in *Judicious and Select Essayes,* 1650; in *Three Discourses,* 1702, with a slightly different title, 1751, 2:21–70; in *Works,* 1751, 2:21–70; in *Works,* 1829, 8:253–97.

71. *Of a War with Spain and our Protecting the Netherlands. Written by the Command of King James I., in the First Year of his Reign, 1602 [sic].* Printed in *Three Discourses of Sir Walter Ralegh,* 1702, 147–60; in *Works,* 1751, 2:1–20; in *Works,* 1829, 8:299–316.

72. *Opinions delivered by the Earl of Essex, Lord Burleigh, Lord Willoughby, Lord Burrough, Lord North, Sir William Knollys, Sir Walter Raleigh, and Sir George Carew, on the Alarm of an Invasion from Spain in the Year 1596, and the Measures proper to be taken on that occasion.* London: A. Strahan, [1794?], 60 pp. Ralegh's opinion is on pages 41–48 and is reprinted in *Works,* 1829, 8:675–81.

NAVAL WRITINGS

73. "A Discourse of the Invention of Ships, Anchors, Compasse, &c. The first Naturall Warre, the severall use, defects, and supplies of Shipping, the strength, and defects of the Sea forces of England, France, Spaine, and Venice, Together with the five manifest causes of the suddaine appearing of the Hollanders, Written by Sir Walter Rawleigh." Printed in *Judicious and Select Essayes,* 1650, 1–42; in Appendix to *Abridgment of The History of the World,* 1700, 1–16; 1702, 1–18; in *Works,* 1751, 2:71–90; in *Works,* 1829, 8:317–34; in *Old South Leaflets,* General Series, vol. 7, no. 166, Boston, Directors of the Old South Work, 1906, 16pp.

74. *Excellent Observations and Notes, Concerning the Royall Navy and Sea-service. Written By Sir Walter Rawleigh and by him Dedicated to the Most noble and Illustrious Prince Henry Prince of Wales.* London, Printed by T. W. for Humphrey Moseley, 1650. 46 pp. Also in *Judicious and Select Essayes*

(1650), with separate title-page and pagination; in *Works*, 1751, 2:91–107; in *Works*, 1829, 8:335–50. Often attributed to Arthur Gorges.

75. *A Relation of Cadiz Action, in the Year 1596.* First printed in the Appendix to *Abridgment of The History of the World*, 1700, 17–25; 1702, 19–25; reprinted in Cayley, *Life*, 1805, 1:290–301; in *Works*, 1829, 8:667–74; in Edwards, *Life*, 1868, 2:146–56; in Hersey, *Selections*, 1916, 73–83; and in Hadow, *Selections*, 1917, 167–77.

POLITICAL WRITINGS

76. *The Interest of England with Regard to Foreign Alliances. Explained in Two Discourses. (1). Concerning a Match propounded by the Savoyan, between the Lady Elizabeth and the Prince of Piemont. (2). Touching a Marriage between prince Henry of England and a Daughter of Savoy. By Sir Walter Rawleigh, Knt. Now first Published from his original Manuscript.* London, Printed for the Editor, and Sold by J. Newbery, 1750. 54 pp. Reprinted in *Works*, 1751, 1:249–80; in *Works*, 1829, 8:223–52.

77. *The Prerogative of Parliaments in England: Proued in a Dialogue (pro & contra) betweene a Councellour of State and a Justice of Peace. Written by the worthy (much lacked and lamented) Sir Walter Raleigh Knight, deceased. Dedicated to the Kings Maiestie, and to the House of Parliament now assembled. Preserued to be now happily (in these distracted Times).* Published and Printed at Midelburge, 1628. 65 pp. Brushfield reports an edition from Hamburg, 1628. Reprinted in all editions of the *Remains* from 1657; in *Works*, 1751, 1:171–248; in *Works*, 1829, 8:151–221; in the *Harleian Miscellany*, 1744–46 and later eds. Ralegh's poem, "The Authours Epitaph, made by himselfe," appears on the verso of page 65.

78. *The Prerogative of Parliaments in England . . .* with "deceased" omitted and ending "Printed 1640." 65 pp. and Ralegh's "Epitaph" poem on page [66].

79. *The Perogative [sic] of Parliaments in England . . . ,* 1640. 65 pp. and Ralegh's "Epitaph" poem on page [66].

80. *Sir Walter Raleigh: The Prerogative of Parliaments in England; The Priviledges [sic] and Practice of Parliaments; Sir John Dodderidge: Opinions of Sundry Learned Antiquaries; Henry Elsynge: The Manner of Holding Parliaments in England.* In *Classics of English Legal History in the Modern Era*, selected by David S. Berkowitz and Samuel E. Thorne. New York and London: Garland, 1979. 66, 46, 96, 298 pp. Four facsimiles in one volume.

81. *Seat of Government.* First published in the *Remains*, 1651, 59–68, and in subsequent editions. Reprinted in *Works*, 1751, 2:317–20; in *Works*, 1829, 8:538–40.

82. Speeches in Parliament, 1592–1601. In Heywood Townshend, *Historical Collections.* London, Printed for T. Basset, W. Crooke, and W. Cademan, 1680. Reissued in 1682, under the title of *Megalopsychy.* Contains reports of speeches by Ralegh on tin mining and other topics.

POEMS

83. Gascoigne, George. *The Steele Glas.* London: Richard Smith, 1576. [136 pp.]. Includes a prefatory poem entitled "Walter Rawely of the middle Temple, in commendation of the Steele Glasse."

84. Byrd, William. *Psalmes, Sonets, and Songs.* London: Thomas East, 1588. Includes four stanzas of "Farewell false love" as No. 25 of "Sonnets and Pastorals."

85. Spenser, Edmund. *The Faerie Queene.* London: William Ponsobie, 1590. 596 pp. Includes, at the end of this edition of the first three Books of *The Faerie Queene*, Ralegh's sonnets beginning "Methought I saw the grave where Laura lay" and "The prayse of meaner wits this worke like profit brings."

86. Breton, Nicholas (?). *Brittons Bowre of Delights.* London: Richard Jhones, 1591. Includes "Like to an Hermit poore" and "Her face, her tongue, her wit."

87. *The Phoenix Nest.* London: Iohn Iackson, 1593. 102 pp. Reprint. Edited by Hyder Edward Rollins. Cambridge: Harvard University Press, 1931. 241 pp. Includes "Like to a Hermite poore," "Farewell to the Court," "Praised be Diana's faire and

harmless light," "The Excuse," "An Epitaph upon the Right
Honorable Sir Philip Sidney Knight," and a dozen other poems
which Rollins speculates may be a Ralegh group.

88. *Englands Helicon.* London: J. R. for John Flasket, 1600.
Enlarged ed., 1614. Edited by Hugh Macdonald. London,
1925, and Cambridge, Mass., 1950. Includes "The Nimphs
reply to the Sheepheard" in answer to Marlowe's poem "The
Passionate Sheepheard to his loue," and other poems attributed
to Ralegh.

89. Davison, Francis, ed. *A Poetical Rapsody.* 2 vols. London: V. S.
for J. Bailey, 1602. Enlarged eds. 1608, 1611, 1621. All four
edited by Hyder Edward Rollins. Cambridge: Harvard
University Press, 1931–32. Includes "The Lie," "A Poesy to
prove affection is not love," and other poems attributed to
Ralegh in earlier publications.

90. *Diaphantus, or The Passions of Love . . . Whereunto is added,
The passionate mans Pilgrimage.* London: Printed by T. C. for
William Cotton, 1604. Includes, as the title states, the poem
beginning "Give me my scallop shell of quiet."

91. Gibbons, Orlando. *The First Set of Madrigals and Mottets.*
London: Thomas Snodham, 1612. n.p. Includes "What is our
life? a play of passion."

92. Gorges, Sir Arthur. *Lucans Pharsalia.* London: Thorp, 1614.
Includes a prefatory sonnet praising Gorges, Ralegh's cousin
and companion on the expedition to the Azores in 1597.

93. Ralegh, Sir Walter. *The History of the World.* London: Walter
Burre, 1614. 651 and 776 pp. Includes translations of over
sixty brief passages from Homer, Aeschylus, Euripides, Virgil,
Ovid, Lucretius, Horace, Juvenal, Lucan, and other classical
authors.

94. Brathwayte, Richard. *Remains after Death.* London: Iohn Beale,
1618. n.p. Includes "Even such is tyme which takes in trust,"
reputed to have been written the night before Ralegh was
executed, and in fact a variant of the last stanza of "Nature
that washed her hands in milk."

95. Deloney, Thomas. *The Garland of Good-Will.* London: Printed
for Robert Bird, 1631. n.p. Entered in the Stationers Register in
1593. Includes in the third part "As you came from the holy
land/Of Walsingham" and "Farewell false love" in five stanzas.

96. Cotgrave, John. *Wits Interpreter, the English Parnassus*. London: Printed for N. Brooke, 1655. 548 pp. Twice includes, on pp. 40 and 68, the poem beginning "Our passions are most like to floods and streams," the first time under the title "To his Mistresse by Sir Walter Raleigh." In some of the numerous manuscripts, Queen Elizabeth is named in the title. The six-line poem is often conflated with "Wrong not, deare Empresse of my Heart," now usually attributed to Sir Robert Ayton.

97. Rudyerd, Sir Benjamin (?). *Le Prince d'Amour, or the Prince of Love, with a Collection of Several Ingenious Poems and Songs by the Wits of the Age*. London: William Leake, 1660. 184 pp. Includes "The Advice" and attributes it to W. R. The book's dedication declares that the poems long pre-date the Civil War.

98. Donne, John [the younger], ed. *Poems by William Earl of Pembroke [and] by Sir Benjamin Ruddier*. London: Matthew Inman, 1660. 118 pp. Includes "A Prognostication upon Cards and Dice," which begins "Beefore the sixt day of the next new year," here termed anonymous but attributed to Ralegh in many manuscripts.

99. Oldys, William. *Life of Ralegh*, prefixed to the 11th ed. of Ralegh's *History of the World*. London: Printed for G. Conyers, 1736. 232 pp. Quotes or refers to 17 poems attributed to Ralegh.

100. Cooper, Elizabeth. *The Muses' Library*, 268–96. London: Hodges, 1737. 400 pp. Includes 13 poems, some of doubtful attribution.

101. *The Works of Sir Walter Ralegh, Kt., Political, commercial, and Philosophical; together with his Letters and Poems*. 2 vols. 2:391–400. London: Printed for R. Dodsley, 1751. Includes ten poems.

102. Percy, Thomas. *Reliques of Ancient English Poetry*. 3 vols. 1:219–20, 2:299–303. London: Dodsley, 1765. Includes "The Nymph's Reply" and "The Lye."

103. Ellis, George, ed. *Specimens of the Early English Poets*. 3 vols. 2:180–97. London: Bulmer, 1790.

104. Brydges, Sir Egerton. *The Poems of Sir Walter Raleigh, now first collected*. Lee Priory: Private Press, 1813. 71 pp. 2d ed. London: Longman, Hurst, Rees, Orme, and Brown, 1814. 80 pp. Includes numerous poems not by Ralegh.

105. Campbell, Thomas. *Specimens of the British Poets.* 7 vols. 2:289–99. London: Murray, 1819. Includes six poems attributed to Ralegh and "The Lie" but places it among "Anonymous Poems."

106. *The Works of Sir Walter Ralegh.* 8 vols. 8:697–736. Oxford: Oxford University Press, 1829. Reprint. New York: Burt Franklin, [1965]. Includes 39 poems, some of doubtful attribution, and Marlowe's "Passionate Shepherd."

107. Hannah, John, ed. *Poems by Sir Henry Wotton, Sir Walter Raleigh, and Others,* 87–134. London: Pickering, 1845. 76 and 136 pp. Includes eight poems attributed to Ralegh.

108. ———. *The Courtly Poets from Raleigh to Montrose.* London: Bell and Daldy, 1870. 33 and 261 pp. Reissued as *The Poems of Sir Walter Raleigh, collected and authenticated with those of Sir Henry Wotton and other courtly poets from 1540–1650.* London: Bell, 1875. Includes 29 poems attributed to Ralegh, among them "The Ocean to Cynthia," published for the first time, from the Hatfield MS.

109. Bullen, A. H., ed. *Speculum Amantis: Love-poems from rare song-books and miscellanies of the seventeenth century,* 76–77. London: Privately printed, 1889, 1902. 129 pp. Includes "Nature that washed her hands in milk," discovered in Harleian MS 6917.

110. Hersey, Frank W. C. *Selections from the writings of Sir Walter Ralegh.* Boston: Sherman, French, 1909. 57 pp. Includes 12 poems.

111. Macklin, W. Roy, ed. *Sir Walter Raleigh: Selections from His Writings in Prose and Verse,* 15–72. London and Toronto: Dent; New York: Dutton, 1926. 224 pp.

112. Latham, Agnes M. C., ed. *The Poems of Sir Walter Ralegh.* London: Constable; Boston and New York: Houghton Mifflin, 1929. 200 pp. Revised ed. London: Routledge & Kegan Paul; Cambridge: Harvard University Press, 1951. 56, 182 pp. Provides detailed editorial apparatus and the texts; though challenged in parts, still the standard edition of the poems.

113. Bullett, Gerald, ed. *Silver Poets of the Sixteenth Century,* 279–315. London: Dent; New York: Dutton, 1947. 428 pp. Includes 32 poems attributed to Ralegh.

114. Seddon, George. "A Newly-Discovered and Unknown Poem in Sir Walter Raleigh's Autograph: An Address to Queen

Elizabeth." *Illustrated London News and Sketch* 222 (28
February 1953): 330. Presents a photograph of the manuscript,
in Ralegh's hand, of the poem in eight quatrains which begins
"Now we have present made/ To Cynthia."

115. Oakeshott, Walter. *The Queen and the Poet*. London: Faber and
Faber, 1960; New York: Barnes & Noble, 1961. 232 pp.
Contains "an edition of [27] poems which can plausibly be
associated with" Queen Elizabeth, preceded by an analysis of
Ralegh's relationship with her.

116. Lucie-Smith, Edward, ed. *The Penguin Book of Elizabethan
Verse*, 209–18. Harmondsworth, England, and Baltimore:
Penguin Books, 1965. 288 pp. Includes eight of Ralegh's poems.

117. Bender, Robert M., ed. *Five Courtier Poets of the English
Renaissance*, 597–651. New York: Washington Square Press,
1967. 671 pp. Includes 34 of Ralegh's poems.

118. Rudick, Michael. "The Poems of Sir Walter Ralegh: An
Edition." Ph.D. diss., University of Chicago, 1970. 268 pp.
Analyzes the continuing controversy about authorship of the
poems attributed to Ralegh, and provides extensive apparatus
with the texts.

119. Nye, Robert, ed. *A Choice of Sir Walter Ralegh's Verse*. London:
Faber and Faber, 1972. 72 pp.

120. Seymour-Smith, Martin. *Longer Elizabethan Poems*. New York:
Barnes & Noble, 1972. 261 pp. Includes "The Ocean to
Cynthia" by Ralegh, with editorial apparatus.

121. Colman, E. A. M., ed. *Sir Walter Raleigh: Poems*. Sydney,
Australia: Department of English, University of Sydney, 1977.
86 pp.

122. Ralegh, Sir Walter. *The Ocean to Cynthia: His Autographic
Poems*. Omaha: University of Nebraska Abattoir Editions,
1984. 36 pp.

123. Hammond, Gerald. *Sir Walter Ralegh: Selected Writings*, 23–
61. Manchester: Carcanet Press, 1984; Harmondsworth,
England, and Baltimore: Penguin Books, 1986. 296 pp.
Includes 28 of Ralegh's poems, as well as substantial selections
from his prose.

LETTERS

124. *To day a man, To morrow none: or, Sir Walter Rawleighs Farewell to his Lady, The night before hee was beheaded: Together with his advice concerning Her, and her Sonne.* London: Printed for R. H., 1644. 6 pp. Reprinted in all eds. of his *Remains*, his *Works* 1751 and 1829, in Edwards, and in most of the major biographies. Followed here by Ralegh's poems "Even such is time" and "Like hermit poor," this letter was written after his trial in 1603; his execution was not carried out until 1618.

125. *Maxims of State. Written by Sir Walter Raleigh.* London: Printed by W. Bentley, 1651. Varying pages in this edition and all subsequent editions of his *Maxims* and of *Remains of Sir Walter Raleigh* up to the 1702 edition reproduce eight of his letters; subsequent editions reproduce 11.

126. *Cabala, mysteries of state in letters of the great ministers of K. James and K. Charles. Wherein much of the publique manage of affaires is related. Faithfully collected by a noble hand.* London, Printed for M. M., G. Bedell and T. Collins, 1654. 347 pp. Enlarged in 1663 and 1691. Includes some letters by Ralegh.

127. *The Works of Sir Walter Ralegh, Kt., Political, commercial, and Philosophical; together with his Letters and Poems.* 2 vols. 2:359–90. London: Printed for R. Dodsley, 1751. Includes 13 letters.

128. *The Works of Sir Walter Ralegh.* Oxford, at the University Press, 1829. 8 vols. 8:627–66. Facsimile: New York: Burt Franklin, [1965]. Includes 24 letters.

129. Edwards, Edward. *The Life of Sir Walter Ralegh . . . together with his letters; now first collected.* 2 vols. London: Macmillan, 1868. Includes 166 letters by Ralegh in volume 2.

130. Ewen, Cecil Henry L'Estrange. "Raleigh's Letters." *Times Literary Supplement,* 4 March 1939, 136. Prints a hitherto unpublished letter from Ralegh to Dr. David Lewes, written about April 1584.

For lists of more recently discovered letters, see also Pierre Lefranc, *Sir Walter Ralegh écrivain,* pp. 579–85, and Peter Beal,

Index of English Literary Manuscripts, vol. 1, *1450–1625*, part 2, 373–75.

COLLECTED WORKS

The collections titled *Maxims of State* and *Remains of Sir Walter Raleigh* contain most or all of items 1–10 below. Most of these items were first published several decades after Ralegh's death, and his authorship of some of them, notably 1, 3, 4, 6, and 10, has been challenged by modern critics such as Pierre Lefranc. Some of the items were evidently prepared for separate publication, as they are in different type-face and have their own pagination and title-pages, often dated a year or more earlier than the collection of which they form part. Occasionally an item is included twice in the same collection.

1. Maxims of State.
2. His Instructions to his Son, and The Son's Advice to his Father.
3. His Sceptick.
4. Observations concerning the Magnificency and Opulency of Cities.
5. Seat of Government.
6. Observations touching Trade . . . with the Hollander and other Nations.
7. Letters to divers persons of quality.
8. Poems.
9. Speech immediately before he was beheaded.
10. The Prerogative of Parliaments.

131. *Judicious and Select Essayes and Observations. By that Renowned and Learned Knight, Sir Walter Raleigh. Upon The First Invention of Shipping. The Misery of Invasive Warre. The Navy Royall and Sea-Service. With His Apologie for his voyage to Guiana.* London, Printed by T. W. for Humphrey Moseley, 1650. 42, [65], 46, 69 pp.

132. *Sir Walter Rawleigh's Judicious and Select Essayes and Observations upon the first Invention of Shipping. Invasive War. The Navy Royal and Sea-Service. With his Apologie for his*

Voyage to Guiana. London, Printed for A. M., 1667. A re-issue
of the 1650 ed. of *Judicious and Select Essayes.*

133. *Maxims of State. Written by Sir Walter Raleigh. Whereunto is
added, His instructions to his Sonne; and The Son's Advice to
his aged Father.* London, Printed by W. Bentley, 1651. 78, 28,
15, 150 pp. Contains all ten items listed above except 6 and 10.

134. *Maxims of State. With Instructions to his Son, and the Sons
advice to his aged Father. Whereunto Is added Observations
touching Trade and Commerce with the Hollander and other
Nations, Proving that our Sea and Land Commodities inrich
and strengthen other Countries against our own.* London,
Printed for Will. Shears Junior, 1656. 202, 80 pp. Contains all
ten items listed above except 10.

135. *Maxims of State. With Instructions to his Son, and the Son's
Advice to his aged Father, with many Additions thereunto.*
London, Printed for Will. Shears, Junior, 1657. 202 pp.
Contains all ten items listed above except 6 and 10.

136. *Remains of Sir Walter Raleigh; Viz. Maxims of State. Advice to
his Son: his Sons Advice to his Father. His Sceptick.
Observations concerning the causes of the Magnificency and
Opulency of Cities. The Prerogative of Parliaments in England,
proved in a Dialogue between a Councellour of State and a
Justice of Peace. His Letters to divers persons of quality.*
London, Printed for William Sheares, Junior, 1657. 202, 122
pp. Contains all ten items listed above except 6. First use of title
Remains of Sir Walter Raleigh.

137. *Remains of Sir Walter Raleigh* . . . . London, Printed for William
Sheares, 1661. 264, 122 pp. Contains all ten items listed above.

138. *Remains of Sir Walter Raleigh* . . . . London, By Iohn Redmayne
for Margaret Sheares, 1664. 264, 122 pp. Contains all ten
items listed above.

139. *Remains of Sir Walter Raleigh* . . . . London, By Iohn Redmayne
for Margaret Sheares, 1669. 264, 122 pp. Contains all ten
items listed above.

140. *Remains of Sir Walter Raleigh* . . . . London, Printed for Henry
Mortlock, 1675. 396 pp. Contains all ten items listed above.

141. *Remains of Sir Walter Raleigh* . . . . London, Printed for Henry
Mortlock, 1681. 396 pp. Contains all ten items listed above.

142. *Remains of Sir Walter Raleigh* . . . . London, Printed for Henry
Mortlock, 1702. 1–264, 295–342 pp. Added at end of title is

With the addition of some Letters never printed before, raising the number from eight to eleven. Contains all ten items listed above, but "The Speech before he was beheaded" is much enlarged, and an account of the execution added.

143. *Remains of Sir Walter Raleigh* . . . . London, Printed for W. Mears, F. Clay. and D. Browne, 1726. 1–264, 295–342 pp. A reissue of the 1702 ed. by different publishers.

144. *Sir Walter Raleigh's Sceptick, or Speculations. And Observations of the Magnificency and Opulency of Cities. His Seat of Government. And Letters to the Kings Majestie, and others of Qualitie. Also his Demeanor before his Execution.* London, Printed by Will. Bentley for William Hope, 1651. 150 pp. Reissued in the same year, and differing only in the designation: "London, Printed by W. Bentley, 1651."

145. *Three Discourses of Sir Walter Ralegh. I. Of a War with Spain, and our Protecting the Netherlands. Written by the Command of King James I. in the First year of his Reign, 1602 [sic]. II. Of the Original, and Fundamental Cause of Natural, Arbitrary, and Civil War. III. Of Ecclesiastical Power. Published by Phillip Ralegh, Esq; his only Grandson.* London, Printed for Benjamin Barker, 1702. 204 pp. [i.e. 174pp.] The title-page of Part II reads: *A Discourse of the Original and Fundamental Cause of Natural, Arbitrary, Necessary and Unnatural War. Written by Sir Walter Ralegh, Knt.* London, Printed for B. Barker, 1701.

146. *The Works of Sir Walter Ralegh, Kt., Political, Commercial, and Philosophical; together with his Letters and Poems. The whole never before collected together, and some never yet printed, to which is prefix'd a new account of his Life by Tho. Birch, M.A., F.R.S.* London, Printed for R. Dodsley, 1751. 2 vols. Volume 1 contains Birch's Life, Speech . . . on the Scaffold, Orders to . . . Commanders . . . bound for the South Parts of America . . . 1617, The Dutiful Advice of a loving Son to his aged Father, A brief Relation of . . . Ralegh's Troubles: With the taking away the Lands and Castle of Sherburn . . . , A Discourse touching a Match . . . between the Lady Elizabeth and the Prince of Piedmont, A Discourse touching a Marriage between Prince Henry of England, and a Daughter of Savoy; volume 2 contains A Discourse touching a War with Spain . . . , A Discourse of . . . War, A Discourse of the Invention of Ships . . . , Observations concerning the Royal Navy . . . ,

Observations touching Trade . . . with the Hollander . . . , A Voyage for the Discovery of Guiana, An Apology for the Voyage to Guiana, A Letter to Lord Carew touching Guiana, An Introduction to a Breviary of the History of England . . . , The Seat of Government , Observations of the Causes of the Magnificence and Opulence of Cities, The Sceptic, Instructions to his Son, [13] Letters, [10] Poems.

147. *The Works of Sir Walter Ralegh, Kt., now first collected; to which are prefixed the Lives of the Author by Oldys and Birch, in eight volumes* . . . . Oxford, at the University Press, 1829. Contents: vol. 1, 696 pp. The *Lives* by Oldys and Birch, *Trial*, and *Speech on the Scaffold*; vols. 2–7. *History of the World*; vol. 8, 792 pp. *Miscellaneous writings*. Contains all items in the 1751 *Works*, plus A Treatise on the Soul, a Discourse of Tenures which were before the Conquest, [24] Letters, [40] Poems, A Relation of the Cadiz Action, Spanish Alarum, and Appendix containing comments about Ralegh by Aubrey, Howell, Gondomar, etc.

148. *The Works of Sir Walter Ralegh* . . . . 8 vols. New York: Burt Franklin, [1965]. Facsimile of the 1829 *Works*.

DOUBTFUL WORKS

During the seventeenth century, Ralegh's name was used on the title pages of various publications which are no longer considered to be by him, such as *A Breviary of the History of England, The Life of Mahomet*, and *Tubus Historicus*. Other works of questionable authorship are listed below.

149. *All is not Gold that Glisters: Or, A Warning-piece to England, being a Prophecie, written by that famous and learned Knight Sir Walter Rawleigh, the day before he was beheaded on Towerhill, in the Raign of our late Soveraign Lord King James. Fore-telling the great and wonderful things that will befall the King of Scots, the People of this Nation, and change of Religion and Law, and how long the Government shall continue without a King, or House of Lords. Also the landing of an English Army in France this Summer, the taking of the City of Rome, and the beheading of the Pope, and seven of his Cardinals. With*

other remarkable Passages and Presidents [sic]. London, Printed
for G. Horton, 1651. 4 leaves. Authorship termed suppositious
in the British Library catalogue.

150. *The Cabinet-Council: Containing the Cheif [sic] Arts of Empire
and Mysteries of State; Discabineted In Political and Polemical
Aphorisms, grounded on Authority, and Experience; And
illustrated with the choicest Examples and Historical
Observations. By the Ever-renowned Knight, Sir Walter
Raleigh, Published by John Milton, Esq.* London: Printed by
Tho. Newcomb for Tho. Johnson, 1658. 199 pp. Reprinted in
Works, 1751, 1:39–170; and in *Works,* 1829, 8:35–150.
Contains the following preface "To The Reader: Having had
the Manuscript of this Treatise, Written by Sir Walter Raleigh,
many years in my hands and finding it lately by chance among
other Books and Papers, upon reading thereof, I thought it a
kinde of injury to withhold longer the work of so eminent an
Author from the Publick; it being both answerable in Style to
other works of his already Extant, as far as the subject would
permit, and given me for a true Copy by a Learned Man at his
Death, who had Collected several such peices [sic]. John
Milton." Ralegh's authorhip is denied by E. A. Strathmann and
Pierre Lefranc.

151. *Aphorisms of State, grounded on Authority and Experience,
and illustrated with the Choycest Examples and Historical
Observations. By Sr Walter Raleigh Kt.* Printed for Tho.
Johnson, 1661. 199 pp. Contains neither Milton's prefatory
note nor his name on the title-page.

152. *The Arts of Empire and Mysteries of State Discabineted.*
London: Printed by G. Croom, for Joseph Watts, 1692. 238 pp.
Contains Milton's prefatory note.

153. *The Secrets of Government, and Misteries of State, Plainly laid
open, in all the several Forms of Government in the Christian
World.* Published by John Milton, Esq. Printed in the Year
1697. 238 pp. Ralegh's name is not mentioned.

154. *A Discourse of Sea-ports, principally of the Port and Haven of
Dover. Written by Sir Walter Rawleigh, and address'd to Queen
Elizabeth. With useful Remarks, &c. on that subject, by
Command of his late Majesty, K. Charles the Second. Never
before made Publick.* London, 1700. 16 pp. Reissued the
following year with the title: *An Essay on Ways and Means to*

Maintain the Honour and Safety of England, to encrease Trade, Marchandize, Navigation, Shipping, Marriners, and Sea-men in War or Peace. With useful Remarks and observations on our Harbours, Ports, and Havens, Principally those of Kent. By Sir Henry Sheers. London: Printed in the year 1701. Reprinted in *Harleian Miscellany*, 1744, 4:305–13; ibid., 1808–11, ed. Malham, 12 vols. (10:434–45); ibid., 1808–13, by Thomas Park, 10 vols. (4:305–13). The *Discourse* has also been attributed to Sir Dudley Digges.

155. *A Good Speed to Virginia.* London: Printed by Felix Kyngston for William Welbie, 1609. [30] pp. At one time thought to be by Ralegh because a copy was signed "W. Ralegh. Turr [Tower]. Lond.," though the Epistle Dedicatorie is signed R. G. and the Register of the Stationers Company declares the work to be by Robert Gray.

156. *Observations on the Landing of Forces Designed for the Invasion of a Country. With Arguments On the safest and most expedient Courses to be taken on that Occasion. By Sir Clement Edmonds, Knt. Whereupon are added Some Animadversions, With several Examples and Arguments to manifest the great Advantages of A good Fleet in War Between Nations divided by the Sea; And prove that an Army may be landed in an Enemy's Country, unless they have a Naval Power able to oppose it. By Sir Walter Ralegh, Knt.* London, Printed for J. Pridden, 1759. 40 pp. Includes section by Ralegh on pages 21–40.

157. *Observations on the Publick Affairs of Great-Britain. With Some Toughts [sic] on the Treaty Concluded and Signed (on what Terms God knows) at Seville in Spain, between his Catholick Majesty and the King of Great-Britain. In a letter from W Raleigh to Caleb D'anvers, of Gray's-Inn, Esq.* London, Printed for the Author, 1729. 24 pp. Concludes with Ralegh's name.

158. *The Prince, or Maxims of State. Written by Sir Walter Rawley, and presented to Prince Henry.* London, Printed, 1642. 46 pp. Reprinted as *Maxims of State* in all editions of Ralegh's *Remains* except the first edition of 1651; in *Works*, 1751, 1:1–38; in *Works*, 1829, 8:1–34; in Baron John Somers, *A Second Collection of scarce and valuable Tracts*, edition of 1750, 2:213–39; Scott's edition of 1809, 3:281–304. Ralegh's

authorship is strongly argued against by Pierre Lefranc in *Sir Walter Ralegh écrivain* on pages 67–70.

159. *Sir Walter Raleigh's Observations concerning the Causes of the Magnificencie and Opulencie of Cities.* First printed in the *Remains*, 1651, and repeated in subsequent editions except the second ed. of 1651, and the eds. of 1656 and 1657. Reprinted in *Works*, 1751, 2:321–29; and in *Works*, 1829, 8:541–47. Translates Giovanni Botero's 1589 treatise on the subject.

160. *Sir Walter Raleigh's Sceptick, or Speculations.* First printed in Ralegh's *Remains* of 1651, pages 1–31, and in most subsequent editions. Reprinted in *Works*, 1751, 2:331–40; *Works*, 1829, 8:548–56. Has the following half-title: The Sceptick doth neither affirm, neither denie any Position; but doubteth of it, and opposeth his Reasons against that which is affirmed, or denied, to justify his not Consenting. Translates parts of *Hypotyposes* by Sextus Empiricus; Ralegh's authorship is denied by Pierre Lefranc in *Sir Walter Ralegh écrivain*, pages 66–67.

161. *Warrs with Forraign Princes Dangerous to Our Common-Wealth: or, Reason for Foreign Wars answered. With A Summary of all the Exactions upon this State, from the Conquest to Queen Elizabeth. Proving that the Kings of England always preferred Vnjust Peace, before the Justest Warre. By Sr Walter Rawley.* London, Printed for William Shears, 1657. 96 pp. Probably written by Sir Robert Cotton.

162. *Sir Walter Raleigh's Observations touching Trade & Commerce with the Hollander and other Nations as it was presented to K. James. Wherein is proved that our Sea and Land Commodities serve to inrich and strengthen other Countries against our owne. With other Passages of high Concernment.* London: Printed by T. H., 1653. 80 pp. Reprinted in Ralegh's *Remains* of 1656, and in all later eds. except 1657; in *Works*, 1751, 2:109–36; and *Works*, 1829, 8:351–76. *Trade and Commerce* is usually thought to have been written by John Keymer.

163. "Some Collections of Sir Walter Rawleys Presented to King James, taken out of his *Remains*, discovering Englands loss for want of due Improvement of its Native Commodities." This forms pages 13–26 of the following tract: *Englands Interest asserted in the Improvement of its Native Commodities; and more especially the Manufacture of Wool: Plainly shewing its*

exportation Un-manufactured, amounting unto Millions of Loss to His Majesty and Kingdom. With some Brief Observations of that worthy Author Sir Walter Rawley, touching the same. All Humbly presented to His Majesty, and both Houses of Parliament. By a true Lover of His Majesty and Native Country. License by Roger l'Estrange. London: Printed for Francis Smith, and Henry Mortlock, 1669. 36 pp. In the "Second Impression," London, 1671, "Sir Walter Rawley" does not appear on the title page. Reprints part of *Observations Touching Trade & Commerce.*

164. *Select Observations of the Incomparable Sir Walter Raleigh, Relating to Trade, Commerce and Coin. As it was Presented to King James. Wherein is Proved: that our Money, our Sea and Land Commodities, serve to Enrich and Strengthen other Countries against our Own. With other Matters of the highest Moment to the Publick Welfare.* London: Printed for J. S., 1696. 12 pp. Reprinted in William A. Shaw, *Select tracts and documents illustrative of English monetary history 1626–1730,* 133–46. London, 1896.

165. *Sir Walter Raleigh's Observations on the British Fishery, and several other Points relating to Trade and Commerce. By him address'd and presented to King James I.* London, Reprinted [by J. Roberts], 1720. 55 pp. Reprints part of *Observations Touching Trade & Commerce.*

166. "Observations touching Trade and Commerce with the Hollander and other nations," reprinted in John Ramsey MacCulloch, *A Select Collection of Scarce and Valuable Tracts on Commerce,* printed by Lord Overstone for private distribution. London, 1859. 38 pp.

Chapter 2.

RALEGH IN BIOGRAPHY

Adams, W. H. Davenport. *See* Clinton.

167. Adamson, J. H., and H. F. Folland. *The Shepherd of the Ocean: An Account of Sir Walter Ralegh and His Times.* Boston: Gambit, 1969. 464 pp. Sets Ralegh's life in its historical and political contexts and devotes ample space to summarizing his literary work and relationships.

168. Aikin, John, et al. "Ralegh." In *General Biography.* 10 vols. 8:440–45. London: Robinson, 1799–1815.

169. Allibone, S. Austin. "Ralegh." In *A Critical Dictionary of English Literature.* 3 vols. 2:1726–30. Philadelphia: Lippincott, 1858–71. Reprint. Detroit: Gale, 1965.

170. Anderson, James S. M. "Sir Walter Ralegh." In *Addresses on Miscellaneous Subjects,* 266–359. London: Rivington, 1849. 439 pp.

171. Anthony, Irvin. *Ralegh and His World.* New York and London: Scribner, 1934. 339 pp. Stresses influence of Machiavelli on Ralegh and speculates that his poem "The Ocean to Cynthia" included 15,000 lines since lost.

172. Ashe, Samuel A. "Oration on Sir Walter Raleigh." *Proceedings of the North Carolina Press Association,* 1884, 13–30. Published separately. Raleigh, N.C.: Edwards, Broughton, 1885.

173. Asse, Eugene. "Raleigh ou Ralegh, Sir Walter." In *Nouvelle Biographie Générale.* 46 vols. 41:510–21. Paris: Firmin Didot, 1853–66.

174. Aubrey, John. "Life of Sir Walter Ralegh, Knight." In *Letters written by Eminent Persons . . . and Lives of Eminent Men.* 2 vols. Vol. 2, pt. 2, 509–21. London: Longman, 1813. Reprinted, with additions from Aubrey's manuscript, in *Works of Ralegh* (1829). Another ed. *Brief Lives, Chiefly of contemporaries, set down by John Aubrey, between the years 1669 and 1696,* edited by Andrew Clark. Oxford: Clarendon

Press, 1898. Edited by Anthony Powell. New York: Scribner, 1949. Edited by Oliver Lawson Dick. London: Secker and Warburg, 1949. Contains some of the notorious bawdy anecdotes about Ralegh.

175. Bain, John, Jr. "Sir Walter Raleigh. Sketch." In *Tobacco in Song & Story*, 7–19. New York and Boston: Caldwell, 1896. 144 pp. Summarizes Ralegh's life.

176. Belknap, Jeremy. "Walter Raleigh and Richard Grenville." In *American Biography*. 2 vols. 1:206–23. Boston: Thomas and Andrews, 1794–98. Enlarged edition with additions and notes by F. M. Hubbard. 3 vols. 1:289–370. New York: Harper, 1842.

177. Bell-Chambers, Edmund. "Raleigh, Sir Walter." In *A General Biographical Dictionary*. 4 vols. 4:63–66. London: Bell, 1835.

178. Berkenhout, John. "Sir Walter Raleigh." In *Biographia Literaria, or a Biographical History of Literature*, 1, 518–24. London: Dodsley, 1777. 537 pp. Lists twenty-six works attributed to Ralegh, mainly essays.

179. "Biography: Sir Walter Ralegh, born 1552, beheaded 1618." In *Family Magazine* 4 (1838): 6–12.

180. Birch, Thomas. "Life of Ralegh." In *A General Dictionary, Historical and Critical*. 10 vols. 8:678–91. London: Strahan, 1734–41. Reprinted in *Heads and Characters of Illustrious Personages of Great Britain*. London: Knapton, 1743, 1751; London: Baynes, 1813. Re-written and published in *Works of Ralegh* (1751) and in *Works* (1829).

181. Blake, J. L. "Raleigh, Sir Walter." In *A General Biographical Dictionary*, 789–90. New York: French, 1839. 1096 pp.

182. Bolton, Sarah Knowles. "Sir Walter Raleigh." In *Famous Voyagers and Explorers*, 154–234. New York: Crowell, 1893. 509 pp.

183. Boyce, F. B. "The First Empire Builder, Sir Walter Raleigh." *United Empire*, n.s. 18 (1927): 326–32. Reprinted in *Devonian Yearbook* (1929).

184. Brendon, John Adams. "Sir Walter Raleigh." In *Great Navigators and Discoverers*, 102–19. New York: Harcourt, Brace, 1930. 282 pp; London: Harrap, 1937.

185. Brooke-Hunt, Violet. "Sir Walter Raleigh." In *Prisoners of the Tower of London*, 221–37. London: Dent, 1901. 347 pp.

186. Browne, Wynyard. "Sir Walter Raleigh circa 1552–1619 [sic]."
In *The Great Tudors*, edited by Katharine Garvin, 595–610.
London: Nicholson & Watson; New York: Dutton, 1935. 658
pp. Shorter ed. London: Eyre and Spottiswoode, 1956. 296 pp.
Sees Ralegh as both poet and man of action, motivated by
ambition and curiosity.

187. Brushfield, T. N. "Sir Walter Ralegh." *Western Antiquary* 3
(1884): 196–97.

188. Brydges, Sir Egerton. "Sir Walter Raleigh." In *Imaginative
Biography*. 2 vols. 2:1–74. London: Saunders and Otley, 1834.

189. Buchan, John, *Sir Walter Ralegh*. Oxford: Blackwell, 1897. 78
pp.

190. Campbell, John. "Memoirs of Sir Walter Raleigh, Knight." In
*Lives of the British Admirals and other Eminent British Seamen
. . .* 2d ed. 4 vols. 2:42–94. London: Printed for T. Waller,
1750. Praises Ralegh and blames King James I for destroying
him.

191. Cates, W. L. R. "Raleigh or Ralegh, Sir Walter." In *A Dictionary
of General Biography*. 2d ed., 927–28. London: Longmans,
Green, 1875. 1461 pp.

192. Cayley, Arthur. *The Life of Sir Walter Ralegh, Knt.* 2 vols.
London: Cadell and Davies, 1805. Consists of letters and
writings of Ralegh and documents about him, linked by
Cayley's comments.

193. Chalmers, Alexander. "Ralegh, Sir Walter." In *The General
Biographical Dictionary*. 32 vols. 25:500–515. London:
Nichols and Bentley, 1812–17.

194. Chambers, Robert. "Sir Walter Raleigh." In *Cyclopaedia of
English Literature*. 2 vols. 1:243–49. Edinburgh: Chambers,
1844.

195. Chasles, Philarète. "Walter Raleigh." *Revue des deux mondes*,
4th ser. 23 (1840): 279–321.

196. Chidsey, Donald Barr. *Sir Walter Raleigh: That Damned
Upstart*. New York: John Day, 1931. 315 pp.

197. Cibber, Theophilus. "Life of Ralegh." In *The Lives of the Poets
of Great Britain and Ireland*. 5 vols. 1:180–202. London:
Griffiths, 1753.

198. Clark, John Scott. "Sir Walter Raleigh (1552–1618)." In *A
Study of English and American Writers: A Laboratory Method*,

5–12. Chicago and New York: Row, Peterson, 1916. 645 pp. Reprint. New York: AMS Press, 1974.

199. Clarke, F. L. *Sir Walter Raleigh: His Life and Times*. London: Sonnenschein, 1883. 112 pp. Reprint. 1885.

200. Clinton, Walter. "Sir Walter Raleigh." In *Sword and Pen; or English Worthies in the Reign of Elizabeth*, 1–124. Edinburgh: Nimmo; New York: Vertue and Yorston, 1869. 469 pp. Re-issued in 1875 with the title page bearing the author's real name, W. H. Davenport Adams.

201. Collier, R. "Sir Walter Raleigh. Abstract of Lecture by Mr. R. Collier. Read at a Meeting of the Plymouth Institution, March 29, 1877." *Transactions of the Plymouth Institution* 6 (1877): 133–47.

202. Collier, William Francis. "Sir Walter Raleigh." In *A History of English Literature in a Series of Biographical Sketches*, 150–54. London and New York: Nelson, 1894, 1919. 582 pp.

203. Collis, Louise. "Sir Walter Raleigh." In *Seven in the Tower*, 110–52. New York: Roy, 1960. 208 pp.

204. "Cornelia." "Biographical Essay on Sir Walter Ralegh." *Western Miscellany*, 1850, 107–12.

205. Costley, Thomas. "Sir Walter Raleigh." In *My Favourite Authors*, 1–20. London: Simpkin, Marshall, Hamilton, Kent, 1894. 300 pp.

206. Creighton, Louise. *Life of Sir Walter Ralegh*. London: Rivington, 1877. 270 pp. Appraises Ralegh's life sympathetically.

207. ———. "Sir Walter Ralegh." In *Cambridge History of English Literature*. 15 vols. 4:51–65. Cambridge: Cambridge University Press, 1907–27.

208. Crinò, Anna Maria. *Sir Walter Ralegh nella Letteratura e nella Stòria*. Verona: Linotipia Veronese Ghidini e Fiorini, 1963. 115 pp. Uses letters by Florentine ambassadors to England.

209. Cunningham, George Godfrey. "Sir Walter Raleigh." In *Lives of Eminent and Illustrious Englishmen*. 8 vols. 2:356–62. Glasgow: Fullerton, 1837. Reprint. 1853.

210. Davies, J. Hamilton. *A Lecture on the Life and Times of Sir Walter Raleigh, before the Sherborne Literary Institution, on Dec. 9th, 1850*. Sherborne, Dorset: Hallet, 1851. 38 pp.

de Sélincourt, Hugh. *See* Sélincourt, Hugh de.

211. Deshler, Charles D. "Sir Walter Ralegh." In *Afternoons with the Poets*, 89. New York: Harper, 1879. 320 pp.

212. DeWitt, William A. *Illustrated Minute Biographies*, 128. New York: Grosset & Dunlap, 1949. 160 pp. Rev. ed. 1953.

213. D'Israeli, Issac. "The Psychological History of Rawleigh." In *Amenities of Literature*. 3 vols. 2:263–94. London: Edward Moxon, 1841. The first of several editions. Depicts Ralegh as a "moral phenomenon," the architect of his fluctuating fortunes, and "among the founders of our literature."

214. _____. "An Authentic Narrative of the Last Hours of Sir Walter Rawleigh." In *Curiosities of Literature*. 3 vols. 3:124–30. London and New York: Routledge, 1858.

215. _____. "Secret History of Sir Walter Rawleigh." In *Curiosities of Literature*. 3 vols. 3:111–24. London and New York: Routledge, 1858. Delineates Ralegh's character and Stucley's treachery to him.

216. Dodd, Whitwell M. "Raleigh: A Superman." *Quarterly Review* 265 (1935): 63–74.

217. Doran, Joseph Ingersoll. *Sir Walter Raleigh, Address before the Council of the Pennsylvania Society of Colonial Governors, February 6, 1911*. [Philadelphia]: Pennsylvania Society of Colonial Governors, [1911]. 22 pp.

218. Drake, Samuel Gardner. *A Brief Memoir of Sir Walter Raleigh*. Boston: Privately printed, 1862. 35 pp. With additions from the *New England Historical and Genealogical Register*, 16 (1862): 105–18.

219. Ecclestone, Eric. *Sir Walter Ralegh*. Middlesex, England: Harmondsworth; New York: Penguin Books, 1941. 122 pp.

220. Echard, Laurence. "An Account of the Author's [Ralegh's] Life, Tryal and Death." In *An Abridgment of Sir Walter Raleigh's History of the World*, 3d ed. only, i–xxx. London: Philip Raleigh, 1702. approx. 500 pp.

221. Edwards, Edward. "Life of Ralegh." In *Exmouth and its Neighborhood, Ancient and Modern*, 127–235. Exmouth: Bounsall, 1868. 362 pp. Re-issued, without date, under the title of *Devonshire*. Contains a pedigree of the Ralegh family.

222. _____. *The Life of Sir Walter Ralegh*. 2 vols. London: Macmillan, 1868. Based on contemporary documents and letters, which are printed in volume 2.

223. Edwards, Philip W. *Sir Walter Ralegh*. London: Longmans, Green, 1953. 184 pp. Reprint. London: Folcroft Library, 1976. Focuses on his intellectual life and literary techniques.

224. Egerton, H. E. "Sir Walter Raleigh." *United Empire*, n.s. 3 (1912): 42–44.

225. Elliott, Bette. "Now There Was a Man." *State* 44 (1976): 20–22. Inspired by a visit to Ralegh's cell in the Tower of London.

226. Elliott, L. E. "Sir Walter Raleigh and His Times." *Pan American Magazine* 42 (1930): 341–49.

227. "Eminent Men of Devon and Cornwall: Sir Walter Raleigh." *South Devon Literary Chronicle*, 1846, 304–5, 310–13, 325–26, 347–48, 359–61, 370–73.

228. "English Prose Writers No. 5. Sir Walter Raleigh." *Saturday Magazine* 3 (1833): 231.

229. Ewald, Alexander Charles. "Westward Ho!" In *Studies Restudied; Historical Sketches from Original Sources*, 164–205. London: Chatto and Windus, 1885. 374 pp. Reprints an article from *Gentleman's Magazine* (July 1883).

230. Flloyd, T. "Ralegh (Sir Walter)." In *Bibliotheca Biographica*. 3 vols. 3:[102–8]. London, 1760.

231. Fletcher, Charles Robert Leslie and Emery Walker. "Sir Walter Raleigh." In *Historical Portraits: Richard II to Henry Wriothesley: 1400–1600*, 86–89. Oxford: Clarendon Press, 1909. 199 pp.

232. Foley, Caroline A. (Mrs. T. W. Rhys Davids). "Ralegh, Sir Walter." In *Dictionary of Political Economy,* ed. Sir R. H. Inglis Palgrave. 3 vols. 3:259–60. 1894–99. Summarizes Ralegh's ideas about trade and economics.

233. Ford, John. *Linea Vitae: A Line of Life. Pointing out the Immortalitie of a Vertuous Name.* pp. 47–51. [London]: Printed by W. S. for N. Butter, 1620. 129 pp. Includes a passage (excised from some early copies) citing Ralegh as an example of contradictions but praising his deportment at his end.

234. Fuller, Thomas. "Sir Walter Rawleigh." In *The History of the Worthies of England*, pt. 1, 261–62. London: Printed by J. G., W. L., and W. G., 1662. approx. 1000 pp. Abridged by George Sandys as *Anglorum Speculum* (1684); and by J. Freeman (1952). Prints the anecdotes about Ralegh's laying down his cloak for Queen Elizabeth and their exchanging verses scratched on a window.

235. Garnett, Richard, and Edmund Gosse. "Sir Walter Raleigh." In *English Literature: An Illustrated Record*. 4 vols. 2:46–62. London: Heinemann; New York: Macmillan, 1903. Another ed. 1926.

236. Golding, Claud. "Sir Walter Raleigh, Hero of His Own Execution." In *Great Names in History, 356 B.C.–A.D. 1910*, 97–103. London: Harrap, 1935; Philadelphia: Lippincott, 1936. 300 pp.

237. Gordon, George Stuart. "Sir Walter Raleigh." In *Lives of Authors*, 33–43. London: Chatto and Windus, 1950. 207 pp.

238. Gorton, John. "Ralegh or Raleigh (Sir Walter)." In *A General Biographical Dictionary*. 2 vols. 2:719–21. London, 1828.

239. Gosse, Edmund. *Raleigh*. London: Longmans; New York: Appleton, 1886. 248 pp. Reprints. London: Longmans, 1888; Folcroft, Penn.: Folcroft Library, 1974.

240. _____. "Sir Walter Raleigh." *Geographical Journal* 21 (1903): 602–5.

241. Greenblatt, Stephen J. "Sir Walter Ralegh: The Functions of Art in the Life of the Courtier and Adventurer." Ph.D. diss., Yale University, 1969. 289 pp. Sees the major events of Ralegh's life as illustrative of his propensity for self-dramatization.

242. _____. *Sir Walter Ralegh: The Renaissance Man and His Roles*. New Haven and London: Yale University Press, 1973. 209 pp. Argues that Ralegh's life and works are products of his self-dramatizing capacity.

243. Grigson, Geoffrey. "Sir Walter Ralegh." In *Poets in Their Pride*, 17–27. London: Phoenix House, 1962; New York: Basic Books, 1964. 151 pp. Includes three of Ralegh's poems and an account of his life.

244. Grigson, Geoffrey, and C. H. Gibbs-Smith, eds. *People: A Volume of the Good, Bad, Great and Eccentric*, 344–45. New York: Hawthorn Books, 1956. 469 pp.

245. "Gualterio Raleigh o Ralegh." In *Enciclopedia Universal Illustrada Europeo-Americana*. 72 vols. 49:455–57. Barcelona: Espasa, 1907–30.

246. Gunn, Thom. "Sir Walter Ralegh." In *The Concise Encyclopedia of English and American Poets and Poetry*, edited by Stephen Spender and Donald Hall, 270–71. New York: Hawthorn Books, 1963. 415 pp.

247. Hammond, Peter. *Sir Walter Ralegh*. London: Pitkin "Pride of

Britain" Books, 1978. 24 pp. Provides a concise biography, with abundant pictures.

248. Harris, James Morrison. "Discourse on the life and character of Sir Walter Ralegh. Delivered . . . before the Maryland Historical Society, May 19, 1846." In *Publications of the Maryland Historical Society*, vol. 1, no. 6. Baltimore: Maryland Historical Society, 1846. 71 pp.

249. Hatton, Joseph. *The Story of Sir Walter Ralegh and A Day in A Tobacco Factory*, 1–39. Liverpool: Cope's Tobacco Plant, 1894. 69 pp.

250. Haywood, Marshall DeLancey. "Sir Walter Raleigh: An Address Delivered at Old Fort Raleigh in Roanoke Island, North Carolina, at the Celebration of Virginia Dare Day, August 18, 1913." *North Carolina Booklet* 13 (1913): 65–116. Reprinted as *Sir Walter Raleigh: An Address*. Raleigh: Edwards and Broughton, 1913. Reprint. Raleigh: Roanoke Colony Memorial Association, 1937. Sketches the life of Ralegh, with emphasis on the Roanoke Island colonies.

251. Hervey, Frederick, and others. *Naval History of Great Britain*. 5 vols. 1:400–401, 462–65; 2:27–37. London: William Adlard, 1779.

252. Hinchman, W. S. and F. B. Gummere. "Sir Walter Raleigh." In *Lives of Great English Writers from Chaucer to Browning*, 22–43. New York: Houghton Mifflin, 1908. 569 pp.

253. Hoffman, Ann. "Sir Walter Ralegh." In *Lives of the Tudor Age 1485–1603*, 365–72. New York: Harper and Row, 1977. 500 pp.

254. Horne, Charles F., ed. "Sir Walter Raleigh." In *Great Men and Famous Women*. 4 vols. 1:182–89. New York: Selmar Hess, 1894.

255. Hume, Martin A. S. *Sir Walter Ralegh: The British Dominion of the West*. London: Fisher Unwin, 1897. 431 pp. Reprints. London: Fisher Unwin; New York: Longmans, Green, 1898, 1903, 1906. New imprint. London: Fisher Unwin; New York: Knopf, 1926.

256. Hutchinson, Frederick Winthrop. "The Boy Who Loved the Sea." In *The Men Who Found America*, 90–103. Philadelphia: Edward Stern, 1909. 158 pp. Provides a sketch of Ralegh's life.

257. Innes, Arthur Donald. "Sir Walter Raleigh." In *Ten Tudor*

Statesmen, 361–91. London: Grayson, 1906. 295 pp. Another ed. 1934.

258. _____. "Sir Walter Raleigh, Dreamer and Adventurer." In *Leading Figures in English History*, 139–62. London: Rivington, 1931. 361 pp.

259. Irwin, Margaret. *That Great Lucifer: A Portrait of Sir Walter Ralegh*. London: Chatto and Windus; New York: Harcourt, Brace, 1960. 320 pp. Portrays Ralegh among his political and literary contemporaries.

260. Johnston, Sir Harry Hamilton. "Walter Raleigh." In *A Gallery of Heroes and Heroines*, 13–25. London: Wells, Gardner, Darton, 1915. 140 pp.

261. Kingsley, Charles. "Sir Walter Raleigh and His Time." *North British Review* 23 (May 1855): 1–39 (pages 1–16 misnumbered as 315–30). Reprinted in *Eclectic Magazine* (1855); in *Littell's Living Age* (1855); in Kingsley's *Works*. London: Macmillan, 1859; in Kingsley's *Miscellanies*. London: Parker, 1859; in Kingsley's *Sir Walter Raleigh and His Time, with Other Papers*. Boston: Ticknor and Fields, 1859; and in Kingsley's *Plays and Puritans and other Historical Essays*. London: Macmillan, 1873. From reflections on five books involving Ralegh, staunchly defends Ralegh and excoriates James I.

262. Knight, Charles. "Raleigh, Sir Walter." In *The English Cyclopaedia (Biography)*. 6 vols. 5:16–19. 1856–58.

263. Knight, Charles [?]. "Sir Walter Raleigh." In *The Cabinet Portrait Gallery of British Worthies*. 7 vols. 5:71–83. London: Charles Knight, 1845.

264. Lacey, Robert. *Sir Walter Ralegh*. London: Weidenfeld & Nicholson, 1973. 415 pp. New York: Atheneum, 1974, 1979. Seeks to relate Ralegh's poems to various events in his life.

265. Latham, Agnes M. C. *Sir Walter Ralegh*. London: Longmans, Green, 1964. 45 pp. Treats Ralegh's literary work in relation to different aspects of his career.

266. _____. "Sir Walter Ralegh (c. 1554–1618)." In *British Writers: Edited under the Auspices of the British Council*. 8 vols. 1:145–59. New York: Scribner, 1979.

267. Laughton, J. K., and Sidney Lee. "Ralegh, Sir Walter." In *Dictionary of National Biography*, edited by Leslie Stephen and Sidney Lee. 66 vols. 47:186–206. New York: Macmillan;

London: Smith, Elder, 1885–1901. Reprinted in *Representative Biographies of English Men of Letters*, edited by Charles Townsend Copeland and Frank Wilson Cheney Hersey (1909).

268. Lawrence, Eugene. "Sir Walter Raleigh." In *The Lives of the British Historians*. 2 vols. 1:31–163. New York: Scribner, 1855.

269. Lawrence, J. Hamilton. *Sir Walter Raleigh and his Age*. Parkville, Mo.: Park College Press, 1898. 21 pp.

270. Lemonnier, Leon. *Sir Walter Raleigh*. Paris: La Renaissance du Livre, 1931. 242 pp.

271. Lempriere, J. "Raleigh, Sir Walter." In *Universal Biography*. 2 vols. 2:[419–20]. New York: Sargeant, 1810. Enlarged by W. A'. Beckett. 3 vols. 3:569–72. London: Isaac, [1835?].

272. "Life of Ralegh." In *Biographia Britannica*. 7 vols. 5:3467–85. London: Printed for W. Innys, 1747–66.

273. "Life of Ralegh." In *Select Biography, A Collection of Lives of Eminent Men who have been an honour to their Country*. 13 vols. 5:1–177. London: Wetton & Jarvis, 1821.

274. "The Life of Sir Walter Raleigh." In *Lives, English and Forein [sic]: containing the history of the most illustrious persons of our own and other nations, from the year 1550, to the year 1690. By several hands*. 2 vols. 1:74–135. London: Printed for B. Tooke and William Davis, 1704.

275. "The Life of Sir Walter Raleigh." *Universal Museum* 2 (1763): 6–8.

276. "The Life of Sir Walter Raleigh." In *Britannia Triumphant: or, An account of the Sea-fights and Victories of the English Nation, from the earliest times. By a Society of Naval Gentlemen*, 2d ed., 8–17. London: Sold by R. James, 1766. 224 pp. Another ed. 1777.

277. "The Life of Sir Walter Raleigh." In *British Biography . . . from Wickliff . . . to the present time*. 7 vols. 4:33–74. London, 1776–83.

278. "The Life of Sir Walter Raleigh, Knt., with his head curiously engraved." *London Magazine* 24 (1755): 149–53.

279. *The Life of Sir Walter Raleigh, Statesman, Soldier, Traveller, and Historian. The Typical Man of the Elizabethan age; Explorer of Guiana and Founder of Virginia; Court Favourite and Political Martyr*. London: Ward, Lock, [1880?]. 16 pp.

280. "Life of Sir Walter Raleigh. With an elegant head." *Literary Magazine and British Review* 2 (1789): 163–74.

281. *The Lives of Sir Walter Raleigh and Capt. John Smith, with an Account of the Governors of Virginia to 1781*. Shepherds-Town, Va.: n.p., 1817. 121 pp.

282. Lloyd, David. "Observations on the life of Sir Walter Rawleigh." In *The Statesmen and Favourites of England since the Reformation*, 485–92. London: Printed by J. C. for S. Speed, 1665. 823 pp. 2d ed. entitled *State Worthies*. London: Printed by T. Milbourn for S. Speed, 1670. 3d ed. London: Printed for J. Robson, 1766.

283. Lodge, Edmund. "Sir Walter Raleigh." In *Portraits of Illustrious Personages of Great Britain*. 4 vols. 2:6. London: Lackington, 1821. Often reprinted.

284. Low, Sir Sidney, and F. S. Pulling. "Ralegh, Sir Walter." In *The Dictionary of English History*, 884. London: Cassell, 1884. Revised ed., 1928. 1154 pp.

285. Magnus, Sir Philip. *Sir Walter Raleigh*. London: Falcon Educational Books, 1952. 126 pp. Revised eds. London: Collins; New York: Macmillan, 1956; Hamden, Conn.: Archon Books, 1968.

286. Malden, Henry. "Raleigh." In *Distinguished Men of Modern Times*. 4 vols. 1:489–504. London: Charles Knight, 1838. Based on the essay by Malkin.

287. Malkin, Arthur Thomas. "Raleigh." In *The Gallery of Portraits with Memoirs*. 7 vols. 6:1–10. London: Charles Knight, 1833–36. Reproduces Ralegh's portrait from the collection of the Duchess of Dorset; text is the same as Malden's.

288. Mavor, William. "Sir Walter Raleigh: Born 1552—Beheaded 1618. From 5th Edward VI to 15th James I." In *The British Nepos: or, Mirror of Youth*. 5th ed., revised. 108–18. Philadelphia: Byrne, 1803. 375 pp. First published 1798.

289. Meadows, Denis. *Five Remarkable Englishmen: A New Look at the Lives & Times of Walter Ralegh, Capt. John Smith, John Winthrop, William Penn, James Oglethorpe*. 3–48. New York: Devin-Adair, 1961. 245 pp. Emphasizes Ralegh's colonizing efforts.

290. Miller, Helen Hill. "The Renaissance Man." In *Captains from Devon: The Great Elizabethan Seafarers Who Won the Oceans for England*, 151–208. Chapel Hill, N.C.: Algonquin Books of Chapel Hill, 1985. 221 pp. Portrays the diversity of Ralegh's career.

291. Mitchell, Donald Grant. "Walter Raleigh." In *English Lands,*

Letters, and Kings. 4 vols. 2:11–19. New York: Scribner, 1889.

292. Moore, Thomas. "Life of Ralegh." In *History of Devonshire.* 2 vols. 2:228–332. London: Robert Jennings, 1836.

293. Mortimer, Thomas. "The Life of Sir Walter Raleigh." In *The British Plutarch.* 8 vols. 3:22–52. London: Dilly, 1791. Much enlarged in new edition by Francis Wrangham (1816).

294. Mueller, Johann Georg. *Bekenntnisse merkwürdiger Männer von sich selbst.* 6 vols. 5:199–227. Winterthur: n.p., 1793–1822. Describes famous people by utilizing their own words.

295. Napier, Macvey. "The Life and Writings of Sir Walter Raleigh." *Edinburgh Review* 71 (1840): 1–98. Reprinted in *Museum of Foreign Literature, Science and Art* (1840). Combined with Napier's article on Bacon and published as *Lord Bacon and Sir Walter Raleigh.* Cambridge: Macmillan, 1853. While reviewing five works about Ralegh, provides an account of his life.

296. Naunton, Sir Robert. "Rawleigh." In *Fragmenta Regalia, or Observations on the late Queen Elizabeth, Her Times and Favorits [sic],* 30–32. n.p., 1641. 43 pp. Also published in 1642, 1653, 1714, 1807, 1824, 1870, and in translation in Rouen, 1683, Amsterdam, 1703, and in French in London, 1745. Writing *c.* 1630, Naunton depicts Ralegh as "fortune's tennis ball."

297. Oakeshott, Walter Fraser. "Last Elizabethan and the First American." In *Founded upon the Seas,* 167–89. Cambridge: Cambridge University Press, 1942. 200 pp.

298. Ober, Frederick Albion. *Sir Walter Raleigh.* New York and London: Harper, 1909. 303 pp.

299. Oldys, William. *Life of Ralegh,* prefixed to the 11th ed. of Ralegh's *History of the World.* London: Printed for G. Conyers, 1736. Reprinted in *Works of Ralegh* (1829). An anonymous and abridged edition of Oldys's book (probably pirated), titled *The Life of Sir Walter Ralegh, from his Birth to his Death on the Scaffold . . . . The whole compiled from the most approved Authorities and curious Manuscripts.* London: Printed for the Booksellers in Town and Country, 1740. Replete with facts, Oldys's *Life* was the first substantial biography of Ralegh.

300. Partington, C. F., ed. "Raleigh, Sir Walter." In *The British Cyclopedia of Biography.* 2 vols. 2:733–36. London: Orr, 1837–38.

301. Patrick, David, ed. "Sir Walter Raleigh." In *Chambers's*

Cyclopaedia of English Literature. 3 vols. 1:304–13. London:
Chambers; Philadelphia: Lippincott, 1901.

302. Peele, W. J. "Sir Walter Raleigh and His Colonies. The Principal
Events in His Life—A Study in Dates." In *Literary and
Historical Activities in North Carolina, 1900–1905*, 251–66.
Raleigh: North Carolina Historical Commission, 1907. 623 pp.
Lists chronologically the major events of Ralegh's life.

303. Phillips, Edward. "Sir Walter Raleigh." In *Theatrum Poetarum,
or a Compleat Collection of the Poets*, pt. 2, 233. London:
Printed for Charles Smith, 1675. 392, 261 pp. Reprint. New
York: Georg Olms, 1970. Phillips's brief comments were later
enlarged as "Life and Character of Sir Walter Ralegh." In
*Theatrum Poetarum Anglicanorum . . . . By Edward Phillips,
the nephew of Milton . . . (with additions by Sir Egerton
Brydges)*. Canterbury: Printed by Simmons and Kirkby for J.
White, 1800. Reprints. 1824, 1828, 1830, and 1856.

304. Powell, William Stevens, "Sir Walter Raleigh." *American
Heritage*, n.s. 4 (1953): 46–49.

305. Pridham, T. L. "Raleigh." In *Devonshire Celebrities*, 198–204.
Exeter: Eland; London: Bell & Daldy, 1869. 236 pp.

306. Prince, John. "Life of Ralegh." In *Danmonii Orientales
Illustres: or, The Worthies of Devon*, 530–44. Exeter: Printed
by Sam. Farley for Awnsham, John Churchill, Charles Yeo and
Philip Bishop, 1701. 600 pp. 2d ed. London: Printed for Rees
and Curtis, 1810.

307. "Ralegh, Gualtieri." In *Dizionario Biografico Universale*, edited
by Felice Scifoni. 5 vols. 4:747–48. Florence: D. Passigli, 1846.

308. "Raleigh, Sir Walter." In *Chambers's Biographical Dictionary*,
775–76. London: Chambers, 1907. 1006 pp.

309. "Raleigh (Sir Walter)." In *The Biographical Magazine . . . By a
society of gentlemen*, 557–66. London, 1776. 813 pp.

310. "Rawleigh (Sir Walter)." In *A New and General Biographical
Dictionary*. 12 vols. 11:37–45 (1784). New ed. 8 vols. 8:3–6
(1795). Title page of first volume only of 1795 edition reads
The New Biographical Magazine by G. W. Johnson.

311. Rodd, Sir Rennell. *Sir Walter Raleigh*. London and New York:
Macmillan, 1904. 292 pp. Reprints. 1905, 1914, 1928. Deals
more accurately with Ralegh's public career than with his
literary work.

312. Rose, Hugh. "Ralegh, Raleigh, or Rawlegh, (Sir Walter)." In *A

New General Biographical Dictionary. 12 vols. 11:282–85. London: Fellowes, 1853.

313. Ross, George. "Sir Walter Raleigh." In *Studies: Biographical and Literary*, 119–68. London: Simpkin, Marshall, 1867. 168 pp.

314. Routh, C. R. N. "Ralegh, Sir Walter." In *Who's Who in History: England 1485–1603.* 5 vols. 2:222–24. Oxford: Basil Blackwell, 1964.

315. Rowse, A. L. "Sir Walter Raleigh." *Listener* 11 (1934): 794–96.

316. Rowse, A. L. and G. B. Harrison. "Sir Walter Raleigh." In *Queen Elizabeth and Her Subjects*, 79–90. London: Allen and Unwin, 1935. 139 pp. Reprint: Freeport, N.Y.: Books for Libraries Press, 1970. Collects several radio broadcasts.

317. Ruoff, Henry W., ed. "Raleigh, or Ralegh, Sir Walter." In *Masters of Achievement*, 938–39. Buffalo, N.Y.: Frontier Press, 1910. 1038 pp.

318. Sabatini, Rafael. "Sir Walter Ralegh." In *Heroic Lives*, 195–271. London: Hutchinson; New York: Houghton Mifflin, 1934. 416 pp.

319. St. John, James Augustus. *Life of Sir Walter Raleigh.* 2 vols. London: Chapman and Hall, 1868. 2d ed. 1869.

320. Samuel, R. "Sir Walter Raleigh ou Ralegh." In *La Grande Encyclopédie.* 31 vols. 28:108. Paris: Lamirault, 1886–1902.

321. Saunders, Beatrice. "Sir Walter Raleigh." In *Portraits of Genius*, 9–19. London: Murray, 1959. 214 pp.

322. Saunders, J. W. "Ralegh, Sir Walter." In *A Biographical Dictionary of Renaissance Poets and Dramatists, 1520–1650*, 133–34. Sussex: Harvester Press; Totowa, N.J.: Barnes and Noble, 1983. 216 pp.

323. Schmidtchen, Paul W. "Let Valor Be My End!" *Hobbies: The Magazine for Collectors* 71 (1966): 105–6. Sketches Ralegh's life.

324. Schnittkind, Henry Thomas, and Dana Arnold Schnittkind [Henry Thomas and Dana Lee Thomas]. "Sir Walter Raleigh." In *Living Biographies of Famous Men*, 61–75. Garden City, N.Y.: Garden City Publishing, 1944. 300 pp.

325. Sélincourt, Hugh de. *Great Ralegh.* London: Methuen; New York: Putnam, 1908. 310 pp. Wilmington, Del.: Scholarly Press, 1977. Focuses on Ralegh's public life and is unusual in finding humor in *The History of the World.*

326. Seward, William. "Sir Walter Raleigh." In *Anecdotes of some distinguished persons.* 4 vols. 4:333–40. London: Cadell, 1796.

327. [Shirley, John.] *The Life of the Valiant and Learned Sir Walter Raleigh, Knight. With his Tryal at Winchester.* London: Printed by J. D. for Benj. Shirley and Richard Tonson, 1677. 243 pp. No author on title page, but attributed to John Shirley (1648–79) by Anthony à Wood. The *Life* also appeared in the 1677 edition of Ralegh's *History of the World,* in the 1687 edition, and even as an after-insertion in earlier editions such as the 1614.

328. Sigourney, Lydia H. "Sir Walter Raleigh." In *Biographies of the Great and Good,* 70–89. Glasgow and London: Collins, 1855. 248 pp.

329. Sinclair, Andrew. *Sir Walter Raleigh and the Age of Discovery.* Harmondsworth and New York: Penguin, 1984. 127 pp. Reiterates some unproven ideas about Ralegh's writings.

330. "Sir Walter Raleigh." *Southern Review* 4 (1829): 433–65.

331. "Sir Walter Raleigh." *Chambers's Edinburgh Journal* 6 (1837): 266–67; 11 (1842): 339–40.

332. "Sir Walter Raleigh." *National Magazine* 9 (1856): 22–31.

333. "Sir Walter Raleigh." *New Monthly Magazine* 126 (1862): 54–65.

334. "Sir Walter Raleigh." *Leisure Hour* 13 (1864): 459–64. Reprinted in *Eclectic Magazine* (October 1864).

335. "Sir Walter Raleigh." *Chambers's Journal of Popular Literature, Science, and Arts* 45 (1868): 308–11.

336. "Sir Walter Ralegh." *Quarterly Review* 175 (1892): 287–318.

337. "Sir Walter Ralegh." *Times Literary Supplement,* 31 October 1918, 517–18. Commemorates Ralegh on the tercentenary of his death.

338. "Sir Walter Ralegh, Born 1552, beheaded, 1618." *Family Magazine, or Monthly Abstract of General Knowledge* (1837): 6–12.

339. "Sir Walter Raleigh: A Portrait from History." *Tait's Edinburgh Magazine,* n.s. 25 (1858): 453–59.

340. "Sir Walter Rawleigh." *Biographical Magazine* (1794): 9.

341. Sjögren, Gunnar. *Walter Ralegh: Den Siste Elisabetanen.* Stockholm: Askild & Kärnekull, 1975. 244 pp. Swedish account of "the last Elizabethan."

342. Southey, Robert. "Sir Walter Raleigh, 1552–1618." In *Lives of*

the British Admirals with an Introductory View of the Naval History of England. 6 vols. 4:209–447. London: Longman and Taylor, 1833–40. Reprinted in *English Seamen; Hawkins, Greenville [sic], Devereux, Raleigh*, edited by David Hannay, 234–450. London: Methuen, 1904. 450 pp. Favors Ralegh less than most of his biographers in the nineteenth century did.

343. Spender, Edward. "Sir Walter Raleigh." *London Quarterly Review* 30 (1868): 457–76. Appears also in *Littell's Living Age* (1868).

344. Squire, J. C. "Sir Walter Raleigh." In *Books in General*, 3d ser., 228–34. London and New York: Hodder & Stoughton; New York: Doubleday, Doran, 1921. 244 pp.

345. Standing, Percy C. "Sir Walter Raleigh." *Nautical Magazine* 97 (1917): 166–69.

346. Stebbing, William. *Sir Walter Ralegh, a Biography*. Oxford: Clarendon Press, 1891. 413 pp. London: Macmillan, 1891; Oxford: Clarendon Press, 1899; New York: Lemma, 1972.

347. Sullivan, Margaret F. "Concerning Sir Walter Raleigh." *Catholic World* 39 (1884): 626–36.

348. Taylor, Ida Ashworth. *Sir Walter Raleigh*. London: Methuen, 1902. 214 pp. Reprint. New York: Dutton, 1903.

349. Taylor, James. "Raleigh, Sir Walter." In *The Imperial Dictionary of Universal Biography*, ed. John Francis Waller. 14 vols. 12:769–70. London: Mackenzie, 1857–63.

350. Theobald, Lewis. *Memoirs of Sir Walter Raleigh; His, Life, his Military and Naval Exploits, his Preferments and Death: In Which are Inserted the Private Intrigues between the Count of Gondamore, the Spanish Ambassador, and the Lord Salisbury, then Secretary of State*. London: W. Mears, 1719. 40 pp. 2d ed., also 1719, identical except for title page. Dwells chiefly on Ralegh's trials in 1603 and 1618.

351. Thomas, Lowell. "Sir Walter Raleigh." In *The Vital Spark: 101 Outstanding Lives*, 284–86. Garden City, N.Y.: Doubleday, 1959. 480 pp.

352. Thompson, Edward. *Sir Walter Ralegh: The Last of the Elizabethans*. London: Macmillan, 1935. 387 pp. New Haven: Yale University Press, 1936. Pays considerable attention to Ralegh's literary work.

353. Thomson, Mrs. A. T. [Katherine Byerley]. *Memoirs of the Life of Sir Walter Ralegh, with some account of the period in which*

he lived. London: Longmans, 1830. 496 pp. New York and Philadelphia: Carey & Lea, 1831; Philadelphia: Gibon, 1850; New York: Miller, Orton & Mulligan, 1856. (Last two editions give author's initials as M. A. Thomson.) Summarized in *Ladies' Museum* (July 1830).

354. Thoreau, Henry David. *Sir Walter Raleigh*, edited by Henry Aiken Metcalf, introduction by Franklin Benjamin Sanborn. Boston: Bibliophile Society, 1905. 106 pp. Reprint. New York: Gordon Press, 1976. Prints an essay written in the 1840s, surveying Ralegh's life and writings, especially his prose.

355. True, Charles K. *The Life and Times of Sir Walter Raleigh, Pioneer of Anglo-American Colonization.* Cincinnati: Hitchcock and Walden; New York: Nelson & Phillips, 1877. 271 pp.

356. Tytler, Patrick Fraser. *Life of Sir Walter Raleigh. Founded on authentic and original documents, some of them never before published, including a view of the most important transactions in the reigns of Elizabeth and James I; sketches of Burleigh, Essex, Secretary Cecil, Sidney, Spenser and other eminent contemporaries, with a vindication of his character from the attacks of Hume and other writers.* Edinburgh: Oliver and Boyd; Philadelphia: Greenbank, 1833. 468 pp. Reprints. 1836, 1839, 1840, 1844, 1849, 1851, 1853. Exalts Ralegh at the expense of his contemporaries.

357. Untermeyer, Louis. "Sir Walter Ralegh." In *Lives of the Poets*, 63–65. New York: Simon and Schuster, 1959; London: Allen, 1960. 757 pp.

358. Uslar Pietri, Arturo. "La grande y dorada aventura de Sir Walter Raleigh." *Revista Shell* 4 (1955): 30–35. Sketches Ralegh's life.

359. Waldman, Milton. *Sir Walter Raleigh*. London: John Lane; New York: Harper, 1928. 255 pp. 2d ed. London: Collins, 1943. Reprint. London: Collins, [1950].

360. Wallace, Willard M. *Sir Walter Raleigh*. Princeton: Princeton University Press; Oxford: Oxford University Press, 1959. 334 pp. Includes detailed consideration of Ralegh's literary work and the spelling and pronunciation of his name.

361. "Walter Raleigh." *American Literary Magazine* 1 (1847): 1–19.

362. Watkins, John. "Sir Walter Raleigh." In *Characteristic Anecdotes of Men of Learning and Genius*, 43–57. London: James Cundee, 1808. 562 pp.

363. Webb, Alfred. "Raleigh, Sir Walter." In *A Compendium of Irish Biography*. 448–49. Dublin: Gill, 1878. 598 pp.

364. Whibley, Charles. "Sir Walter Ralegh." *Blackwood's Magazine* 204 (1918): 670–86. Reprinted in the author's *Literary Studies*. London: Macmillan, 1919.

365. Whitehead, Charles. *The Life and Times of Sir Walter Ralegh. With copious extracts from his History of the World.* London: Cooke, Ingram, 1854. 309 pp. The *Life* occupies two-thirds of the book.

366. Williams, Charles Harold. "Sir Walter Raleigh or Ralegh." In *Chambers's Encyclopaedia*, new rev. ed. 15 vols. 11:509–10. Oxford, London: Newnes, 1967.

367. Williams, Norman Lloyd. *Sir Walter Raleigh*. London: Eyre and Spottiswoode, 1962. Philadelphia: Dufour Editions, 1963. 295 pp. Reprint. London: Penguin, 1965. Reconstructs Ralegh's life through use of his letters, public documents, diaries, and remarks by his contemporaries, with linking commentary by the author.

368. Williamson, Hugh Ross. *Sir Walter Raleigh*. London: Faber and Faber, 1951; New York: Macmillan, 1952. 215 pp. Reprint. Westport, Conn.: Greenwood, 1978.

369. Wilmer, James Jones. "Walter Raleigh, &c." In *The American Nepos: a collection of the lives of . . . men who have contributed to the discovery . . . of America*, 60–70. Baltimore: Douglas, 1805. 384 pp. 2d ed. Baltimore: Miltenberger and Vance, 1811.

370. Winstanley, William. "The Life of Sir Walter Raleigh." In *England's Worthies. Select Lives of the most Eminent Persons from Constantine the Great, to the death of Oliver Cromwel [sic], late Protector*, 250–61. London: Printed for Nath. Brooke, 1660. 613 pp. 2d ed., omitting all reference to Cromwell. London: Printed by J. C. And F. C. for Obadiah Blagrave, 1684.

371. Winton, John [John Pratt]. *Sir Walter Ralegh*. New York: Coward, McCann and Geoghegan, 1975. 352 pp. Seeks to relate Ralegh's life and literary work, while arguing for the superiority of his prose over his poetry.

372. Wood, Anthony à. "Life of Ralegh." In *Athenae Oxonienses*, 1:369–74. London: Printed for Tho. Bennet, 1691. 2 vols.

Often reprinted. Provides a colorful account characteristic of Wood.

373. Woolf, Virginia. "Sir Walter Raleigh." In *Granite and Rainbow*, 162–66. London: Hogarth Press; New York: Harcourt & Brace, 1958. 240 pp. Originally published in *Times Literary Supplement*, 15 March 1917.

374. _____. "Sir Walter Raleigh." In *Collected Essays*. 4 vols. 3:27–31. New York: Harcourt, Brace & World, 1967.

375. "Worthies of the West: Poets and Literati No. 2, Sir Walter Raleigh." *Philo-Danmonian, A Western Magazine* 1 (1830): 397–410. Quotes extensively from his prose and poems.

376. Wotton, Mabel E., ed. "Sir Walter Raleigh." In *Word Portraits of Famous Writers*, 244–47. London: Bentley, 1887. 337 pp. Emphasizes Ralegh's style of dressing.

377. No entry.

Wrangham, Francis. *See* Mortimer.

378. Wrench, Sir Evelyn. "Founders of Virginia." *National Geographic Magazine* 93 (1948): 433–62. Includes a brief biography of Ralegh, beginning with his life at court.

379. Y., Y. "Sir Walter Raleigh." *Western Antiquary* 1 (1881): 75–76.

380. Zimmermann, Eberhard August Wilhelm von. "Biographie: Sir Walter Raleigh." In *Taschenbuch der Reisen; oder, Unterhaltende Darstellung der Entdeckungen des 20 Jahrhunderts in Rücksicht der Länder-, Menschen- und Producten-kunde*, 2:293–319. Leipzig: n.p., 1817. 18 vols.

Chapter 3.

RALEGH IN ENGLAND, IRELAND, AND EUROPE: PARTICULAR TOPICS

381. Addis, John, Jr. "Raleigh At His Prison Window." *Notes and Queries*, 3d ser. 11 (1867): 55–56. Discusses the story, from the *Journal de Paris* of May 1787, of Ralegh's burning the manuscript continuation of his *History of the World* when he noted how unreliable witnesses are.

382. Ahier, Philip. *The Governorship of Sir Walter Ralegh in Jersey, 1600–1603, together with some local Raleghana*. St. Helier, Jersey: Bigwoods Printers, 1971. 253 pp. Reproduces documents connected with Ralegh's governorship, during which he visited the island only twice.

383. Aikin, Lucy. "1618." In *Memoirs of the Court of King James the First*. 2 vols. 2:86–108. London: Longman, 1822. Boston: Wells and Lilly, 1822. Describes the disastrous last year of Ralegh's life.

384. Akrigg, G. P. V. *Jacobean Pageant; or the Court of James I*, 34–47, 324–33. Cambridge, Mass.: Harvard University Press, 1962. 431 pp. Traces Ralegh's decline from the execution of Essex in 1601 to his own.

385. Alexander, J. J. "Devon County Members of Parliament, Part 4: The Tudor Period (1485–1603)." *Report and Transactions of the Devonshire Association for the Advancement of Science, Literature and Art* 47 (1915): 357–71.

386. Allen, John William. "Raleigh." In *English Political Thought 1603–1660*, 63–67. London: Methuen, 1938. 525 pp. Argues that although Ralegh believed in total freedom of action for the monarch, he approved of the custom of making law and imposing taxation only by Parliament.

387. *The Arraignment and Conviction of Sr. Walter Rawleigh, At the Kings Bench-Barre at Winchester, on the 17 of November,*

1603. Before the right Honorable the Earle of Suffolke, Lord Chamberline, the Earle of Devonshire, Lord Henry Howard, Lord Cecill, Lord Wottom, Sir John Stanhope, Lord Chiefe Justice of the Common-Pleas, Popham and Andrewes, Justice Gandy, Justice Warberton, Sir William Wade, Commissioners. London: Printed by William Wilson for Abel Roper, 1648. 38 pp. Also contains "The Proceedings against" Ralegh in 1618, an account of his execution, and his letter to King James.

388. B. "Raleigh Suspected of Complicity in the Gunpowder Treason." *Athenaeum* (1858): 297–98. Dismisses the charge and publishes a newly noticed letter by Ralegh denying any arrangements with Captain Edmund Whitelock.

389. B., C. R. "Sir Walter Raleigh at Sherborne." *Gentleman's Magazine* 40 (1853): 434–42; 41 (1854): 17–23.

390. B., W. A. "The Ralegh Tercentenary." *Field* 66 (1918): 374.

391. Bagwell, Richard. *Ireland Under the Tudors, With a Succinct Account of the Earlier History.* 3 vols. London: Longmans, 1885–90. Reprint. London: Holland Press, 1963. Discusses, in the third volume, Ralegh's role in the Desmond War, the establishment of his estates in Munster, and their destruction in the Tyrone Uprising.

392. Baird, C. W. "A Relic of One of the 'Regicide' Judges." *Magazine of American History*, 1886, 345–46. Describes a copy of Ralegh's *History* which Colonel John Dixwell, one of the judges who condemned Charles I to death, bequeathed to the Reverend James Pierpont in New Haven.

393. Bakeless, John. *Christopher Marlowe: The Man in His Time.* New York: William Morrow, 1937. 404 pp. Discusses Marlowe's friendship with Ralegh.

394. ———. *The Tragicall History of Christopher Marlowe.* 2 vols. 1:127–40, passim. Cambridge, Mass.: Harvard University Press, 1942. Discusses Marlowe's involvement with Ralegh and his circle and denies that Ralegh had any part in Marlowe's murder.

395. Baker, Herschel. *The Race of Time: Three Lectures on Renaissance Historiography*, 35–41. Toronto: University of Toronto Press, 1967. 110 pp. Notes Ralegh's juxtaposition in his *History* of the truth of Scripture and the deceptiveness of the natural world.

396. Baker, Marian Elizabeth. *English Factional Politics, 1596–1599.*

Abstract of Master's thesis, University of Illinois, 1932. 10 pp. Discusses Ralegh's involvement in the disputes between the Cecil and Essex factions.

397. Bald, R. C. *John Donne: A Life*, 82–83, 86–92. New York: Oxford University Press, 1970. 627 pp. Discusses Ralegh's service in the Cadiz and Islands expeditions and suggests Donne may have been in one of the ships in the squadron led by Ralegh.

398. Baring-Gould, Sabine. "Sir 'Judas' Stukeley." In *Devonshire Characters and Strange Events*, 278–85. London and New York: John Lane, 1908, 1913. 813 pp. Discusses the career of Sir Lewis Stukeley, who acquired the nickname "Sir Judas" because he arrested his cousin Ralegh after his return from Guiana in 1618 and received £500 to obtain evidence damaging to Ralegh.

399. Baring-Gould, Sabine, and R. Twigge. *An Armory of the Western Counties*, 40. Exeter: Commin, 1898. 115 pp. Discusses two branches of the Ralegh family in the sixteenth century.

400. Barlow, Jem. "Raleigh's House at Youghal." *Landmark* 5 (1923): 805–7. Describes Youghal and the house where Ralegh reputedly lived.

401. Barnham, James C. "Drake and Raleigh." *Western Antiquary* 2 (1862): 79. Claims that Ralegh introduced the potato to Europe.

402. Barrington, Michael. " 'The Most High Spirited Man on Earth': Sir Richard Grenville's Last Fight, September 1591." *Mariner's Mirror* 36 (1950): 350–53.

403. Barrow, John. "Sir Walter Raleigh: 1570–96." In *Memoirs of the Naval Worthies of Queen Elizabeth's Reign*, 377–418. London: John Murray, 1845. 495 pp.

404. Bates, William. "Raleigh At His Prison Window." *Notes and Queries* 11 (1867): 201–2. Reprints the story of Ralegh's burning the manuscript continuation of his *History of the World*.

405. Batho, G. R. "The Wizard Earl in the Tower, 1605–21." *History Today* 6 (1956): 344–51. Describes Henry Percy's activities while imprisoned in the Tower concurrently with Ralegh.

406. _____. "The Library of the 'Wizard' Earl: Henry Percy, Ninth

Earl of Northumberland (1564–1632)." *Library*, 5th ser. 15 (1960): 246–61.

407. _____, ed. *The Household Papers of Henry Percy, Ninth Earl of Northumberland (1564–1632)*. London: Officers of the Royal Historical Society, 1962. 190 pp. Occasionally refers to Ralegh and his servants.

408. Bayley, A. R. "Sir Walter Raleigh and Brixton." *Notes and Queries* 154 (1928): 337–38. Declares that until about 1887 a Jacobean house called the Raleigh House stood in Brixton, but it was probably the home of Captain George Ralegh.

409. _____. "Sir Walter Raleigh and Brixton." *Notes and Queries* 155 (1928): 31. Adds to the preceding item that the "Raleigh House" was a square red-brick Jacobean structure, with later additions.

410. Beau, Jean. "La Religion de Sir Walter Ralegh." *Revue Anglo-Américaine* 11 (1934): 410–22. Argues that Ralegh's intellectual independence may have prevented his believing in anything more particular than in a moral force governing the universe, until his lengthy incarceration led him to believe in a providential God not limited by any sectarian dogma.

411. Bedwell, C. E. A. *A Brief History of the Middle Temple*, 34–36. London: Butterworth, 1909. 132 pp.

412. Bell, Douglas. *Elizabethan Seamen*, 273–91. London: Longmans, Green, 1936. 323 pp. Describes Ralegh's downfall and execution.

413. Bellot, Hugh H. L. *The Inner and Middle Temple*, 288–90. London: Methuen, 1902. 412 pp.

414. Benians, E. A. "Raleigh: Died 29 October 1618." *Geographical Journal* 52 (1918): 277–87. Pays tribute to Ralegh for seeing that England's road to greatness lay in overseas colonizing, although that also led to his undoing.

415. Bentham, Thomas. "Ralegh's Burial Place." *Times Literary Supplement*, 20 December 1923, 896. Argues for Beddington, Surrey, as opposed to St. Margaret's, Westminster.

416. Bethell, Samuel L. *The Cultural Revolution of the Seventeenth Century*, 41, 45–48. London: Dobson, 1951. 161 pp. Discusses Ralegh's concept of the universe.

417. Birch, T. *The Court and Times of James the First*. 2 vols. 1:95–106. London: Colburn, 1848. Includes two Chamberlain letters

that mention Ralegh's execution.

418. "Birthplace of Sir Walter Ralegh." *Penny Magazine* 4 (1835): 52.

419. No entry.

420. Black, John Bennett. *The Reign of Elizabeth, 1558–1603.* Oxford: Clarendon Press, 1936. 448 pp. Reprints. 1937, 1945, 1949, 1952. 2d ed. 1959. Occasionally refers to Ralegh.

421. Blathwayt, Margaret. "Ralegh and the Potato." *Wide Awake* 28 (1889): 313–23.

422. Boas, F. S. "New Light on Sir Walter Raleigh." *Literature* [later *Times Literary Supplement*], 11 August 1900, 96–98; 18 August 1900, 113–14.

423. ———. *Marlowe and His Circle,* 84–91. Oxford: Clarendon Press, 1929. 159 pp. Discusses the Cerne Abbas investigation of Ralegh's religion and Marlowe's association with Ralegh and the "School of Night."

424. ———. "The 'Atheism' of Chomley, Raleigh, and Marlowe." In *Christopher Marlowe: A Biographical and Critical Study,* 253–64. Oxford: Clarendon Press, 1940. 336 pp. Discusses Marlowe's hostility to religion and finds it in contrast to Ralegh's beliefs in the divinity of the soul and the underlying truth of scripture.

425. Bonar, James. *Theories of Population from Raleigh to Arthur Young.* London: Allen & Unwin; New York: Greenberg, [1931]. 253 pp. Maintains that Ralegh's founding of Virginia was "a eugenic contribution" to the future U.S.A., and that his *History of the World* prefigures ideas of Liebnitz and Charles Darwin about the individual and the species.

426. Borrow, George. "Sir Walter Raleigh; Tried at Winchester, Upon an Indictment of High Treason, in the First Year of the Reign of James I." In *Celebrated Trials and Remarkable Cases of Criminal Jurisprudence,* edited by Edward Hale Bierstadt. 2 vols. 1:37–101. New York: Payson and Clarke, 1928.

427. Boulind, R. H. "The Crompster in Literature and Pictures." *Mariner's Mirror* 54 (1968): 3–17. Observes that in his "Discourse of the Invention of Ships," Ralegh describes the English crompster or hog, a heavily armed, highly maneuverable ship for use along coasts.

428. Bounsall, W. M. *Devonshire: containing historical, biographical, and descriptive notices . . . with notices of the*

pedigree of the Rolle, Raleigh, and Courtenay families, 129–235. Exeter: Drayton, [c. 1862]. 362 pp. Discusses Ralegh's pedigree and life.

429. Bovill, E. W. "The *Madre De Dios.*" *Mariner's Mirror* 54 (1968): 129–52. Discusses the capture of this Portugese galleon, an expedition which Ralegh was removed from commanding because of Queen Elizabeth's anger at his marriage, although he was sent to Dartmouth to stop the plundering of the ship.

430. Bowen, Catherine Drinker. "The Lion and the Throne: The Trial of Sir Walter Ralegh." *Atlantic Monthly* 198 (1956): 63–73. Discusses the 1603 treason trial of Ralegh in which he was found guilty and ordered beheaded.

431. ———. *The Lion and the Throne: The Life and Times of Sir Edward Coke (1552–1634)*, 190–224. Boston: Little, Brown, 1957. 652 pp. Includes a fuller account of Ralegh's treason trial than in the preceding item.

432. ———. "Trial of Sir Walter Ralegh." Excerpts from *The Lion and the Throne*, in *Voices in Court: A Treasury of the Bench, the Bar, and the Courtroom*, edited by William H. Davenport, 308–29. New York: Macmillan, 1958. 588 pp.

433. ———. *Francis Bacon: The Temper of a Man*, 164–66. Boston: Little, Brown, 1963. 245 pp. Defends Bacon's involvement in Ralegh's execution.

434. Bowers, R. H. "Ralegh's Last Speech: The 'Elms' Document." *Review of English Studies*, n.s. 2 (1951): 209–16. Reproduces, from the Pierpont Morgan library, a version made by Edmund Elms of Ralegh's last speech before his execution.

435. Boxer, C. R. "The Taking of the *Madre De Deus*, 1592." *Mariner's Mirror* 67 (1981): 82–84. Employs hitherto unused Portuguese sources, which reveal the roles of Fernão de Mendoça and Duarte Gomes de Solis.

436. Bradridge, C. Kingsley. "A Great Devonian: Sir Walter Raleigh." *Devonia* 3 (1905): 141–45.

437. Bremer, Francis, Jr. "Thomas Hariot: American Adventurer and Renaissance Scientist." *History Today* 29 (1979): 639–47. Traces Hariot's association with Ralegh from 1583 to 1618.

438. Brenan, Gerald. *A History of the House of Percy*. 2 vols. 2:164–68. London: Freemantle, 1902. Describes the relationship of Ralegh and Northumberland.

439. Brewer, David J. *The World's Best Orations.* 10 vols. 4:1348–54, 9:3280–83. St. Louis: Kaiser, 1899. Includes Coke's prosecution of Ralegh and Ralegh's "Speech on the Scaffold."

440. Brushfield, T. N. "Notes on the Ralegh Family." *Report and Transactions of the Devonshire Association for the Advancement of Science, Literature, and Art* 15 (1883): 163–79.

441. ———. "London and Suburban Residences of Sir W. Ralegh." *Western Antiquary* 4 (1884): 83–87, 109–12; 7 (1887): 73–74. Notes that in John Thorpe's *Book of Plans,* preserved in the Soane Museum in Lincoln's Inn Fields, there is a sketch of a large house, lettered "Sr. Walter Rawley," St. James, and identifies eleven houses where Ralegh resided or may have.

442. ———. "Sir Walter Ralegh." *Western Antiquary* 3 (1884): 196–97. Observes that the order for Ralegh's arrest after his return from Guiana was signed by King James on 9 June 1618 and again on 11 June.

443. ———. "Sir W. Ralegh: A Plea for a Surname." *Report and Transactions of the Devonshire Association for the Advancement of Science, Literature, and Art* 18 (1886): 450–61. Presents evidence that until 1583 Ralegh's autograph appears as "Rauley" or some slight variant, but from the year of his knighthood he regularly signed his name "Ralegh."

444. ———. "The Birthplace of Sir Walter Ralegh." *Report and Transactions of the Devonshire Association for the Advancement of Science, Literature, and Art* 21 (1889): 312–30. Reports that the letter in Ralegh's own writing, stating that he was born at Hayes Barton, is now in the Royal Albert Memorial Museum at Exeter.

445. ———. "Sale of Important Properties." *Western Antiquary* 8 (1889): 238–39. Explains that, though Fardell in Devonshire was the home of the Raleghs for several centuries, Sir Walter's father left it and moved to Hayes: hence, despite local tradition, Fardell was not Sir Walter's seat.

446. ———. "Ralegh v. Raleigh." *Athenaeum,* no. 3401 (1892): 919–20. Again cites much evidence for the spelling Ralegh.

447. ———. "Raleigh, Walter v. Slade, Roger." *Devon Notes and Queries* 1 (1900): 33–35. Describes a chancery suit.

448. ———. "Remarks on the Ancestry of Sir Walter Ralegh." *Report and Transactions of the Devonshire Association for the*

Advancement of Science, Literature, and Art 32 (1900): 309–40.

449. ———. "Sir Walter de Ralegh, knight, ob. 1301." *Report and Transactions of the Devonshire Association for the Advancement of Science, Literature, and Art* 34 (1902): 455–81.

450. ———. "The History of Durham House." *Report and Transactions of the Devonshire Association for the Advancement of Science, Literature, and Art* 35 (1903): 539–80. Discusses Ralegh's principal residence in London.

451. ———. "Ralegh and Camden." *Devon Notes and Queries* 3 (1904): 124–25. Claims that the defacing of Camden's bust was not done by Ralegh.

452. ———. "Sir Walter Ralegh and Buried Treasure." *Report and Transactions of the Devonshire Association for the Advancement of Science, Literature, and Art* 36 (1904): 95.

453. ———. "Three State Documents Relating to the Arrest and Execution of Sir Walter Ralegh in 1618." *Report and Transactions of the Devonshire Association for the Advancement of Science, Literature, and Art* 37 (1905): 284–324; 38 (1906): 416–90. Reprint. *Raleghana*, pt. 7. Analyzes King James's *Declaration*, Stukeley's *Appollogie*, and his *Petition*.

454. ———. "Was Sir Walter Ralegh a Lawyer?" *Devon Notes and Queries* 4 (1906): 46–48.

455. ———. "The Execution of Sir Walter Ralegh and Some of the Events that Followed It." *Report and Transactions of the Devonshire Association for the Advancement of Science, Literature, and Art* 34 (1907): 242–63. Reprint. *Raleghana*, pt. 8.

456. ———. "The Execution of Sir W. Ralegh: 'Written by one of his Captains.'" *Devon and Cornwall Notes and Queries* 5 (1908): 212–13.

457. ———. "Ralegh Miscellanea." *Report and Transactions of the Devonshire Association for the Advancement of Science, Literature, and Art* 41 (1909): 179–214.

458. ———. "Ralegh Miscellanea: Part II." *Report and Transactions of the Devonshire Association for the Advancement of Science, Literature, and Art* 42 (1910): 361–82.

459. Bryant, Arthur. *The Elizabethan Deliverance*. London: William

Collins, 1980. 232 pp. Discusses Ralegh's part in expeditions against the Armada, and to Roanoke and Guiana.

460. Brydges, Sir Egerton. "The Secret Correspondence of Robert Cecil with James VI of Scotland, published 1766." In *Censura Literaria*. 10 vols. 2:193–206. London: Longmans, 1805–9. Reveals Cecil's plots against Ralegh.

461. Buckley, George T. "The Atheism of Sir Walter Raleigh." In *Atheism in the English Renaissance*, 137–52. Chicago: University of Chicago Press, 1932. 163 pp. Specifies that the first charge of atheism against Ralegh came from a Jesuit spy in 1592, but the hearing at Cerne Abbas in 1594 produced no evidence of atheism against Ralegh, nor did his trial in 1603. Argues that though he may in youth have had religious doubts, in maturity he was a Christian apologist, as his writings attest.

462. B[urtt], J. "Sir Walter Raleigh at Sherborne." *Gentleman's Magazine* 2 (1853): 435–43; 1 (1854): 17–23. Describes Ralegh's acquisition of this residence and his disputes and lawsuits with his steward, John Meere.

463. Butler, Jon. "Sir Walter Raleigh in Defense of Quaker Orthodoxy: A Phineas Pemberton Letter of 1694." *Quaker History* 66 (1977): 106–15. Notes that Pemberton sought to discredit George Keith with the Quakers in London by citing Ralegh's *History* to expose Keith as an incompetent and dangerous scholar.

464. Cadwallader, Laura Hanes. *The Career of the Earl of Essex From the Islands Voyage in 1597 to His Execution in 1601*. Philadelphia: University of Pennsylvania, 1923. 128 pp. Considers Ralegh's role in the Islands Voyage of 1597 commanded by Essex.

465. Callender, Geoffrey. "Raleigh's Boyhood." *Times Literary Supplement*, 28 March 1918, 153. Believes that Ralegh as a small boy did not move to Exeter with his family but grew up at the farmhouse at East Budleigh.

466. ———. "The Battle of Flores." *History*, n.s. 4 (1919): 91–102. Criticizes Grenville's role in the battle but acknowledges that his fame is assured because of Ralegh's vivid *Report of the Fight about the Azores*.

467. Campbell, Lily B. "The Use of Historical Patterns in the Reign of Elizabeth." *Huntington Library Quarterly* 1 (1937): 135–67. Describes Elizabethan attitudes towards history as revealed

in the Preface to Ralegh's *History of the World*.

468. _____. *Shakespeare's "Histories": Mirrors of Elizabethan Policy*, 78–84, 122–23. San Marino, Calif.: Huntington Library, 1947. 346 pp. Reprint. 1958. Praises Ralegh's *History of the World* as the epitome of the historiographical tradition.

469. Canning, Albert S. G. "Spenser and Raleigh," 49–56. In *Literary Influence in British History: A Historical Sketch*. London: Unwin, 1904. 280 pp. Concludes that Spenser condoned Ralegh's suppression of Catholics in Ireland.

470. Carlyle, Thomas. "Execution of Ralegh." In *Historical Sketches of Notable Persons and Events in the Reigns of James I and Charles I*, 140–41. New York: Scribner, 1898. 354 pp. Reprinted in *Devonian Year Book* (1920).

471–472. No entries.

473. Castle, W. C. "Loss of the *Revenge*." *Journal of the Royal United Service Institute* 1 (1926): 38–41. Describes the battle but does not mention Ralegh's account.

474. Caulfield, Richard. *Council Book of the Corporation of Youghal*. Guildford, Surrey: Billings, 1878. 1191 pp. Provides picture and description of Ralegh's house in Ireland, and some Ralegh records.

475. Cavendish, Richard, ed. *Legends of the World: A Cyclopedia of the Enduring Myths, Legends, and Sagas of Mankind*. London: Orbis Publishing; New York: Schocken Books, 1982. 433 pp. Discusses the Eldorado myth that Ralegh pursued in Guiana.

476. Cecil, Algernon. "Ralegh." In *A Life of Robert Cecil, First Earl of Salisbury*, 192–212. London: Murray, 1915. 406 pp.

477. Chamberlain, John. *The Letters of John Chamberlain*, edited by Norman Egbert McClure. 2 vols. 2:175–80. Philadelphia: American Philosophical Society, 1939. Mentions Ralegh in many letters and discusses events around his execution.

478. Chamberlin, Frederick. *Elizabeth and Leycester*, 266. New York: Dodd, Mead, 1939. 487 pp. Cites a letter by Ralegh.

479. Chaudhuri, Sukanta. *Infirm Glory: Shakespeare and the Renaissance Image of Man*, 60–63. Oxford: Clarendon Press, 1981. 231 pp. Using Ralegh's *History of the World* and *A Treatise of the Soul*, he argues that Ralegh remained skeptical of man's ability to know truth through reason and characterizes his vision as "other-worldly."

480. Chidsey, Donald Barr. *Sir Humphrey Gilbert: Elizabeth's*

Racketeer. New York: Harper, 1932. 204 pp. Describes the nautical and privateering world in which Ralegh and his half-brother grew up.

481. Chope, R. Pearse. "New Light on Sir Richard Grenville." *Report and Transactions of the Devonshire Association for the Advancement of Science, Literature, and Art* 49 (1917): 210–82.

482. Chute, Marchette. *Ben Jonson of Westminster*, 198–200. New York: Dutton, 1953. 380 pp. Reprint. 1960. Discusses the friendship of Bacon and Ralegh.

483. Clapham, John. *Elizabeth of England: Certain Observations Concerning the Life and Reign of Queen Elizabeth*, edited by Evelyn Plummer Read and Conyers Read, 92–94. Philadelphia: University of Pennsylvania Press, 1951. 125 pp. Discusses Ralegh's role at court.

484. Clements, H. G. J. "Local Vestiges of Sir Walter Raleigh." *Report and Transactions of the Devonshire Association for the Advancement of Science, Literature, and Art* 6 (1873): 223–31.

485. Collier, J. Payne. "Additional Information Respecting the Life and Services of Sir Walter Raleigh." *Archaeologia* 34 (1852): 149–59. Reprints documents dealing with the *Ark Raleigh*, Ralegh's role as Vice-Admiral, and the grants to him of Sherborne Castle and a wine license.

486. _____. "Continuation of New Materials for a Life of Sir Walter Raleigh." *Archaeologia* 34 (1852): 160–70. Publishes letters by Ralegh and documents from the 1590s.

487. _____. "Sir Walter Raleigh, his Character, Services and Advancement; with new Particulars of his Life." *Archaeologia* 34 (1852): 137–48. Reproduces documents covering the period from Ralegh's Middle Temple days to the time of his knighthood.

488. _____. "Conclusion of New Materials for a Life of Sir Walter Raleigh." *Archaeologia* 35 (1853): 213–22. Reprinted separately. London: Nichols, 1853. Provides letters and documents relating chiefly to Ralegh's years in the Tower.

489. _____. "Sir Walter Raleigh and Sir Francis Vere." *Archaeologia* 35 (1853): 368–78. Reprint. London: Nichols, 1853. Discusses Ralegh's relations with Vere concerning renewal of his wine license and the expeditions against Cadiz in 1596 and the Islands Voyage in 1597.

490. _____. "Documents, Etc. Regarding Sir Walter Raleigh." *Notes and Queries*, 3d ser. 5 (1864): 108–9. Includes a letter by Ralegh about the sighting of the Armada and two letters to him from John Gilbert.

491. _____. "Particulars Regarding Sir Walter Raleigh." *Notes and Queries*, 3d ser. 5 (1864): 7–8. Reports previously unpublished Raleghana.

492. _____. "Sir Walter Raleigh. Additional Papers." *Notes and Queries*, 3d ser. 5 (1864): 207–8.

493. _____. "Sir Walter Raleigh. New Particulars." *Notes and Queries*, 3d ser. 5 (1864): 352. Reprints documents including the order that Ralegh be paid for letters brought to Whitehall in 1581, and theorizes that George Gascoigne induced Ralegh to turn from the law to the army.

494. Collins, D. C. *A Handlist of News Pamphlets 1590–1610*. London: South-West Essex Technical College, 1943. 129 pp. Considers Ralegh's *Report of the Fight about the Azores* almost a government blue book meant to be read in England and abroad, and cites a Spanish notice of it.

495. Collis, Louise. "Raleigh." In *Seven in the Tower*, 110–52. London: Faber and Faber, 1958. 208 pp. Reprint. New York: Roy, 1960.

496. Corbett, Julian S. *The Successors of Drake*. London and New York: Longmans, Green, 1900. 464 pp. Reprints. 1916, 1919. Maintains that however high Ralegh's reputation became later, many of his contemporaries regarded him as a Jonah and a marplot who lacked staunchness at sea.

497. _____. "The Elizabethan Origin of Ralegh's Instructions." In *Fighting Instructions, 1530–1816*, 27–45. London: Navy Records Society, 1905. 366 pp. Maintains that the instructions to Ralegh's fleet in 1617, except those dealing specifically with the Guiana voyage, followed early Elizabethan precedent.

498. _____, ed. *Papers Relating to the Navy During the Spanish War 1585–1587*. London: Navy Records Society 1898. 363 pp. Includes documents referring to Drake's bringing home the Lane colony and to various activities of Ralegh's.

499. Cottell, W. H. "Sir Walter Ralegh." *Western Antiquary* 6 (1886): 79. Prints a letter of 10 October 1597 from Amyas Cottell to Lady Ralegh, which reports that the Lord Warden was well.

500. Cotton, William, and Henry Woollcombe. *Gleanings from the*

Municipal and Cathedral Records Relative to the History of the City of Exeter. Exeter: Townsend, 1877. 208 pp., 38 pp. Contains an account of Sir Henry Ralegh de Ralegh and how he came to be buried in Exeter Cathedral.

501. Covington, Nina Holland. "Spelling of Raleigh." *North Carolina Booklet* 23 (1926): 86–87. Claims that Sir Walter never spelled his name Raleigh and that his name was pronounced "Rawly."

502. Croker, Thomas Crofton, ed. *The Popular Songs of Ireland.* London: Colburn, 1839. 340 pp. Argues that Ralegh introduced the potato at Youghal.

503. Cunningham, Dolora G. "The Ralegh Group and the History of Elizabethan Skeptical Thought." In *American Philosophical Society Yearbook,* 1969, 551–52.

504. Danchin, F. C. "Etudes Critiques sur Christopher Marlowe II: Quelques Documents concernant les Dramaturges Thomas Kyd et Christopher Marlowe, et Sir Walter Raleigh et son Entourage." *Revue Germanique* 9 (1913): 566–87. Considers the 1593–94 charges that Ralegh was an atheist.

505. Davies, T. E. "Sir Walter Raleigh." *Devon and Cornwall Notes and Queries* 27 (1956): 22. Reports that in the Baptismal Registers of the Church of St. Mary, Beddington, Surrey, appears the entry: "1565 April 16 Elizabeth Throgmorton."

506. Day, George H. "The Trial of Sir Walter Ralegh." *Connecticut Bar Journal* 32 (1958): 142–59. Draws largely on Jardine's account.

507. Day, Robert. "Notes on Youghal." *Journal of the Royal Society of Antiquaries of Ireland,* 5th ser. 13 (1904): 325. Claims that Ralegh introduced the potato there and sat under yew-trees at Myrtle Grove, smoking tobacco.

508. *A Declaration of the Demeanor and Cariage of Sir Walter Raleigh, Knight, as well in his Voyage, as in, and sithence his Returne; And of the true motiues and inducements which occasioned his Maiestie to Proceed in doing Iustice vpon him, as hath bene done.* London: Printed by Bonham Norton and John Bill, 1618. 68 pp. Several imprints appeared in 1618, including one partly in smaller type, of only 63 pp., and a Dutch translation (see *Verclaringe*) in 1619. The *Declaration* was reprinted in the *Harleian Miscellany* and Somers' *Collection of Tracts,* both 1809, and in Spedding's *Lord*

Bacon's Life and Letters, 1872, though in a letter on page 378 Bacon makes clear that King James was in large part the author of this attempted justification of his actions against Ralegh.

509. Delderfield, Eric R. *The Raleigh Country*. Exmouth: Raleigh Press, 1949. 96 pp. Other eds. 1950, 1953, 1959, 1966. Describes South Devon, with numerous illustrations.

510. ———. "Sherbourne Castle; Sir Walter Raleigh's Castle." In *West Country Historic Houses and Their Families*. 2 vols. 2:97–102. Newton Abbot, Devon: David & Charles, 1968. Provides an account with pictures.

511. Denton, W. "Sir Walter Raleigh." *Notes and Queries* 11 (1855): 262. Discusses a document signed in 1616 by Ralegh, his wife and his son Walter, conveying property in Surrey to Thomas Plummer for £600, apparently to finance his Orinoco voyage.

512. Dickson, Sarah Augusta. *Panacea or Precious Bane: Tobacco in Sixteenth Century Literature*, 167–74. New York: New York Public Library, 1954. 227 pp. Relates legends concerning Ralegh and tobacco.

513. "Different Spelling of Ralegh's Name." *Proceedings of the Massachusetts Historical Society* 15 (1876–77): 383–85. Claims that the "i" was added to Ralegh by Sir Walter's son Carew.

514. Dixon, W. Hepworth. *Her Majesty's Tower*. 4 vols. 1:334–92. London: Hurst and Balckett, 1869–71. Many subsequent editions. Describes Ralegh's life in the Tower of London.

515. Dodds, M. H. "Sir Walter Raleigh." *Notes and Queries* 159 (1930): 14. Reports references to Ralegh in the accounts of the ninth Earl of Northumberland.

516. Dorris, George E. "Sir Walter Enjoying." *Notes and Queries*, n.s. 12 (1965): 381–82. Observes that Aubrey's scandalous "swisser swatter" anecdote about Ralegh was set to music by Henry Purcell in a catch published in 1701.

517. Douglas, W. O. "Too Many Short Cuts; Trial of Sir Walter Raleigh." *New Republic* 129 (1953): 9–11.

518. Drake, Henry H. "Drake, Tobacco, and Potatoes." *Western Antiquary* 2 (1882): 88. Maintains that Francis Drake brought back tobacco and the potato with the Roanoke colonists in 1586.

519. Drake, Sir William Richard. "Notes upon the Capture of 'The Great Carrack' in 1592." *Archaeologia* 33 (1849): 209–40.

Reprinted separately. London: Nichols, 1850. Reprints and discusses some documents concerning this successful expedition, command of which was taken from Ralegh after he had planned it.

520. Du Cann, Charles Garfield Lott. "The King Versus Raleigh." In *English Treason Trials*, 89–115. London: Muller, 1964. 272 pp. American title. *Famous Treason Trials*. New York: Walker, 1965.

521. Dukes, W. B. "Ralegh's *History of the World.*" *Times Literary Supplement*, 25 January 1934, 60. Discusses changes in the portrait on the title page.

522. Dunaway, Philip, and George De Kay, eds. *Turning Point: Fateful Moments That Revealed Men and Made History*, 112–14. New York: Random House, 1958. 432 pp. Cites Ralegh's letter to his wife in 1603 after he had been sentenced to death.

523. Duncan, Ronald. *Devon and Cornwall*, 47–51. London: Batsford, 1966. 191 pp.

524. Durant, David N. *Arbella Stuart: A Rival to the Queen.* London: Weidenfield and Nicolson, 1978. 242 pp. Argues that whether Ralegh was involved in the "Main" plot to place Arabella (Arbella) on the throne or not—for which plot he was condemned to death in 1603—its success would have suited him.

525. E., G. "Raleigh—Pronunciation." *Notes and Queries* 195 (1950): 481. Asserts that while the spelling of Ralegh's name varied, it was regularly pronounced "Rawly" in his era.

526. Eagleston, Arthur John. *The Channel Islands under Tudor Government, 1485–1642: A Study in Administrative History.* Cambridge: Cambridge University Press, 1949. 194 pp. Briefly discusses Ralegh's governorship of Jersey, where tradition credits him with initiating the trade between Jersey and Newfoundland.

527. Eccles, Mark. *Christopher Marlowe in London*, 62–63. Cambridge, Mass.: Harvard University Press, 1934. 185 pp. Notes that one of the participants in Essex's rebellion saved his own life by purchasing a pardon from Ralegh.

528. _____. "Marlowe in Kentish Tradition." *Notes and Queries* 169 (1935): 39–41. Mentions that in a 1640 entry in a commonplace book compiled by Henry Oxinden, Ralegh is

termed "an atheist in his younger days," a remark attributed to Simon Aldrich, a minister at Canterbury.

529. _____. "Sir Walter Ralegh." In *Brief Lives: Tudor and Stuart Authors. Studies in Philology* Texts and Studies Series 80 (1982): 110–11. Reports Ralegh's being robbed, posting bail for a servant, and other matters discovered in the Public Record Office in England.

530. Edwards, Edward. *Diocesan Records and Historical Searchers: Being a correspondence with the Right Reverend the Lord Bishop of Salisbury and the Registrars of the See and Chapter, in relation to a recent Life of Sir Walter Ralegh . . . with a brief elucidatory statement.* London: Clay and Taylor, 1868. 24 pp. Describes the author's difficulties in obtaining access to the records of the Chapter Library at Salisbury while writing his biography of Ralegh.

531. _____. "New Facts in the Biography of Ralegh, Drawn from the Papers of the Marquis of Salisbury at Hatfield House." *St. Paul's Magazine* 2 (1868): 185–97. Summarizes facts included in the author's biography of Ralegh.

532. Eliot, John. *The Monarchie of Man, printed from the author's manuscript in the Harleian Collection, No. 2228,* edited by A. B. Grosart. 2 vols. London: Chiswick Press, 1879. Praises Ralegh's conduct at his execution, which Eliot witnessed.

533. Ellis-Fermor, Una M. "Marlowe in the Eyes of his Contemporaries." In *Christopher Marlowe,* appendix II, 156–68. London: Methuen, 1927. 172 pp. Considers the charges of atheism brought against Ralegh.

534. Emden, Cecil Stuart. "Sir Walter Ralegh: His Friends at Oriel." In *Oriel Papers,* 9–21. Oxford: Clarendon Press, 1948. 223 pp. Reports that Ralegh appears to have entered Oriel College in late 1571 or early 1572 and left in 1574.

535. Esler, Anthony. *The Aspiring Mind of the Elizabethan Younger Generation.* Durham: Duke University Press, 1966. 266 pp. Sees desire for power and hunger for glory as traits of Ralegh's generation, though he later expressed disillusionment with them.

536. "The Execution of Sir Walter Raleigh." In *The Dying Speeches and Behaviour of the Several State Prisoners that have been Executed the last 300 years. With their several characters from*

the best historians as Cambden, Spotswood, Clarendon, Sprat,
Burnet, &c., and a table shewing how the respective sentences
were executed, and which of them were mitigated, or pardon'd.
Being a proper supplement to the State-tryals, 59–67.* London:
Printed for Brotherton and Meadows, 1720. 495 pp.

537. F., R. J. "Raleigh Family." *Western Antiquary* 5 (1886): 298.
Cites inscription on the grave of Elizabeth Raleigh,
granddaughter of Sir Walter, at Church of St. Martin Cheriton,
Kent (in July issue Brushfield observes that she had to be Sir
Walter's great-granddaughter).

538. Falls, Cyril. *Elizabeth's Irish Wars.* London: Methuen, 1950.
362 pp. Occasionally mentions Ralegh.

539. Ferguson, Arthur B. *Clio Unbound: Perception of the Social and
Cultural Past in Renaissance England,* 68–77. Durham: Duke
University Press, 1979. 443 pp. Discusses Ralegh's interest in
the relationship between first and second causes in history.

540. Fink, Zera S. *The Classical Republicans: An Essay in the
Recovery of a Pattern of Thought in Seventeenth-Century
England,* 23–24. Evanston, Ill.: Northwestern University Press,
1945. 229 pp. Considers Ralegh's ideas on the power of the
populace in government.

541. Firth, Charles. "Sir Walter Raleigh's *History of the World.*"
Proceedings of the British Academy 8 (1918): 427–46. Argues
that Ralegh combined Ciceronian and providential concepts of
history.

542. Fisher, Lois H. *A Literary Gazetteer of England.* New York:
McGraw-Hill, 1980. 740 pp. Describes over thirty places
associated with Ralegh.

543. Flood, William H. Grattan. "The Warden's House, Youghal."
Journal of the Royal Society of Antiquaries of Ireland, 5th ser.
14: (1904): 73–74. Says that Orpen was correct in identifying
Myrtle Grove as Ralegh's house, that Ralegh lived less than six
months in Youghal, that his duties as mayor were performed by
deputy, and that Sir Richard Boyle did not acquire College
House by deed of 1602 but by illegal gift in 1604 while Ralegh
was in the Tower.

544. Floyer, J. K. "Two Devonshire Papists in the Time of Queen
Elizabeth." *Report and Transactions of the Devonshire
Association for the Advancement of Science, Literature, and
Art* 50 (1918): 611–20. Concerns Ralegh at Youghal.

545. Foard, James T. "Some Phases in the Life of Sir Walter Raleigh." *Manchester Quarterly* 21 (1895): 97–130.

546. Forman, W. Courthope. "Sir Walter Raleigh and Brixton." *Notes and Queries* 154 (1928): 411–12. Says Ternant confuses Raleigh Hall with Raleigh House, which stood in twelve acres exactly opposite the Cornwall Road and is also demolished.

547. Fowler, Joseph. "Sir Walter Ralegh's Sojourn in 'Fortune's Fold.' " In *Mediaeval Sherborne*, 369–401. Dorchester: Longmans, 1951. 409 pp. Discusses Ralegh's residence at Sherborne.

548. Francis, René. *The Story of the Tower of London*, 178–83. London: Harrap, 1915. 268 pp. Says that Ralegh was imprisoned in the Bloody Tower.

549. Franklin, Charles [Frank Hugh Usher]. "Sir Walter Raleigh." In *World-Famous Trials*, 133–52. New York: Taplinger; London: Odhams, 1966. 320 pp.

550. French, J. Milton. "Raleigh, Frobisher and the Great Carrack of Spain." *Notes and Queries* 174 (1938): 327–30. Reprints the bill and answer to an action brought in 1616 by a member of Frobisher's family claiming that Ralegh had failed to repay Frobisher his proper share in the spoils of the capture of the *Madre de Dios* by Ralegh's fleet in 1592.

551. French, Peter J. *John Dee: The World of an Elizabethan Magus*, 171–72. London: Routledge and Kegan Paul, 1972. 243 pp. Discusses Ralegh's relationship with John Dee.

552. Fussner, F. Smith. "Sir Walter Ralegh and Universal History." In *The Historical Revolution: English Historical Writing and Thought, 1580–1640*, 191–210. New York: Columbia University Press, 1962. 343 pp.

553. Fynmore, R. J. "Sir Walter Raleigh and Queen Elizabeth at Sandgate." *Notes and Queries*, 12th ser. 5 (1919): 96. Describes the queen's visit in August 1573 to Saltwood Castle, where she and Ralegh danced the saraband, and she rode from Sandgate on a pillion behind Ralegh; town accounts show that ten pence was paid for shoeing Ralegh's horse.

554. Gardiner, S. R. "Raleigh's Last Voyage." In *History of England from the Accession of James I to the Outbreak of the Civil War*. 10 vols. 3:108–55. London: Longmans, Green. 1893. Considers Ralegh's 1617 voyage to Guiana and his execution.

555. Gemmill, William N. "The Trial of Sir Walter Raleigh." *Case*

and Comment 23 (1916): 175–80. Maintains that, during his 1603 treason trial, Ralegh's insistence on being brought face to face with his accusers was a pioneering act, because that principle had not yet been established.

556. Gerard, John. *The Herball or Generall historie of plantes*, 289. London: Norton, 1597. 1392 pp. Mentions that Ralegh was the first Englishman of rank to smoke tobacco, a habit that spread rapidly.

557. Gillespie, James Edward. *The Influence of Overseas Expansion on England to 1700*, 76–81. New York: Columbia University Press, 1920. 367 pp. Discusses Ralegh's role in the tobacco habit.

558. Gordon, Delahay. "The History of the Life and Death of Sir Walter Ralegh." In *A General History of the Lives, Trials, and Executions of All the Royal and Noble Personages, that have Suffered in Great Britain* . . . 3 vols. 3:1–331. London: Burd, 1760.

559. Gordon, J. E. "Sir Walter Raleigh and the Three G.P.s of Salisbury." *Practitioner* 201 (1968): 382–87.

560. Gorges, Raymond. "Alcyon: Sir Arthur Gorges," and "The Lord Proprietor of Maine: Sir Ferdinando Gorges." In *The Story of a Family through Eleven Centuries, Being a History of the Family of Gorges*, 57–78, 119–39. Boston: Privately printed, 1944. 289 pp. Describes Ralegh's association with these two men.

561. Gosling, William Gilbert. *The Life of Sir Humphrey Gilbert: England's First Empire Builder*. London: Constable, 1911. 304 pp. Treats Ralegh's close relationship with his half-brother and his part in Gilbert's overseas activities.

562. Gosse, Edmund. "Tercentenary of Sir Walter Ralegh's Death." *Fortnightly Review* 104 (1918): 715–23. Reprinted as "The Shepherd of the Ocean," *Devonian Yearbook* (1919), and in *Some Diversions of a Man of Letters*. London: Heinemann; New York: Scribner, 1919, 1920. Prints an address delivered at the Mansion House on 29 October 1918.

563. Graham, Winston. *The Spanish Armadas*. London: Collins; Garden City, N.Y.: Doubleday, 1972. 288 pp. Discusses Ralegh's involvement in expeditions against the Spanish fleet, especially at Cadiz.

564. Green, A. Wigfall. *Sir Francis Bacon: His Life and Works*, 214–

16. Denver, Colorado: Alan Swallow, 1952. 296 pp. Defends Bacon's role in the execution of Ralegh.

565. Greenlaw, Edwin. "Spenser and British Imperialism." *Modern Philology* 9 (1912): 347–70. Discusses the influence of Ralegh and Sidney on Spenser's political views and his concept of the Irish problem as seen in *The Fairie Queene* and *The View of Ireland.*

566. _____. "Ralegh and British Imperialism." *Proceedings of the State Literary and Historical Association of North Carolina* 25 (1918): 30–41. Maintains that to deal with the menace of Spain, which he feared and hated, Ralegh felt that England would have to become a great sea power and develop colonies.

567. _____. "Spenser and the 'Party and Progress.'" In *Studies in Spenser's Historical Allegory.* Baltimore: Johns Hopkins; London: Oxford University Press, 1932. 220 pp. Assesses the influence of Sidney, Ralegh, and Fulke Greville on Spenser's political opinions and suggests that, next to Sidney, Ralegh had the greatest influence.

568. Griffiths, G. M. "An Account Book of Raleigh's Voyage, 1592." *National Library of Wales Journal* 7 (1952): 347–53. Documents the events involved in the expedition that captured the *Madre de Dios.*

569. Guiney, Louise I. "Sir Walter Raleigh of Youghal in the County of Cork." *Atlantic Monthly* 66 (1890): 779–86. Describes the house of the warden at Youghal once belonging to Ralegh and associated with Spenser.

570. Gules, Wyvan. "Sir Walter Ralegh." *Western Antiquary* 2 (1882): 67. Reports that his signatures read "W. Ralegh."

571. H., J. J. "Raleigh of Downton, Wilts." *Wiltshire Notes and Queries* 7 (1912): 332–33. Concerns the heraldic arms of Sir Carew Raleigh.

572. H., J. R. "Sir Walter Raleigh, East Londoner." *Notes and Queries,* 12th ser. 5 (1919): 51. Says that a house near the Artichoke Tavern was reputedly where Ralegh smoked his first pipe in England.

573. _____. "Sir Walter Raleigh and Queen Elizabeth at Sandgate." *Notes and Queries,* 12th ser. 6 (1920): 20. Claims that Ralegh and Elizabeth could have danced the saraband because it was well known in Tudor England.

574. Hale, J. R., ed. "Introduction." In *The Evolution of British Historiography from Bacon to Namier*. Cleveland, Ohio, and New York: World Publishing, 1964. 380 pp. Reprint. London: Macmillan, 1967. Sees Ralegh as a transitional historiographer, who bridged the gap between old traditions and new.

575. Hamilton, A. H. A. "The Jurisdiction of the Lord Warden of the Stannaries in the Time of Sir Walter Raleigh." *Report and Transactions of the Devonshire Association for the Advancement of Science, Literature, and Art* 8 (1876): 380–83. Reprinted in *Quarter Sessions from Queen Elizabeth to Queen Anne*. London: Low, 1878. Shows what Ralegh's wardenship involved, based on records in the County of Devon archives.

576. Handover, Phyllis M. *The Second Cecil: The Rise to Power 1563–1604 of Sir Robert Cecil, Later First Earl of Salisbury*. London: Eyre & Spottiswoode, 1959. 332 pp. Argues against the traditional view that Ralegh was a victim of Cecil's unscrupulousness, but acknowledges that Cecil's desire to advance James's pro-Spanish policy caused Cecil to turn against Ralegh.

577. Hardy, B. C. *Arbella Stuart: A Biography*. New York: Dutton, 1913. 340 pp. Argues that Ralegh was not involved in the "Main" plot of 1603 to place Arbella (Arabella) on the throne.

578. Hargrave, Francis. "The Trial of Sir Walter Raleigh, Kt. at Winton, for High Treason, the 17th of November, 1603." In *A Complete Collection of State Trials and Proceedings for High Treason, and Other Crimes and Misdemeanours* 2 vols. 1:211–32. London: Wright, 1776. Provides portions of the official transcript of the proceedings, Ralegh's letter of apology to King James after the failure of the Guiana effort, his letters to the king and his wife the night before his execution, and his speech from the scaffold.

579. Harington, Sir John. "A Briefe View of the State of the Church of England as it stood in Q. Elizabeth's and King James his Reigne to the yeere 1608." In *Nugae Antiquae*. Ed. Thomas Park. 2 vols. 2:124–27, 129, 151–53. London: Vernor, Hood, Cuthell, Martin, 1804. First published in 1653. Alleges that Ralegh contrived to bring into the Queen's displeasure two bishops whose property at Sherborne and Wilscombe he coveted.

580. Harman, Edward George. *Gabriel Harvey and Thomas Nashe,* 197–200. London: Ouseley, 1923. 275 pp. Claims that part of *A Report of the Fight about the Azores* is by Bacon.

581. Harper, Charles G. "Otterton—East Budleigh—Sir Walter Raleigh." In *The South Devon Coast,* 53–61. London: Chapman & Hall, 1907. 304 pp. Includes an account of Hayes Barton and anecdotes of the region.

582. Harris, Carrie Jenkins [Charles Edward Lloyd]. *State Trials of Mary, Queen of Scots, Sir Walter Raleigh, and Captain William Kidd, Condensed and Copied from the State Trials of Francis Hargrave, Esq., London, 1776, and of T. B. Howell, Esq., F.R.S., F.S.A., London, 1816, With Explanatory Notes,* 61–126. Chicago: Callaghan, 1899. 260 pp.

583. Harris, Victor. *All Coherence Gone: A Study of the Seventeenth-Century Controversy over Disorder and Decay in the Universe.* London: Frank Cass; Chicago: University of Chicago Press, 1949. 255 pp. Reprint. 1966. Sees Ralegh's *History of the World* as arguing that man is the source of decay in the world.

584. Harrison, George H. R. "Raleigh Pedigree, Extracted from the Records of the College of Arms." *Miscellenea Genealogica et Heraldica,* 1869, 2:155–57. Reissued in a quarto of three leaves. Reproduces signatures of ten family members, all spelled "Ralegh."

585. Hart, W. H. "Expenses Laid out in Trial of Ralegh, 1603." *Proceedings of the Society of Antiquarians,* 2d ser. 1 (1860): 58–63.

586. Haynes, Alan. "The Cadiz Expedition of 1596." *History Today* 23 (1973): 161–70.

587. _____. "The Islands Voyage, 1597." *History Today* 25 (1975): 689–96. Discusses the Azores expedition led by Ralegh and Essex.

588. Heath, Sidney. *The South Devon and Dorset Coast,* 191–97. London: Unwin, 1910. 445 pp.

589. Hedley, Oliver. *Prisoners in the Tower.* London: Pitkin Pictorials, [1972]. 24 pp.

590. Helm, P. J. *England Under the Yorkists and Tudors 1471–1603,* 304–6, 357–59. London: Bell, 1968. 372 pp.

591. Henderson, Philip. "Sidney and Bruno." *Times Literary*

Supplement, 9 October 1937, 735. Claims that the charge of atheism against men like Ralegh was apt to be made about any free and rational inquiry into established religion.

592. _____. "Sir Walter Ralegh's School of Atheism." In *And Morning in His Eyes: A Book about Christopher Marlowe*, 145–65. London: Boriswood, 1937. approx. 345 pp. Surveys Ralegh's career to the mid 1590s, in connection with the School of Night.

593. _____. "The School of Night." In *Christopher Marlowe*, 35–54. London: Longmans, Green, 1952. 162 pp. Reprint. New York: Barnes & Noble; Brighton: Harvester Press, 1974. Discusses Marlowe's association with Ralegh and the School of Night, and Ralegh as a probable model for Tamburlaine.

594. Hennell, Sir Reginald. *The History of the King's Bodyguard of the Yeomen of the Guard*. Westminster: Constable, 1904. 343 pp. Discusses the role of captain of the guard, a position twice held by Ralegh.

595. Hennessy, John Pope. *Sir Walter Ralegh in Ireland*. London: Kegan, Paul, Trench, 1883. 263 pp. Includes nineteen letters by Ralegh (copied without acknowledgment from Edwards's edition) amid a denunciation of the English presence in Ireland, written by the then-owner of Ralegh's house in Youghal.

596. Herbert, H. W. "Sir Walter Raleigh and His Wife." *Godey's Ladies' Book* 42 (1851): 55–59.

597. Heron, Robert [John Pinkerton]. *Letters of Literature*, 213. London: Robinson, 1785. 515 pp. Tells the anecdote of Ralegh's burning the manuscript continuation of his *History of the World* because he despaired of arriving at objective truth after hearing a friend describe an incident that they had both witnessed.

598. Hickson, Mary Agnes. "Historic Truth and Sham Legends." *Journal of the Royal Society of Antiquaries of Ireland* 28 (1898): 65–66. Claims that the legend that Ralegh was involved in exterminating Italian and Spanish troops at Smerwick in 1580 is not supported by contemporary records, and that Ralegh was in either Limerick or Cork at the time.

599. Hill, Christopher. "Intellectual Origins of the English Revolution—III: Sir Walter Ralegh and History." *Listener* 67 (1962): 1023–26. Argues that while Ralegh did not deny that God acted throughout history as the first cause, he

concentrated on second causes and insisted that they were sufficient for historical explanation. Notes Ralegh's patriotism, sympathy for the poor, belief in the middle class, and commitment to the rule of law.

600. _____. "Intellectual Origins of the English Revolution—IV: Ralegh and the Revolutionaries." *Listener* 67 (1962): 1066–68. Notes that Ralegh was read and much appreciated by Sir John Eliot, Pym, and other leaders of the English Revolution.

601. _____. "Intellectual Origins of the English Revolution—VI: A Single Revolution." *Listener* 67 (1962): 17–19. Sees Ralegh, Bacon, and Coke not as original thinkers but as men whose skepticism challenged traditional beliefs.

602. _____. "Ralegh—Science, History, and Politics." In *Intellectual Origins of the English Revolution*, 131–224. Oxford: Clarendon Press, 1965. 333 pp. Examines the influence of Ralegh's thought on the seventeenth century and argues that he was a Modern in his promotion of scientific experimentation.

603. Hill, T. H. "Raleigh—Pronunciation." *Notes and Queries* 196 (1951): 64. Maintains that the correct pronunciation is "Rawly."

604. Hinton, Edward M. "Walter Raleigh." In *Ireland through Tudor Eyes*, 46–48. Philadelphia: University of Pennsylvania Press; London: Oxford University Press, 1935. 111 pp. Reprint. Folcroft, Penn.; Folcroft Library Editions, 1974.

605. "The History of the Tryal of the Famous Sir Walter Raleigh, kt., at Winchester, upon an Indictment of High Treason, in the First Year of the Reign of King James I, Anno Dom 1602 [sic], to which are added some very uncommon Proceedings subsequent to the same, as an Illustration of the History of those Times." In *The History of the Most Remarkable Tryalls in Great Britain and Ireland in Capital Cases*. 2 vols. 2:69–160. London: Printed for Bell, Pemberton and Brown, 1715.

606. Holman, E. B. "Hayes-Barton: The Birthplace of Raleigh." *Craftsman* 17 (1910): 417–24. Provides a description and four pages of photographs.

607. Hopkins, R. Thurston. "Colaton Raleigh and East Budleigh." In *The Literary Landmarks of Devon and Cornwall*, 65–75. London: Palmer, 1926. 270 pp.

608. "House of Sir Walter Ralegh in Youghal." *Artist* 23 (1898): 14.

609. Howe, P. A. "The Ralegh Papers at Sherborne Castle." *History*

Today 21 (1971): 213–14. Discusses documents, including the original lease of Sherborne by Queen Elizabeth to Ralegh, and a will drawn up by him in 1597.

610. Howell, T. B., and T. J. Howell. "The Trial of Sir Walter Raleigh, Knt., at Winchester for High Treason. James I, 17th Nov., A.D. 1603." In *Cobbett's Complete Collection of State Trials . . . From the Earliest Period to the Present Time*. 34 vols. 2:1–60. London: Bagshaw, 1809–26. Also contains accounts of Ralegh's second trial in 1618 and execution.

611. Hughes, G. B. "Ralegh and the Farm of Wines." *Country Life* 147 (1970): 194–95.

612. Hull, Eleanor. *A History of Ireland and Her People*. 2 vols. 1:382–83, 431–37. London: Harrap, 1926.

613. Hume, Martin. "Un gran diplomático español: El Conde de Gondomar en Inglaterra." In *Españoles e Ingleses en el siglo XVI (Estudios Históricos), Biblioteca de Derecho y de Ciencias Sociales*, 271–310. Madrid: Libreria General de Victoriano Suárez; London: Eveleigh Nash, 1903. 311 pp. Discusses Count Gondomar's role in limiting Ralegh's freedom of action in his voyage to Guiana in 1617 and Gondomar's diplomatic victory in bringing about the execution of Ralegh after his return to England.

614. ———. "True Stories of the Past: Sir Walter's Homecoming." *Nash's Magazine*, 1910, 459–66. Treats Ralegh's return from his last voyage.

615. Hutchins, John. "Sir Walter Rauleigh's Stabb." In *The History and Antiquities of the County of Dorset*. 4 vols. 4:217–19. London: Nichols, 1870. Reprints an anonymous account of an alleged attempt at suicide by Ralegh on 20 July (?) 1603 while confined in the Tower.

616. Hutchinson, John. *A Catalogue of Notable Middle Templars*, 202. London: Society of Middle Temple, 1902. 284 pp.

617. Ingram, John H. *Christopher Marlowe and His Associates*. London: Grant Richards, 1904. 305 pp. Maintains that Ralegh was the friend with the greatest influence on Marlowe and discusses their literary relationship.

618. Jackson, B. Daydon. "Ralegh and the Introduction of the Potato." *Gardeners' Chronicles* 27 (1900): 161–62, 178–80.

619. Jacox, Francis. "At the Tower Window with Sir Walter Ralegh. A Vexed Question." *Bentley's Miscellany* 54 (1863): 240–47.

Reprinted in *Recreations of a Recluse*. London: Bentley, 1870.
Also the topic of three items in *Notes and Queries*, 3d ser. 11
(1867): 55, 187, 201, headed, "Raleigh at His Prison Window."

620. Jacquot, Jean. "La Période elisabethaine." In *George Chapman
1559–1634*, 4–32. Paris: Les Belles Lettres, 1951. 308 pp.
Considers the "School of Night."

621. Jaggard, William. "Sir Walter Ralegh's Library." *Notes and
Queries* 166 (1934): 138–39. Notices three pamphlets by
Robert Gray.

622. [James I]. *By the King. A Proclamation declaring His Maiesties
pleasure concerning Sir Walter Rawleigh, and those who
aduentured with him*. London: Bonham Norton and John Bill,
1618. 1 folio. Reprinted in Cayley's *Life of Ralegh* (1805) and
in *Works of Ralegh* (1829). Proclaiming the King's displeasure
at Ralegh's activities on his Guiana expedition, this document
was signed at Greenwich on 9 June 1618 and a similar one at
Westminster on 11 June; both were issued some days before
Ralegh's return.

623. Jardine, David. "Raleigh's Trial." In *Criminal Trials*. 2 vols.
1:389–520. London: Knight, 1832–35. Re-issued with new title
page. London: Nattali, 1847. Also contains accounts of
Ralegh's imprisonment, his voyage to Guiana, and his
execution.

624. Jayne, Sears. *Library Catalogues of the English Renaissance*,
148–49. Berkeley and Los Angeles: University of California
Press, 1956. 225 pp. Notes a list of 494 volumes, mainly of
history and geography, which were probably part of Ralegh's
library in the Tower.

625. Johnson, F. R. *Astronomical Thought in Renaissance England:
A Study of the English Scientific Writings from 1500 to 1645*.
Baltimore: Johns Hopkins Press, 1937. 357 pp. Sees the
enthusiasm for astronomy by Ralegh and his circle as part of a
widespread trend.

626. Johnson, George William. *Gardener* 10 vols. 1:8. London:
Bohn, 1849. Tells of Ralegh's role in introducing the potato to
Britain.

627. Jorgensen, Paul A. "Theoretical Views of War in Elizabethan
England." *Journal of the History of Ideas* 13 (1952): 469–81.
Examines theories of population control in Ralegh's *Discourse
of War*.

628. Judson, Alexander C. *The Life of Edmund Spenser*. Baltimore: Johns Hopkins Press, 1945. 238 pp. Discusses Ralegh's relationship with Spenser from as early as 1579.

629. Kabat, Lillian Trena Gonan. "*The History of the World*: Reason in the Historiography of Sir Walter Raleigh." Ph.D. diss., University of Southern California, 1968. 178 pp. Claims that Ralegh's providential view of history is seen only in the Preface to *The History* and that the bulk of the work reveals Ralegh's faith in reason and science.

630. Kargon, Robert H. "Science and Atomism in England: From Hariot to Newton." Ph.D. diss., Cornell University, 1964. 251 pp.

631. ———. "Thomas Hariot, the Northumberland Circle and Early Atomism in England." *Journal of the History of Ideas* 27 (1966): 128–36.

632. ———. *Atomism in England from Hariot to Newton*. Oxford: Clarendon Press, 1966. 168 pp. Maintains that the rise of atomism as a mechanical philosophy was largely through the circle including the ninth Earl of Northumberland, Thomas Hariot, and Ralegh.

633. Kelly, Henry Ansgar. *Divine Providence in the England of Shakespeare's Histories*, 300–304. Cambridge, Mass.: Harvard University Press, 1970. 344 pp. Finds Ralegh's explanation of divine providence in the Preface to his *History* to be incoherent.

634. Kendrick, T. D. *British Antiquity*. 109. London: Methuen, 1950. 171 pp. Claims that because Ralegh in his *History of the World* omits the British from a list of nations descended from the Trojans, he disbelieved that myth.

635. Kenyon, John. "The Seventeenth Century." In *The History Men: The Historical Profession in England Since the Renaissance*, 18–38. London: Weidenfeld and Nicolson, 1983. 322 pp. Discusses Ralegh as the first Whig historian.

636. King, Horatio. "Incidents in Sir Walter Raleigh's Life." *Magazine of American History* 17 (1887): 251–53. Reprinted in *Turning on the Light*. Philadelphia: Lippincott, 1895. Believes that "the strongest presumptive evidence" supports the story that Ralegh burnt the manuscript continuation of his *History of the World*.

637. Kingsford, C. Lethbridge, ed. "The Taking of the *Madre de Dios*, Anno 1592." *Publications of the Navy Record Society* 40

(1910): 85–121. Discusses the event, using accounts by Francis Seall, who took part in the expedition, and by others.

638. Knott, John. "Sir Walter Ralegh's 'Royal Cordial.'" *Dublin Journal of Medical Science* 121 (1906): 63–70, 131–43. Discusses the contents and use of Ralegh's specific in the treatment of Prince Henry and the supposed therapeutic value of its ingredients.

639. _____. "Sir Walter Ralegh's 'Royal Cordial' (With Some Sidelights on the Clinical Medicine and Therapeutics of his Generation, and Incidental Glances at its Political and Social Morality." *American Medicine*, n.s. 6 (1911): 157–67, 218–24. Expands the preceding item.

640. Kocher, Paul H. "Marlowe's Atheist Lecture." *Journal of English and Germanic Philology* 39 (1940): 98–106. Reprinted in *Marlowe: A Collection of Critical Essays*, edited by Clifford Leech. Englewood Cliffs, N.J.: Prentice-Hall, 1964. Reproduces the document presented by Richard Baines to the Privy Council in 1593 containing blasphemies attributed to Marlowe in a lecture allegedly given to a group including Ralegh.

641. _____. "Backgrounds for Marlowe's Atheist Lecture." In *Renaissance Studies in Honor of Hardin Craig*, edited by Baldwin Maxwell, et al., 112–32. Stanford: Stanford University Press, [1941]. 339 pp. Discusses possible sources for the lecture that Marlowe allegedly gave to Ralegh and his circle.

642. _____. *Christopher Marlowe: A Study of His Thought, Learning, and Character*, 7–18. Chapel Hill: University of North Carolina Press, 1946. 344 pp. Reprint. New York: Russell & Russell, 1962. Maintains that Marlowe's atheism owes nothing to Ralegh, who was basically orthodox in religion.

643. _____. *Science and Religion in Elizabethan England*, 58–61. San Marino, Calif.: Huntington Library, 1953. 340 pp. Finds Ralegh to have been a complete skeptic briefly, if at all, though distrustful of the miraculous.

644. Lacey, Robert. *Robert Earl of Essex*. New York: Atheneum; London: Weidenfeld and Nicolson, 1971. 338 pp. Devotes considerable attention to the relationship of Essex with Ralegh.

645. Laing, David. "Sir W. Raghlies Petition to the Queene." In "Extracts from the Hawthornden MSS." *Archaeologia Scotica* 4 (1857): 236–38.

646. Lamborn, E. A. G. "The Achievement of Sir Walter Ralegh." *Notes and Queries* 185 (1943): 338–41. Claims that heraldic evidence shows Ralegh descended from William the Marshal, Earl of Pembroke.

647. Latham, Agnes M. C. "Ralegh's Letters." *Times Literary Supplement*, 4 February 1939, 74. Discusses 15 of Ralegh's letters to the Gilberts.

648. _____. "Sir Walter Ralegh's Farewell Letter to his Wife in 1603: A Question of Authenticity." *Essays and Studies* 25 (1939): 39–58. Argues that the letter is authentic but doubts that it reached Elizabeth Ralegh.

649. _____. "A Birth-date for Sir Walter Ralegh." *Etudes Anglaises* 9 (1956): 243–45. Concludes from three lawsuits in which Ralegh had to state his age that he was born between June and November 1554.

650. _____. "Sir Walter Ralegh's Will." *Review of English Studies*, n.s. 22 (1971): 129–36. Discusses the recently discovered will, made in July 1597, which confirms the existence of Ralegh's illegitimate daughter.

651. Lawless, Donald S. "Sir Warham St. Leger (d. 1631)." *Notes and Queries*, n.s. 26 (1979): 411–12. Identifies Sir Warham as testifying aginst Ralegh after his last voyage to Guiana.

652. Lawless, Emily. *With Essex in Ireland*. London: Smith, Elder; New York: John W. Lovell, 1890. 299 pp. Refers to Ralegh twice.

653. Lee, Sidney. *The French Renaissance in England*, 306–7. New York: Scribner, 1910. 494 pp. Concerns Ralegh and the French artist Le Moine.

654. Le Febvre, N. *A Discourse upon Sr. Walter Rawleigh's Great Cordial*. London: Printed by J. F. for Octavian Pulleyn, Junior, 1664. 110 pp. Translated into French as *Discours sur le Grand Cordial de Sr Walter Rawleigh* (1665). Discusses the medicine Ralegh devised for Prince Henry.

655. Lefranc, Pierre. "Un Inédit de Raleigh sur la conduite de la guerre (1596–1597)." *Etudes Anglaises* 8 (1955): 193–211. Transcribes a Cotton manuscript in the British Museum, noted by Brushfield, to which Ralegh's name is affixed, and concludes that it was indeed written by him in 1596 or 1597, about the war with Spain.

656. _____. "La date du mariage de Sir Walter Ralegh: Un document inédit." *Etudes Anglaises* 9 (1956): 193–211. Offers evidence to show that Ralegh married in 1588, four years earlier than traditionally believed.

657. _____. "A Miscellany of Ralegh Material." *Notes and Queries*, n.s. 4 (1957): 24–26. Describes manuscripts in the Cecil Papers at Hatfield House, the Public Record Office, and MS Jones B 60.

658. _____. "Un Inédit de Ralegh sur la succession." *Etudes Anglaises* 13 (1960): 38–46. Discusses and transcribes two Ralegh manuscripts, a letter to the Queen and a paper about the dangers of announcing her successor, written c. 1592 and found in the Cecil Papers at Hatfield House.

659. _____. "Ralegh in 1596 and 1603: Three Unprinted Letters in the Huntington Library." *Huntington Library Quarterly* 29 (1966): 337–45. Reproduces a letter written by Ralegh to Arthur Gorges about the taking of Cadiz in 1596 and two letters exchanged by Ralegh and Henry Cobham in 1603.

660. Lemprière, R. R. "Messire Walter Raleigh, gouverneur de Jersey, 1600–03." *Bulletin Societé Jersiaise* 44 (1919): 96–106.

661. *Leicesters Commonwealth* [44]. London: n.p., 1641. Reprint. Edited by D. C. Peck. Athens, Ohio: Ohio University Press, 1985. 323 pp. First published in 1584 under the title *The copie of a leter, wryten by a master of arte of Cambrige, to his friend in London*. Declares that Ralegh was present while the French ambassador Simiers was escorted back to France c. 1579–1580.

662. Lloyd, Rachel. "The Atheism of Sir Walter Raleigh." In *Dorset Elizabethans at Home and Abroad*, 233–92. London: John Murray, 1967. 332 pp. Believes that Ralegh in the 1590s was an atheist but during his imprisonment became quite orthodox, as his *History* clearly reveals.

663. Luke, Mary M. *Gloriana; The Years of Elizabeth I.* New York: Coward, McCann & Geoghegan, 1973. 734 pp. Frequently refers to Ralegh.

664. Lynam, Edward. *Richard Hakluyt and His Successors*, 175–77. London: Hakluyt Society, 1946. 192 pp. Compares Hakluyt and Ralegh as colonizers.

665. Lyon, Walter Hastings, and Herman Block. *Edward Coke, Oracle of the Law.* Boston and New York: Houghton Mifflin,

1929. 385 pp. Provides detailed accounts of Coke's role as Attorney General in the 1603 trial of Ralegh and in the implementing of the death sentence when Ralegh returned from Guiana in 1618.

666. "M" [Talbert Matthews?]. "Sir Walter Ralegh's Library." *Notes and Queries* 166 (1934): 230. Suggests that Collier may have forged the Ralegh signature in a copy of *A Good Speed to Virginia.*

667. M., G. "Sir Walter Raleigh. His Connection with Munster." *Journal of the Cork Historical and Archeological Society,* 2d ser. 26 (1920): 54–59.

668. M., M. "Sir Walter Raleigh and Cornwall." *Cornish Notes and Queries* 1 (1906): 60.

669. M., R. B. "Ralegh and Defoe." *Devon and Cornwall Notes and Queries* 20 (1938): 137. Reports on sources of information about the genealogy of the two men and considers Defoe's claim that he was related to Ralegh.

670. "Mc." "Sir Walter Raleigh, East Londoner." *Notes and Queries,* 12th ser. 4 (1918): 296–97; 5 (1919): 15–16. Asserts that Ralegh had a residence in Mile End near Ratcliff Cross and Stairs, and, according to strong popular tradition, a residence in Blackwall, and is also connected with Limehouse because his half-brother Sir Humphrey Gilbert lived there from 1573 to 1578.

671. McClure, Norman Egbert. "Harington's Epigrams." *Times Literary Supplement,* 19 May 1927, 355. Sees an objection to identifying Ralegh as "Paulus" in Sir John Harington's epigrams, because Harington later wrote to Bishop Sill, defending Ralegh against the charge of atheism.

672. McCollum, John I., Jr. "Ralegh's *The History of the World.*" *Carrell* 5 (1964): 1–6. Examines the composition and influence of Ralegh's *History.*

673. McDonnell, Robert. "Sir Walter Raleigh in Ireland." *New Ireland Review* 19 (1903): 210–18.

674. MacDonnell, Sir John. "Sir Walter Raleigh." In *Historical Trials,* edited by R. W. Lee, 171–93. Oxford: Clarendon Press, 1927. 234 pp.

675. McElwaine, Sir Percy. "A Rawleighe Escapade." *Report and Transactions of the Devonshire Association for the Advancement of Science, Literature, and Art* 87 (1955): 111–

15. Alleges that George and John Ralegh apparently engaged in piracy in the capture of a Portuguese vessel, the *Covington*, in 1557.

676. McElwee, William. *The Wisest Fool in Christendom: The Reign of King James I and VI*. London: Faber and Faber; New York: Harcourt Brace, 1958. 296 pp. Seeks to explain the King's despicable treatment of Ralegh as based on envy.

677. McIlwain, Charles Howard. *The High Court of Parliament and its Supremacy*, 338–43. New Haven, Conn.: Yale University Press, 1910. 409 pp. Uses Ralegh to illustrate the decline in fortunes of the nobility in the Renaissance.

678. McLean, Antonia. *Humanism and the Rise of Science in Tudor England*. London: Heinemann Educational Books; New York: Neale Watson Academic Publications, 1972. 258 pp. Discusses the role of Ralegh and his circle in the expansion of knowledge in his time, during which 26 books were dedicated to him.

679. MacLean, John. "Ralegh Arms." *Notes and Queries*, 3d ser. 4 (1863): 33–34. Claims that the variations in the arms used by Ralegh indicate that he was uncertain which arms he was entitled to use.

680. MacLure, Millar. *George Chapman: A Critical Study*, 7–16. Toronto: University of Toronto Press, 1966. 241 pp. Examines Ralegh's relationship with Chapman.

681. Malthy, William S. *The Black Legend in England: The Development of Anti-Spanish Sentiment, 1558–1660*. Durham: Duke University Press, 1971. 180 pp. Notes how Ralegh, who rarely missed an opportunity to attack Spain, contributed to the Black Legend.

682. Manwaring, George E. "Ralegh's Burial Place: The Case for St. Margaret's." *Times Literary Supplement*, 22 November 1923, 790; 10 January 1924, 23; 21 February 1924, 112. Argues for St. Margaret's, Westminster, as Ralegh's burial place because Lady Ralegh's letter in which she stated her intentions of burying him at Beddington was not sent; the letter by John Chamberlain on 7 November 1618 confirms that Ralegh was buried at St. Margaret's; absence of the word "buried" beside Ralegh's name in the register is not unusual; and his son Carew was buried there on 1 January 1667.

683. Marshall, George. "Sir Walter Raleigh and Queen Elizabeth at Sandgate." *Notes and Queries*, 12th ser. 5 (1919): 273. Points

out that Ralegh could hardly have been with Queen Elizabeth at Sandgate in 1573 because he was still in France, and doubts if the saraband dance was known in England at that time.

684. Mee, Arthur. "The Boyhood Home of Sir Walter Raleigh: East Budleigh." In *Devon, Cradle of Our Seamen*, 165–68. London: Hodder and Stoughton, 1938. 500 pp.

685. ———. "The Home of Sir Walter Raleigh: Sherborne." In *Dorset, Thomas Hardy's Country*, 212–23. London: Hodder and Stoughton, 1939. 335 pp.

686. Menzies, Sutherland [Mrs. Elizabeth Stone]. "Raleigh and Queen Elizabeth." In *Royal Favourites*. 2 vols. 1:271. London: Maxwell, 1865.

687. Mistichelli, William John. "Tragic Perspective and Style in Sir Walter Ralegh's *The History of the World*." Ph.D. diss., Syracuse University, 1978. 217 pp. Notes Ralegh's emphasis on the degeneration of the world and God's retributive justice and classifies Ralegh's perspective as tragic.

688. Montague, F. C. *The Political History of England*. 12 vols. 7:79–82. London, Longmans, Green, 1907. Relates Ralegh's trial and execution.

689. Morales Lezcano, Victor. "La guerra contra España en la filosofía de Sir Walter Raleigh y Francis Bacon." *Revista de Indias* 28 (1968): 125–41.

690. Morgan, A. E. "The Ralegh Tercentenary at Exeter." *Devonian Year Book*, 1919, 65–68.

691. Morley, Henry. "Of Spenser and Raleigh Until 1586." In *English Writers* 10 vols. 9:99–106, 313–15, 373–82. London: Cassell, 1887–93.

692. Morton, Grenfell. "The Massacre of Smerwick." In *Elizabethan Ireland*, 57–59. London: Longman, 1971. 166 pp. Provides a short description of the event and Ralegh's role in it.

693. Naish, G. P. B. "Raleigh's Cloak—An Historical Revision." *Mariner's Mirror* 41 (1955): 63. Notes variants in the legend from its origin in Fuller's *Worthies* (1662) to the present.

694. Neale, J. E. *Queen Elizabeth*, 325–28. New York: Harcourt, Brace, 1934. 402 pp. Discusses Ralegh's fall from favor because of his affair with Elizabeth Throckmorton and mentions him passim.

695. ———. *The Elizabethan House of Commons*. London:

Jonathan Cape, 1949. 455 pp. Includes discussion of Ralegh's changing constituencies and his role in Parliament.

696. _____. *Elizabeth I and Her Parliaments 1584–1601*, 412–15. London: Jonathan Cape, 1957. 452 pp. Discusses Ralegh's career in Parliament.

697. Nevinson, Henry Woodd. "Shepherd of the Ocean." In *Essays in Freedom and Rebellion*, 60–66. New Haven: Yale University Press, 1921. 213 pp. Describes Ralegh's character, greatness, and failures.

698. Newbon, C. E. "A Raleigh Letter." *Times Literary Supplement*, 14 November 1918, 556. Reproduces from Harleian MS 6994 a Ralegh letter of 29 March 1586 to the Earl of Leicester.

699. Nicholl, Charles. *The Chemical Theatre*, 15–17. London: Routledge and Kegan Paul, 1980. 292 pp. Considers Ralegh's interest in alchemy.

700. Nicolson, Marjorie Hope. "Kepler, the Somnium, and John Donne." *Journal of the History of Ideas* 1 (1940): 259–80. Reprinted in *Science and Imagination*. Ithaca, N.Y.: Cornell University Press, 1956. Shows how Kepler's dream could have interested Hariot and Ralegh.

701. Norman, Philip. "Sir Walter Raleigh, East Londoner." *Notes and Queries*, 12th ser. 5 (1919): 15–16. Reports owning a view taken in 1873 of a picturesque old tenement on the back of which is written "Sir Walter Raleigh's House, Blackwall."

702. Northcote, Lady Rosalind. *Devon: Its Moorlands, Streams, & Coasts*. London: Chatto & Windus; Exeter: James G. Commin, 1919. 322 pp. Describes Hayes Barton and gives an account of Ralegh's life. Notes on page 203 that at St. Mary's Church in Bideford the Indian brought back by Sir Richard Grenville from America and called "Raleigh" was baptized and buried a year later.

703. Oakeshott, Walter. *The Queen and the Poet*. London: Faber and Faber, 1960. 232 pp. New York: Barnes & Noble, 1961. Analyzes Ralegh's relationship with Queen Elizabeth, presenting in evidence 27 of his poems.

704. _____. "Sir Walter Ralegh's Library." *Library*, 5th ser. 23 (1968): 285–327. Discusses a list, mostly in Ralegh's hand, of 515 items in his library at least as late as 1606.

705. _____. "Love's Martyr." *Huntington Library Quarterly* 39

(1975): 29–49. Discusses Ralegh's relationship with Essex in light of Robert Chester's *Love's Martyr* (1601).

706. O'Connor, G. B. "Raleigh." In *Elizabethan Ireland*, 161–62. Dublin: Sealy, Bryers, & Walker, 1906. 294 pp.

707. Orpen, Goddard H. "Ralegh's House, Youghal." *Journal of the Royal Society of Antiquaries of Ireland*, 5th ser. 13 (1903): 310–12. Relates the tradition that Ralegh probably obtained the house in 1587, was there fitfully till 1589, and sold it in 1602 to Sir Richard Boyle.

708. _____. "Ralegh's House at Youghal." *Journal of the Royal Society of Antiquaries of Ireland*, 5th ser. 13 (1903): 345–52. Revises the author's previous article by claiming that Ralegh's house was one called Myrtle Grove and tracing the error to a piece by "O'G" in the *Dublin Penny Journal* of 23 May 1833.

709. P., C. J. "Sir Walter Raleigh's Shoes." *Notes and Queries* 151 (1926): 243. Reports that a descendant of William Rawle (died 1789) possesses the shoes reputedly worn by Ralegh at his execution.

710. P., M. A. "The Raleigh or Rawleigh Family." *Devon and Cornwall Notes and Queries* 7 (1912): 223. Asks if Ralegh ever owned a house at or near Dartmouth and offers a few notes about the Raleighs of Buckland Filleigh and Sleepwash.

711. _____. "Raleigh Inscriptions in St. John's-in-the-Wilderness." *Devon and Cornwall Notes and Queries* 8 (1914): 100–103. Discusses the families of two older brothers of Sir Walter and the inscriptions on grave stones at St. John's-in-the-Wilderness.

712. _____. "Abstract of Will of John Raleighe of Fforde in the Countie of Devon, Esquier." *Devon and Cornwall Notes and Queries* 8 (1915): 181–83. Reports that the 1585 will of John Raleighe, an older step-brother of Sir Walter, makes no mention of him.

713. Page, John T. "Sir Walter Raleigh, East Londoner." *Notes and Queries*, 12th ser. 5 (1919): 51.

714. Parfitt, E. "Sir Francis Drake *v.* Sir Walter Raleigh and the Introduction of the Potato Plant." *Western Antiquary* 2 (1882): 61–62. Claims that Ralegh introduced the potato into Ireland when he planted it on his estate at Youghal on his return from Virginia in 1584. This claim began a long controversy about Ralegh and the potato. See *Western Antiquary* 2 (1882): 67, 79,

84, 143, and Parfitt, "Sir Walter Ralegh and the Introduction of the Potato."

715. _____. "Sir Walter Raleigh and Alehouses." *Western Antiquary* 2 (1882): 136. Declares that Ralegh received funds under the grant from the Queen to sell wines.

716. _____. "Sir Walter Ralegh and the Introduction of the Potato." *Western Antiquary* 4 (1884): 95–96. Changes the author's earlier claim, asserting here that the potato was brought into Ireland from Ralegh's expedition, but by Hariot.

717. Parks, George Bruner. *Richard Hakluyt and the English Voyages.* New York: American Geographical Society, 1928. 289 pp. 2d ed. New York: Ungar, 1961.

718. Partington, Wilfred, comp. *Smoke Rings and Roundelays: Blendings from Prose and Verse Since Raleigh's Time.* London: John Castle, 1924. 320 pp. Mentions Ralegh frequently.

719. Peck, D. C. "Raleigh, Sidney, Oxford, and the Catholics, 1579." *Notes and Queries,* n.s. 25 (1978): 427–31. Says that Ralegh was intimately associated with the Oxford-Howard circle of Catholic courtiers in the late 1570s, but finds no proof that he was ever a Catholic.

720. Pengelly, William, and M. W. "Raleigh." *Western Antiquary* 2 (1882): 26. Asserts that Ralegh's name should be pronounced to rhyme with "squally," and the preferred spelling, out of many, should be Raughlie.

721. Penrose, Boies. *The Sherleian Odyssey, Being a Record of the Travels and Adventures of Three Famous Brother During the Reigns of Elizabeth, James I, and Charles I,* 24–27. London: Simpkin, Marshall, 1938. 289 pp.

722. Pérez Bustamante, Ciriaco. *Españoles e Ingleses en América durante el siglo XVII. El Conde de Gondomar y su intervención en el proceso, prisión y muerte de Sir Walter Raleigh.* Santiago: Tip. Paredes, 1928. 48, 148 pp. Appendix separately numbered. Provides an account of Gondomar's role in helping to bring down Ralegh, and appends letters and documents written by Gondomar that relate to Ralegh's last voyage and execution.

723. Phillipps, Samuel M. "The Trial of Sir Walter Raleigh." In *State Trials.* 2 vols. 1:57–83. London: Walker, 1826.

724. Phillpotts, Eden. "Hayes Barton." *Studies in Philology* 15

(1918): 68–72. Describes Ralegh's birthplace.

725. _____. "Hayes Barton." In *A West Country Pilgrimage*, 7–14. London: Parsons; New York: Macmillan, 1920. 115 pp.

726. Phipps, Paul Frederick. *Sir Walter Ralegh's Patronage of Poets and Scholars*. Master's thesis, University of North Carolina at Chapel Hill, 1950. 105 pp. Views Ralegh as a sympathetic and generous patron to Spenser, Arthur Gorges, Thomas Churchyard, and perhaps other poets, and especially to geographers and mathematicians such as Hakluyt, Hariot, Dee, and Hues.

Pinkerton, John. *See* Heron, Robert.

727. Poe, Clarence. "The Tercentenary of Sir Walter Raleigh's Death." *South Atlantic Quarterly* 18 (1918): 1–5.

728. Pollard, A. F. "The Elizabethans and the Empire." *Proceedings of the British Academy* 10 (1921): 139–56. Reprinted separately. London: British Academy, [1921]. Argues that Elizabethan expansion was more of the mind than of territory, but that the Tudor discovery of sea power changed world history.

729. Porter, Mary. "Sir Walter's Garden." *Temple Bar Magazine*, 1887, 392–98. Muses about Ralegh in Youghal.

730. Potter, G. R. "Shakespeare's Will and Raleigh's *Instructions to his Son*." *Notes and Queries* 158 (1930): 364–65. Points out that, like Shakespeare, Ralegh in his will made limited provision for his widow; and in *Instructions to his Son* he urges leaving most of one's estate to one's children, thereby keeping property in the family name.

731. Powell, William S. "John Pory on the Death of Sir Walter Raleigh." *William and Mary Quarterly*, 3d ser. 9 (1952): 532–38. Discusses Ralegh's execution as described in correspondence by Pory, who was in London at the time.

732. _____. *John Pory, 1572–1636: The Life and Letters of a Man of Many Parts*, 69–73. Chapel Hill: University of North Carolina Press, 1977. 187 pp. Incorporates the preceding item.

733. Quinn, David Beers. *The Elizabethans and the Irish*. Ithaca: Cornell University Press, 1966. 204 pp. Shows the relationship between Elizabethan colonization projects in Ireland and America, both of which involved Ralegh.

734. R., J. B. "Ralegh Notes: The Seals of Sir Walter Ralegh." *Report*

and *Transactions of the Devonshire Association for the Advancement of Science, Literature and Art* 37 (1905):79–80.

735. "Ralegh and King James I." *Gentleman's Magazine* 17 (1842): 152–53.

736. Ralegh, Carew. *A Brief Relation of Sir Walter Ralegh's Troubles; with the taking away of the Lands and Castle of Sherborn, in Dorset, from him and his Heirs; being his indubitable Inheritance.* London: Printed for W. T., 1669. 11 pp. Reprinted in *A Selection from the Harleian Miscellany* (1793); Cayley's *Life of Ralegh* (1805); *Somers Tracts* (1809); *Harleian Miscellany* (1810); and *Works of Ralegh* (1829). Requests the House of Commons to reinstate Ralegh's son in possession of the Sherborne property.

737. "Ralegh's Tobacco Box." *Western Antiquary* 6 (1886): 144. Reports that Ralegh's very large tobacco box was in a museum at Leeds in 1719.

738. *The Ralegh Tercentenary Meeting at the Mansion House, October 29th, 1918, together with General Programme of Arrangements for the Tercentenary Commemoration.* London: Jones, 1918. n.p.

739. "Raleigh and the Middle Temple." *Law Times* 180 (1935): 371–72. Reports a lecture by Bruce Williamson on Ralegh's link with the Middle Temple, and the Treasurer's observation that Philip Amadas who sailed in command of one of Ralegh's ships in 1584 was a Middle Templar and was fined for being absent from his legal studies without leave.

740. *Raleigh-Hakluyt Quartercentenary Exhibition: Sir Walter Raleigh and Richard Hakluyt; an Exhibition Held in the King's Library, British Museum, July-September 1952.* London: [British Museum], 1952. 34 pp.

741. "Raleigh in 1918." *Nation* 107 (1918): 505–6.

742. "Raleigh's Tobacco Box," "Mr. Swinburne on Raleigh," and "Fate of an Early Smoker." In *Tobacco Talk and Smokers' Gossip*, 11, 97, 127. London: George Redway, 1884. 148 pp. Relates some amusing anecdotes about Ralegh.

743. "Raleigh Tercentenary." *Nature* 102 (1918): 176–78.

744. "Rare Maps 'Under the Hammer:' Relics of Gilbert and Raleigh." *Illustrated London News*, 24 March 1928, 482–83. Describes and pictures three maps to be auctioned at Sotheby's

from the library of the ninth Earl of Northumberland: one is the map prepared by Dr. John Dee for Sir Humphrey Gilbert to illustrate possible passages through North America to the Pacific, another is of the Orinoco River, and the third is Smith's map of Virginia.

745. Rattansi, P. M. "Alchemy and Natural Magic in Raleigh's *History of the World.*" *Ambix* 13 (1966): 122–38. Argues that the *History* shows the wide interest in alchemical investigations in the early seventeenth century.

746. Reichel, Oswald J. "Ralegh and Drake Inscriptions in St. John's-in-the-Wilderness." *Devon and Cornwall Notes and Queries* 8 (1914): 81–83.

747. Reinecke, George F. "John Ford's 'Missing' Raleigh Passage." *English Language Notes* 6 (1969): 252–54. Provides the passage praising Ralegh and apparently censored from Ford's philosophical essay, *A Line of Life* (1620).

748. Reynell-Upham, W. U. "Raleigh and Exeter." *Devon and Cornwall Notes and Queries* 10 (1918): 41–42. Reports that, according to the city archives, Walter Ralegh the elder paid £4, four times the usual fee, to receive the freedom of Exeter and that he owned a town house in its parish of St. Mary Major.

749. ———. "Raleigh's Boyhood." *Times Literary Supplement,* 21 March 1918, 142. Claims that Ralegh grew up in Exeter after moving there at the age of two with his family.

750. Roberts, John. "The Younger Sir John Gilbert (*c.* 1575–1608)." *Report and Transactions of the Devonshire Association for the Advancement of Science, Literature and Art* 100 (1968): 205–17. Discusses this nephew of Ralegh who sailed on several of his expeditions and apparently caused him much trouble.

751. Robinson, Gregory. "The Loss of H.M.S. *Revenge,* 1591." *Mariner's Mirror* 38 (1952): 148–50. Charges that Barrington's article in volume 36 relied too much on Ralegh's matchless prose and Tennyson's poem, while neglecting reports by Sir William Monson and the *Naval Tracts,* and doubts that Grenville made the speech or intended to blow up the *Revenge.*

752. Rosenberg, Eleanor. "Giacopo Castelvetro: Italian Publisher in Elizabethan London and His Patrons." *Huntington Library Quarterly* 6 (1943): 119–48. Points out that one of Castelvetro's publications, Stella's *Columbeid* (1585), was

dedicated to Ralegh as backer of the Virginia expedition, probably at the instigation of Hakluyt, who was propagandizing for Ralegh.

753. ———. *Leicester: Patron of Letters*, 11. New York: Columbia University Press, 1955. 395 pp. Considers Ralegh as literary patron.

754. Ross, William Lennox Lascelles Fitzgerald (Baron de Ros). "In the Tower." In *Memorials of the Tower of London*, 158–76. London: John Murray, 1866. 298 pp.

755. Rowe, J. Brooking. "Ralegh Notes: The Seals of Sir Walter Ralegh." *Report and Transactions of the Devonshire Association for the Advancement of Science, Literature, and Art* 37 (1905): 79–80.

756. Rowse, A. L. *Sir Richard Grenville of the Revenge, an Elizabethan Hero*. Boston and New York: Houghton-Mifflin; London: Jonathan Cape, 1937, 1949. 365 pp. Discusses in chapters 10–13 the voyages to America and Ralegh's involvement with Grenville.

757. ———. "Sir Walter Raleigh and National Defense." *Spectator* 162 (1939): 767–68.

758. ———. *Tudor Cornwall: Portrait of a Society*. London: Jonathan Cape, 1941. 462 pp. Discusses in chapter 15 Ralegh's role in moves against Spain.

759. ———. "The Tudor Character." In *The English Spirit; Essays in History and Literature*, 88–96. London: Macmillan, 1944; New York: Macmillan, 1945. 275 pp. Revised ed. New York: Funk and Wagnalls, 1967. Praises Ralegh's achievements and refers to him passim.

760. ———. *The England of Elizabeth: The Structure of Society*. New York: Macmillan, 1951. 547 pp. Reprint. Madison: University of Wisconsin Press, 1978. Makes numerous references to Ralegh in connection with government, religion, law, economics, and other spheres.

761. ———. "American Colonisation." In *The Expansion of Elizabethan England*, 206–37. London: Macmillan; New York: St. Martin's Press, 1955. 449 pp. New York: Harper & Row, 1965. Discusses Ralegh's efforts at colonization on Roanoke.

762. ———. "Sir Walter Raleigh: Last of the Elizabethans." *Listener*, 7 July 1955, 17–18.

763. ———. "Sir Richard Grenville's Place in English History." *Proceedings of the British Academy* 43 (1958): 76–95. Frequently mentions Ralegh.

764. ———. *The Elizabethans and America*. London: Macmillan; New York: Harper, 1959. 221 pp. Includes an account of Ralegh's role in the Elizabethan effort to colonize America.

765. ———. "Of Raleigh and the First Plantation." *American Heritage* 10 (1959): 4–19, 105–11.

766. ———. *Ralegh and the Throckmortons*. London: Macmillan; New York: Harper and Row, 1962. 348 pp. American title: *Sir Walter Ralegh, His Family and Private Life*. Reprint. London: Reprint Society, 1964; Westport, Conn.: Greenwood, 1975. Based largely on the diary of Ralegh's brother-in-law, Arthur Throckmorton, which became available only recently and which provides the earliest evidence of Ralegh's secret marriage to Elizabeth and the birth of their first child, a son named Damerie.

767. ———. *The Elizabethan Renaissance: The Life of the Society*. London: Macmillan, 1971; New York: Scribner, 1972. 336 pp. Cites examples from Ralegh's career to illustrate the social history of the period.

768. ———. *The Elizabethan Renaissance: The Cultural Achievement*. London: Macmillan; New York: Scribner, 1972. 412 pp. Notes Ralegh's contributions in literature and science.

769. ———. "Sir Walter Ralegh and Essex," and "Gunpowder Plot: the Wizard Earl and Ralegh." In *The Tower of London in the History of England*, 107–41. New York: Putnam, 1972. 280 pp.

770. ———. *Shakespeare the Man*, 71–72. New York: Harper and Row, 1973. 284 pp. Argues that Shakespeare's sonnet 25 alludes to Ralegh's fall from the Queen's favor as a result of his marrying.

771. ———. "Ralegh as Writer." In *Discoveries and Reviews: from Renaissance to Restoration*, 179–81. New York: Barnes and Noble, 1975. 283 pp. While reviewing Lefranc's book favorably, argues for 1591, not 1588, as date of Ralegh's marriage.

772. ———. *Eminent Elizabethans*, 143–49. London: Macmillan; Athens: University of Georgia Press, 1983. 199 pp. Argues that in Sir John Harington's *Epigrams*, Paulus signifies Ralegh.

773. Rukeyser, Muriel. *The Traces of Thomas Hariot.* New York: Random House, 1971. 366 pp. Discusses the long friendship and scientific collaboration between Hariot and Ralegh.

774. Rushworth, John. "An. 1618." In *Historical Collections,* 4–5, 9. London: Newcomb for Thomason, 1659. 774 pp.

775. Russell, Sandra Joanne. "Ralegh's Universe." Ph.D. diss., Columbia University, 1963. 276 pp. Discusses the orthodoxy of Ralegh's thought.

776. S., W. S. L. "Sir Walter Ralegh's Estimation of Spain." *Western Antiquary* 7 (1888): 320. Quotes Ralegh on the power of Spain and of Turkey.

777. Safford, William Edwin. "The Potato of Romance and of Reality." *Journal of Heredity* 16 (1925): 113–26. Reprinted in *Smithsonian Institution Annual Report, 1925.* Washington: Government Printing Office, 1926. Exposes defects in the legend of Ralegh's having introduced the potato into Ireland.

778. Salaman, Redcliffe N. "The Introduction to Europe: The Raleigh and Other Legends." In *The History and Social Influence of the Potato,* 142–58. Cambridge: Cambridge University Press, 1949. 685 pp. Examines various legends about the potato, concludes that it had been introduced into Spain by 1570, but that Ralegh may well have contributed, at least indirectly, to its introduction into Ireland c. 1586.

779. Salisbury, A. "A Draught of a Jacobean Three-Decker: The *Prince Royal?*" *Mariner's Mirror* 47 (1961): 170–77. Reports that the earliest draught in the National Maritime Museum is of a three-decked ship-of-war, possibly Ralegh's *Prince Royal* of 1609.

780. Salmon, A. L. *Literary Rambles in the West of England,* 15–18. London: Chatto & Windus, 1906. 340 pp.

781. Sánchez Cánton, F. J. "Como se enteró el Conde de Gondomar de la ejecución de Sir Walter Raleigh." *Real Academia de la Historia, Boletín, Madrid* 113 (1943): 123–39. Discusses how the Spanish diplomat was involved in Ralegh's execution.

782. Sanderson, William. *An Answer to a scurrilous pamphlet, intituled, Observations upon a compleat history of the lives and reignes of Mary Queen of Scotland, and of her son King James of Great Britain, France and Ireland, the sixth. The libeller without a name, set out by G. Bedell and T. Collins two booksellers: but the history vindicated by the authour William*

Sanderson Esq. London: Printed for the author, 1656. [32 pp.]
Responds to the *Observations*, which defend Ralegh and are
usually attributed to Carew Ralegh in answer to some
statements made by Sanderson.

783. Sandison, Helen Estabrook. "Arthur Gorges: Spenser's Alcyon
and Ralegh's Friend." *Publications of the Modern Language
Association* 43 (1928): 645–74. Argues that Ralegh influenced
his cousin Gorges to become Spenser's patron.

784. ———. "Ralegh's Orders Once More." *Mariner's Mirror* 20
(1934): 323–30. Argues that Ralegh's Orders 1–16 in *Judicious
Essays* are sailing instructions going back to the 1570s but that
the remaining 23 orders concern fighting and are by him.

785. ———. "Manuscripts of the 'Islands Voyage' and 'Notes on the
Royal Navy' (in Relation to the Printed Versions in Purchas and
in Ralegh's 'Judicious Essays')." In *Essays and Studies in Honor
of Carleton Brown*, 242–52. New York: New York University
Press; London: Oxford University Press, 1940. 336 pp. Argues
that Ralegh's mention of a "Maritimall voyage" in the *Notes*
refers not to a lost work by him but to Arthur Gorges' *Islands
Voyage.*

786. Schoeck, R. J. "The Elizabethan Society of Antiquaries and Men
of Law." *Notes and Queries*, n.s. 1 (1954): 417–21. Cites
Ralegh as a member following his association with the Middle
Temple.

787. [Scott, Thomas]. *A Choice Narrative of Count Gondamor's
Transactions during his Embassy in England by . . . Sir Robert
Cotton . . . Exposed to publick Light, for the Benefit of the
whole Nation. By a Person of Honour.* London, Printed for
John Garfield, 1659. 31 pp. Quotes Gondamar as gloating over
bringing "to an ignominious death that old Pirate [Rawleigh]."

788. ———. *A Narrative of the wicked Plots carried on by Seignior
Gondamore, for Advancing the Popish Religion and Spanish
Faction.* London: Printed by T. B., 1679. approx. 16 pp.
Reprinted in *Harleian Miscellany* (1808). Denounces the
Spanish diplomat who helped to have Ralegh executed.

789. Seeley, John R. *The Growth of British Policy.* 2 vols. 1:222–24,
285–93. Cambridge: Cambridge University Press, 1895.
Considers Ralegh's Spanish policy and his last voyage.

790. Shapiro, I. A. "The 'Mermaid Club.'" *Modern Language*

Review 45 (1950): 6–17. Discounts the belief that Ralegh organized such a club in the Mermaid Tavern and that Shakespeare was a member.

791. Shirley, John W. "Scientific Experiments of Sir Walter Raleigh, the Wizard Earl and the Three Magi in the Tower, 1603–1617." *Ambix* 4 (1949): 52–66.

792. ———. "Sir Walter Raleigh's Guiana Finances." *Huntington Library Quarterly* 13 (1949): 55–69.

793. ———. *Thomas Harriot: A Biography*. Oxford: Clarendon Press, 1983. xii, 507 pp. Frequently discusses Ralegh's relationship with Hariot.

794. ———, ed. *Thomas Harriot: Renaissance Scientist*. Oxford: Clarendon Press, 1974. 181 pp. Includes essays by Shirley on "Sir Walter Ralegh and Thomas Harriot," 16–35, and David Beers Quinn on "Thomas Hariot and the New World," 36–53.

795. Sieveking, J. Giberne. "Sir Walter Ralegh, an Adventurer of the 16th Century; His Home Then and Later." *Gentleman's Magazine*, n.s. 72 (1904): 88–99. Describes Hayes Barton and draws on parish records.

796. "Sir Walter Raleigh." *Historical Magazine* 3 (1859): 308–9. Discusses the pronunciation of Ralegh's name.

797. "Sir Walter Raleigh and His Trial." *Law Times* 182 (1936): 393–95.

798. "Sir Walter Raleigh's Birthplace." *Chambers's Journal*, 5th ser. 8 (1891): 609–12. Describes Hayes Barton.

799. "Sir Walter Raleigh's House." *Western Antiquary* 7 (1887): 61. Pleads that Ralegh's house at Brixton Rise be saved from demolition [but it was not].

800. "Sir Walter Raleigh's House at Youghal." *Journal of the Cork Historical and Archaeological Society* 1 (1892): 129.

801. Skelton, R. A. "Ralegh as a Geographer." *Virginia Magazine of History and Biography* 71 (1963): 131–49. Shows Ralegh as a geographer and as a patron or developer of geographical records, such as John White's drawings and maps, but also as an adherent to the Ptolemaic cosmology.

802. Slafter, Carlos, ed. *Sir Humfrey Gylberte and His Enterprise of Colonization in America . . . .* Boston: Prince Society, 1903. 335 pp. Includes Ralegh's letters to Walsingham and Gilbert.

803. Smith, John Jay. "Sir Walter Raleigh." In *Celebrated Trials of*

*All Countries and Remarkable Cases of Criminal
Jurisprudence*, 180–210. Philadelphia: Carey and Hart, 1835.
596 pp.

804. Smith, Lacey Baldwin. *The Elizabethan Epic*. London: Jonathan
Cape, 1966. 286 pp. Boston: Houghton Mifflin, 1972.
Compares Ralegh with Essex as examples of Elizabethan
dynamism ruined by megalomania.

805. [Smollett, Tobias]. "The Life and Various Voyages of Sir Walter
Raleigh, and of several Adventurers under his Direction." In *A
Compendium of Authentic and Entertaining Voyages*. 6 vols.
3:120–80. London: Dodsley, 1756. Favors Ralegh and scorns
King James's enmity to him.

806. Sokol, Barnett J. "Thomas Harriot—Sir Walter Ralegh's Tutor—
on Population." *Annals of Science* 31 (1974): 205–12. Shows
that Hariot made pre-Malthusian calculations about
overpopulation and "almost undoubtedly" shared them with
Ralegh.

807. _____. "Thomas Hariot's Notes on Sir Walter Raleigh's
Address from the Scaffold." *Manuscripts* 26 (1974): 198–206.
Says that B.M. Add. Ms. 6789, f. 533, contains all the points in
Ralegh's last speech, apparently jotted down at the time Ralegh
spoke it.

808. Somers, John, Baron Somers. *A Collection of scarce and
valuable Tracts* . . . . 4 vols. London: Cogan, 1748.

809. _____. *A Second Collection* . . . . 4 vols. London: Cogan,
1750.

810. _____. *A Third Collection* . . . . 4 vols. London: Cogan, 1751.

811. _____. *A Fourth Collection* . . . . 4 vols. London: Cogan, 1752.
Includes Ralegh material as follows: Marriage of Prince Henry,
1st Coll. 1:412–21; Maxims of State, 2d Coll. 2:213–39;
Arraignment and Conviction, 3d Coll. 1:450–65; Fight about
Azores, 3d Coll. 1:373–82; Proceedings against Ralegh, 28
October 1618, 3d Coll. 1:465–70; Ralegh's letter to the King
the night before his death, 3d Coll. 1:470–71; Letter to his wife
before his death, 3d Coll. 1:471–72.

812. _____. *A Collection of scarce and valuable Tracts* . . . , revised,
edited, augmented, and arranged by Walter Scott, 2d ed. 13
vols. London: Cadell & Davies, 1809–15. An alphabetical
index to this edition, in *Catalogue of the London Library*,
1914, 2:947–59, cites: Arraignment and Conviction, 2:408 ff.;

Carew Raleigh's Brief relation of Sir W. R.'s troubles, 2:451;
His Majesty's reasons for proceedings against R., 2:421 ff.;
Politique discourse about . . . marriage for P. Henry, 2:199;
Prince or Maxims of State, 3:281; Proceedings against Ralegh,
with his Excuse, 2:438; Reflections on late and present effects
of proc. in Eng., 10:178; Reflections on present state of nation,
10:203; Report of Fight about Azores, 1:465.

813. Sorenson, Frederick. "Sir Walter Ralegh's Library." *Notes and
Queries* 166 (1934): 102–3. Reports that a copy of Robert
Gray's *Good Speed to Virginia* (1609) in the Newberry Library
bears Ralegh's autograph, indicating that it was in his library in
the Tower.

814. _____. "Sir Walter Ralegh's Marriage." *Studies in Philology* 33
(April 1936): 182–202. Investigates why the Queen was so
angry at discovering Ralegh's marriage.

815. Sowerby, A. Millicent. "Note on *A Declaration of the demeanor
and cariage of Sir W. Raleigh, 1618*." *Papers of the
Bibliographical Society of America* 34 (1940): 358.

816. Spedding, James. "Alleged Confession of Intended Piracy by Sir
Walter Raleigh." *Gentleman's Magazine* 33 (1850): 360–63.
Reprinted in Spedding's *Reviews and Discussions* (1879).

817. Spivey, Thomas Sawyer. *The Trial for High-Treason of Sir
Walter Raleigh, 1603, and His Execution, October 29, 1618,
with Criticism*. Washington, D.C.: Antique Publishing, 1911.
45 pp. Provides a verbatim transcript of the trial and comments
on its injustice.

818. Stanford, Michael J. G. "A History of the Ralegh Family of
Fardel and Budleigh in the Early Tudor Period." Master's thesis,
London University, 1955. 374 pp.

819. _____. "The Raleghs Take to the Sea." *Mariner's Mirror* 48
(1962): 18–35. Describes the nautical and privateering
activities of Ralegh's family in the mid-sixteenth century, and
their influence on Walter.

820. Stapleton, Laurence. "Halifax and Raleigh." *Journal of the
History of Ideas* 2 (1941): 211–24. Considers that Ralegh's
political writings reflect moderate secular opinion in his time
and that they possibly influenced Lord Halifax.

821. Stephen, George A. "Ralegh Tercentenary, Oct. 29, 1918, a
Select Annotated List." *Norwich Public Library's Readers'
Guide* 7 (1918): 57–58.

822. Stephen, Sir Harry Lashington. *State Trials, Political and Social.* 2 vols. 1:1–71. London: Duckworth; New York: Macmillan, 1899, 1902. Reproduces records of the trials of Ralegh.

823. _____. "The Trial of Sir Walter Raleigh." *Transactions of the Royal Historical Society*, 4th ser. 2 (1919): 172–87. Publishes his lecture delivered in connection with the Ralegh Tercentenary.

824. Stern, Virginia. *Gabriel Harvey: His Life, Marginalia, and Library*, 126, 193–94. Oxford: Clarendon Press, 1979. 293 pp. Comments on Harvey's admiration for Ralegh, as evidenced in marginalia to two books.

825. Stevens, Henry. *Thomas Hariot, the Mathematician, the Philosopher and the Scholar.* London: Privately printed, 1900. [7]-213 pp. Frequently treats of Ralegh's relationship with Hariot.

826. Stibbs, John H. "Raleigh's Account of Grenville's Fight at the Azores in 1591." *North Carolina Historical Review* 27 (1950): 20–31. Says that Ralegh emphasizes Grenville's heroism and neglects his strategy and tactics.

827. Stirling, Brents. *The Populace in Shakespeare*, 120. New York: Columbia University Press, 1949. 203 pp. Describes Ralegh's views on the Brownists.

828. Stone, J. M. "Giordano Bruno in England." In *Studies from Court and Cloister: Being Essays, Historical and Literary, Dealing Mainly with Subjects Relating to the XVIth and XVIIth Centuries*, 158–77. Edinburgh and London: Sands, 1905. 379 pp. Maintains that, following Bruno's stay in England from 1583–1585, Ralegh seems to have disseminated Bruno's ideas, leading to the charges of atheism brought against Ralegh at Cerne in 1594.

829. Stone, Lawrence. *An Elizabethan: Sir Horatio Palavicino*, 212–20. Oxford: Clarendon Press, 1956. 345 pp. Discusses the *Madre de Dios*.

830. Stopes, Charlotte Carmichael. "Sea Dreams and Actions." In *The Life of Henry, Third Earl of Southampton, Shakespeare's Patron*, 96–113. Cambridge: Cambridge University Press, 1922. 544 pp. Describes the Islands Voyage and frequently mentions Ralegh.

831. Storr, Annie. "Sir Walter Raleigh and Brixton." *Notes and Queries* 154 (1928): 297. Solicits support for her conviction

that Ralegh had property in Lambeth. See replies in same
volume by A. R. Bayley, 337; by G. W. Wright, 375; by W.
Courthope Forman, 411–12; and by A. R. Bayley in volume
155:31.

832. Strachey, Lytton. *Elizabeth and Essex: A Tragic History.*
London: Chatto & Windus, 1928. 287 pp. New York:
Harcourt, Brace, 1928. Limited ed. London: Chatto & Windus;
New York: Crosby Gaige, 1928. Treats in detail the rivalry
between Essex and Ralegh for superiority at Elizabeth's court.

833. Strathmann, Ernest A. "*The History of the World* and Ralegh's
Skepticism." *Huntington Library Quarterly* 3 (1940): 265–87.
Argues that Ralegh's *History* demonstrates the sincerity of his
religious views.

834. _____. "Sir Walter Ralegh on Natural Philosophy." *Modern
Language Quarterly* 1 (1940): 49–61. Finds that Ralegh's views
on magic, astrology, and the scientist's duty to his fellow men
show his belief that any kind of knowledge can contribute to
bettering man's lot.

835. _____. "Ralegh as a Transition Figure." *Huntington Library
Quarterly* 5 (1942): 190–92. Assesses Ralegh as opposing
Aristotelianism, promoting the new science, and skeptical
about human authority.

836. _____. "Ralegh and the Catholic Polemists." *Huntington
Library Quarterly* 8 (1945): 337–58. Says that following
Elizabeth's anti-Catholic proclamation of 1591, several
Catholic writers denounced Ralegh as a prominent anti-Spanish
favorite of the Queen's.

837. _____. "John Dee as Ralegh's 'Conjuror.' " *Huntington Library
Quarterly* 10 (1947): 365–72. Considers whether Dee, not
Thomas Hariot, was the conjuror referred to in Robert Parsons'
attack on Ralegh and his "school of atheism" but concludes
that he probably was not.

838. _____. "Ralegh on the Problems of Chronology." *Huntington
Library Quarterly* 11 (1948): 129–48. Observes that in *The
History of the World* Ralegh accepts the Bible as authoritative
but expresses skepticism when assigning dates.

839. _____. "The Idea of Progress: Some Elizabethan
Considerations." *Renaissance News* 2 (1949): 23–25. Argues
that although Ralegh's *History of the World* espouses the
providential theory of history and the mutability of human

fortunes, he also believed that education and science could improve man's lot.

840. _____. *Sir Walter Ralegh: A Study in Elizabethan Skepticism.* New York: Columbia University Press; Oxford: Oxford University Press, 1951. 292 pp. Reprints. New York: Farrar, Straus, & Giroux, 1973; New York: Octagon, 1973. Maintains that the charges of atheism levelled against Ralegh stem largely from Catholic polemics against him, his own arrogance, and his unpopularity, and that those writings which are certainly by him reveal his Christian orthodoxy.

841. _____. "Ralegh Plans His Last Voyage." *Mariner's Mirror* 50 (1964): 261–70. Reprints and discusses a previously unexamined manuscript, Folger G.b. 10, about Ralegh's last voyage to Guiana.

842. Strugnell, W. B. "Sir Francis Drake and Sir Walter Raleigh; the Cultivation of Tobacco in England." *Western Antiquary* 3 (1884): 190–91. Postulates that Ralegh and Drake probably sent some tobacco seed to Richard Pates of Cheltenham, an area which became famous for the tobacco it produced.

843. Stucley, Sir Lewis. *To the Kings most Excellent maiestie. The humble petition and information of Sir Lewis Stucley, Knight, Vice-admirall of Deuon, touching his owne behauiour in the charge commited vnto him, for the bringing vp of Sir Walter Raleigh, and the scandalous aspersions cast vpon him for the same.* London: Bonham Norton and Iohn Bill, 1618. 17 pp. Reprinted in *Harleian Miscellany* (1809); Somers's *Tracts* (1809); and *Works of Ralegh* (1829). Attempts to defend himself against the charge that he betrayed Ralegh.

844. Sturt, Mary. "The Execution of Raleigh." In *Francis Bacon*, 196–200. New York: Morrow, 1932. 246 pp.

845. Tannebaum, Samuel A. *The Assassination of Christopher Marlowe (A New View).* New York: Tenny Press, 1928. 75 pp. Reprint. Hamden, Conn.: Shoe String Press, 1962. Theorizes that Marlowe's murder was instigated by Ralegh to escape being implicated in atheism and to regain the power he lost in 1592.

846. Taylor, Eva G. R., ed. *The Original Writing and Correspondence of the Two Richard Hakluyts.* 2 vols. London: Hakluyt Society, 1935. Contains several items addressed to Ralegh.

847. "Tercentenary of Raleigh." *Law Times*, 146 (1918): 10. Reports that the Middle Temple gave a dinner on 29 October 1918, the tercentenary of the death of Ralegh, a member of that society.

848. Ternant, Andrew de. "Sir Walter Raleigh and Brixton." *Notes and Queries* 154 (1928): 375. Declares that although legends connected Ralegh and Queen Elizabeth with Raleigh Hall, a journalist had shown that no houses stood on the site in Ralegh's day.

849. Theobald, Bertram G. *Francis Bacon Concealed and Revealed*, 39–80. London: Palmer, 1930. 389 pp. Considers Ralegh, Bacon and Spenser.

850. Theobald, [Lewis]. *Memoirs of Sir Walter Raleigh; His Life, his Military and Naval Exploits, his Preferments and Death: In which are Inserted, The Private Intrigues between the Count of Gondamore, the Spanish Ambassador, and the Lord Salisbury, then Secretary of State*. London: Printed for W. Mears, 1719. 40 pp. Dwells chiefly on Ralegh's trials in 1603 and 1618.

851. Tillyard, E. M. W. *The Elizabethan World Picture*, 51–55. New York: Macmillan, 1943. 108 pp. Considers Ralegh's discussion of the stars in the *History*.

852. Tobin, F. G. "Ralegh and Drake Inscriptions in St. John's-in-the-Wilderness." *Devon and Cornwall Notes and Queries* 8 (1914): 46–47. Reports that buried outside this church, formerly called St. Michael's, are George Ralegh (d. 1597), Walter's eldest brother, and Johan Ralegh (d. 1629).

853. Tounson, Robert. "A Letter relating to the last behaviour of Sir Walter Rawleigh, written by Dr. Rob. Tounson of Westminster, and afterwards Bp. of Sarum, to Sir John Isham." In *Walteri Hemingford, Historia de Rebus Gestis Edvardi I . . . ,* edited by Thomas Hearne. 2 vols. in 1 (191 and 736 pp.) 1:184–86. Oxford: Sheldonian Theatre, 1731. Stresses how cheerful Ralegh was in the face of being executed.

854. Trevor-Roper, H. R. "Books in General." *New Statesman and Nation* 42 (1951): 230. Denounces the trial of Ralegh.

855. ———. "The Last Elizabethan: Sir Walter Raleigh." In *Men and Events, Historical Essays*, 103–7. London and New York: Macmillan, 1957. 324 pp.

856. ———. "Another Unpublished Letter of Edward Gibbon." *Bodleian Library Record* 9 (1978): 374–75. Reproduces a letter in which Gibbon asked Thomas Becket to send him the works

of Ralegh, whose life Gibbon briefly considered writing.

857. *The Tryal of Sir Walter Raleigh, Kt., with his Speech on the Scaffold*. London: Printed for S. Redmayne, 1719. 50 pp. Reprinted in Cayley's *Life of Ralegh* (1805), and in *Works of Ralegh* (1829).

858. Tupper, Frederick. "Raleigh and Roosevelt." *Nation* 108 (1919): 344–45. Compares the two men.

859. *Verclaringe ende verhael hoe de Heere Wouter Raleighe, Ridder, hem ghedreghen heeft, soo wel in sijne Voyaghe als in ende sedert sijne wedercomste. Ende vande ware motijven ende redenen, die sijne Majesteyt bewoghen hebben, teghens hem te procedern, by forme van Justitie: ghelijck gheschiedt is*. Naer de Copye tot London, by Bonham Norton. In's Graven-Hage, By Aert Meuris, Boeck-verkooper inde Pape-straet, inden Bybel, 1619. 40 pp. Translates into Dutch the *Declaration* justifying Ralegh's execution and adding Stucley's *Petition*.

860. Vere, Sir Francis. *The Commentaries of Sr. F. V., being diverse pieces of service, wherein he had command, written by himself*. Cambridge: Dillingham, Field, 1657. 209 pp. Reprinted in Edward Arber, *English Garner* (1895). Includes accounts of the Cadiz expedition and the Islands voyage.

861. Vines, Alice Gilmore. *Neither Fire nor Steel: Sir Christopher Hatton*. Chicago: Nelson-Hall, 1978. 248 pp. Describes Hatton's attempts, by sending gifts to Queen Elizabeth, to offset Ralegh's rise to favor with her.

862. Vivian, J. L. "Raleigh of Fardell." In *Visitations of the County of Devon, Comprising Heralds' Visitations of 1531, 1564, and 1620*. Exeter: Eland, 1895. 899 pp. Includes the pedigree of the Ralegh family.

863. Waddington, Raymond B. *The Mind's Empire: Myth and Form in George Chapman's Narrative Poems*. Baltimore and London: Johns Hopkins University Press, [1974]. 221 pp. Considers Chapman's dedicating *The Shadow of Night* to Matthew Roydon and his advocacy of Ralegh's imperialist ventures in "De Guiana" as attempts to align himself with the Ralegh circle.

864. Wagner, Anthony R. *The Historic Heraldry of Britain*, 74. Oxford: Oxford University Press, 1939. 118 pp. Describes Ralegh's coat-of-arms.

865. Walker, P. R. "Sir Walter Ralegh at the Tower." In *The Tower of*

London: Its Buildings and Institutions, edited by John Charlton, 95–99. London: Department of the Environment, 1978. 160 pp. Notes the changes in architecture made for Ralegh's imprisonment.

866. Walling, R. A. J. *The Story of Plymouth*, 87–91, 94–98. New York: Morrow, 1950. 312 pp. Describes Stukeley's betrayal of Ralegh.

867. Wallis, Helen M. "The First English Globe: A Recent Discovery." *Geographical Journal* 117 (1951): 275–90. Claims that Ralegh provided Emery Molyneux with some of the information he used when making his globes, which show Virginia.

868. ———. "Further Light on the Molyneux Globes." *Geographical Journal* 121 (1955): 304–11. After returning to Amsterdam in 1593, Jodocus Hondius, the engraver of the Molyneux globes, produced a revised globe, which shows Ralegh's discoveries in Guiana; a specimen survives in the Middle Temple in London.

869. Waters, David W. *The Art of Navigation in England in Elizabethan and Early Stuart Times*. New Haven: Yale University Press; London: Hollis and Carter, 1958. 696 pp. Discusses Ralegh's role as an inspirer, employer, and supporter of navigators and scientists.

870. Watkin, Hugh R. "Birthplace of Ralegh." *Devon and Cornwall Notes and Queries* 15 (1928): 174–75. Suggests that Hayes Barton was built in or soon after 1528, when Walter Ralegh the elder migrated from Fardell, and that it was thoroughly repaired in 1627 and in 1862.

871. Watson, R. G., and A. Mackie. "Introduction of the Potato." *Western Antiquary* 2 (1882): 84. Claims that Hawkins introduced the potato to Europe before Ralegh introduced it to Ireland.

872. Wernham, R. B. *After the Armada: Elizabethan England and the Struggle for Western Europe, 1588–1595*. Oxford: Clarendon Press; New York: Oxford University Press, 1984. 613 pp. Discusses Ralegh's role in the international events of those years.

873. Westropp, Thomas J. "Notes on Askeaton, County of Limerick." *Journal of the Royal Society of Antiquaries of Ireland*, 5th ser. 13 (1903): 159. Notes its associations with Ralegh and Spenser.

874. _____. "Notes on the Antiquities of Ardmore." *Journal of the Royal Society of Antiquaries of Ireland*, 5th ser. 13 (1903): 360. Reports that the church lands, manor, lordship, castle, and town of Ardmore were leased to Ralegh in 1591 for 101 years.

875. _____. "Raleigh's House, Youghal." *Journal of the Royal Society of Antiquaries of Ireland*, 5th ser. 13 (1903): 425. Notes that it strongly resembles Hayes farm, where Ralegh was born.

876. Wheeler, Adrian. "Raleigh in America." *Notes and Queries*, 9th ser. 12 (1903): 251. Cites passage from John Aubrey's *Brief Lives* to show that Ralegh's name was pronounced "Raw-ly."

877. White, Peter. *Sherborne Old Castle, Dorset.* [London]: Department of the Environment, Ancient Monuments, and Historic Buildings, [*c.* 1971]. 12 pp. Gives the history of the castle once lived in by Ralegh, and a plan of its ruins.

878. Whitfeld, Henry Francis. *Plymouth and Devonport in Times of War and Peace*, 47–48, 79–81. Plymouth: Chapple, 1900. 560, 48 pp.

879. Whitlock, Baird. *John Hoskyns, Serjeant-at-Law.* Washington, D.C.: University Press of America, 1982. 736 pp. Discusses Ralegh's long friendship with Hoskyns, who was also a prisoner in the Tower of London while Ralegh was incarcerated there.

880. Whitmarsh, J. "Sir Walter Ralegh in Wiltshire." *Western Antiquary* 4 (1885): 189–90. Notes that after being exiled from Elizabeth's court, Ralegh is said to have lived for some time in his brother Carew's brick manor-house at Whiteborne.

881. Williams, Arnold Ledgerwood. "Christopher Marlowe and the Ralegh Circle." Master's thesis, University of North Carolina at Chapel Hill, 1930. 82 pp. Shows that in 1592–94 a group nominally headed by Ralegh met for intellectual discussion and that Marlowe was involved, but less closely with Ralegh than with other members.

882. Williams, Franklin B., Jr. "Thomas Rogers on Ralegh's Atheism." *Notes and Queries*, n.s. 15 (1968); 368–70. Reproduces from a Folger manuscript five previously unpublished stanzas of a poem about Ralegh's conviction for treason in 1603, which urge him to acknowledge God's existence, and attributes the poem to Thomas Rogers.

883. Williams, Neville. *Elizabeth: Queen of England*, 257–60. London: Weidenfeld & Nicolson, 1967. 388 pp.

884. _____. *All the Queen's Men: Elizabeth I and Her Courtiers.*
London: Weidenfeld and Nicolson; New York: Macmillan,
1972. 272 pp. Frequently refers to Ralegh, especially in chapter
7, "The Shepherd of the Ocean," which describes his coming to
the court and his subsequent rise to favor with the Queen.

885. _____. *The Sea Dogs: Privateers, Plunder & Piracy in the
Elizabethan Age.* London: Weidenfeld and Nicolson, 1976. 278
pp. and 165 plates.

886. Williamson, George. "Mutability, Decay, and Seventeenth-
Century Melancholy." *English Literary History* 2 (1935): 121–
50. Claims that Ralegh believed in the progressive degeneration
of the world, citing his *History of the World.*

887. Williamson, James Alexander. *The Evolution of England*, 249–
51. Oxford: Clarendon Press, 1931. 493 pp. Praises Ralegh as a
strategist.

888. Williamson, John Bruce. *Sir Walter Ralegh and His Trial; A
Reading Delivered Before the Honourable Society of the Middle
Temple, November 13, 1935.* London: Pitman, 1936. 40 pp.
Summarizes Ralegh's life and comments on his trial in 1603.

889. Williamson, J. W. *The Myth of the Conqueror: Prince Henry
Stuart, A Study of Seventeenth-Century Personation*, 56–60,
87–90. New York: AMS Press, 1978. 219 pp. Portrays Henry
as the focus of myths depicting him as the future conqueror of
Spain and Catholicism and restorer of virility to the Stuart
throne; as such, he was cultivated by Ralegh, who wrote *The
History of the World* partly to warn him against succumbing to
flattery.

890. Wilson, Derek. *The Tower, 1078–1978*, 136–37, 148–60.
London: Hamish Hamilton, 1978. 257 pp. Describes Ralegh's
imprisonment.

891. Wilson, Elkin Calhoun. *England's Eliza*, 304–47. Cambridge,
Mass.: Harvard University Press, 1939. 479 pp. Reprint. New
York: Octagon Books, 1966. Discusses how Queen Elizabeth
was idealized in the poetry of her era, particularly in Ralegh's
"Ocean to Cynthia."

892. _____. *Prince Henry and English Literature.* Ithaca: Cornell
University Press, 1946. 187 pp. Describes Ralegh's friendship
with Henry and the works which Ralegh wrote for him on
ships, statesmanship, and *The History of the World.*

893. Wilson, Frank P. "Spenser and Ireland." *Review of English*

Studies 2 (1926): 456–57. Discusses whether Spenser left
Ireland with Ralegh in 1589 or remained into 1590.

894. Wilson, Violet A. *Queen Elizabeth's Maids of Honour and
Ladies of the Privy Chamber*, 167–75. London: John Lane;
New York: Dutton, 1922. 284 pp. Discusses Ralegh's affair and
marriage with Elizabeth Throckmorton.

895. Winstanley, William. *Lives of the most famous English poets . . .
from the time of K. William the Conquerer, to . . . King James
II.* London: Printed by Clark for Samuel Manship, 1687. 221
pp. Includes in the Epistle to the Reader, xii–xiii, the story of
Ralegh's burning his manuscript continuation of *The History of
the World*.

896. Winthrop, Robert C. "The Confession and Execution of Sir
Walter Raleigh." *Proceedings of the Massachusetts Historical
Society* 13 (1873): 83–98. Reprinted as a pamphlet of 16 pp.
Reproduces "The Confession and Execution" found in a
commonplace book of Adam Winthrop, the father of John
Winthrop, governor of Massachusetts in 1630.

897. ———. "Remarks on Ralegh's Note of Remembrance."
Proceedings of the Massachusetts Historical Society 20 (1882):
40–42. Describes the notes that Henry Stevens discovered and
that he believed Ralegh used to prompt him in his speech from
the scaffold.

898. Wotton, Mabel E. "Ralegh's Burial Place." *Times Literary
Supplement*, 14 February 1924, 96. Maintains that Ralegh's
body was left in St. Margaret's, Westminster, only briefly before
being buried in Beddington in Surrey.

899. Wraight, A. D. *In Search of Christopher Marlowe: A Pictorial
Biography.* London: Macdonald; New York: Vanguard Press,
1965. 376 pp. Frequently discusses Ralegh, especially in
connection with the "School of Night" (pages 132–75), and
considers that Tamburlaine was probably modelled in part on
Ralegh.

900. Wright, G. W. "Sir Walter Raleigh and Brixton." *Notes and
Queries* 154 (1928): 375. Notes three deeds connecting the
Ralegh family with Ravensburie manor in Surrey.

901. Yates, Frances A. *John Florio: The Life of an Italian in
Shakespeare's England*, 69–75, 108–9. Cambridge: Cambridge
University Press, 1934. 364 pp. Notes that French ambassador
Mauvissiere sent messages to Ralegh through Florio and

suggests Ralegh may have met Giordano Bruno through the ambassador.

902. _____. *The Occult Philosophy in the Elizabethan Age*, 101–6. London: Routledge and Kegan Paul, 1979. 217 pp. Discusses Ralegh's admiration for John Dee, his interest in hermeticism, and his role in the cult of Elizabeth-as-Cynthia.

903. Youings, Joyce. *Ralegh's Country: The South West of England in the Reign of Queen Elizabeth I*. Raleigh: America's Four Hundredth Anniversary Committee, N.C. Department of Cultural Resources, 1986. 74 pp. Examines the Ralegh family's background and social standing in southwest England.

904. Zane, John Maxcy. *The Story of Law*, 320–25. Garden City, N.Y.: Garden City Publishing, 1927. 486 pp. Considers the actions of Donne and Coke during Ralegh's trial.

Chapter 4.

RALEGH IN THE AMERICAS:

PARTICULAR TOPICS

905. Adams, Randolph Greenfield. "An Effort to Identify John White." *American Historical Review* 41 (1935): 87–91. Offers evidence that John White was both the artist and the governor of Roanoke.

906. Adamson, Jack H. *The Golden Savage Land*, 14–29. Salt Lake City: University of Utah, 1967. 36 pp. Considers Ralegh's voyages to Virginia and Guiana.

907. Albertson, Catherine F. S. *Roanoke Island in History and Legend*. Elizabeth City, N.C.: Independent Press, 1934. 28 pp. Reprints. 1934, 1936, 1939. Describes the Ralegh colonies, the White Doe legend, and the island's later history.

908. Alexander, Philip F., ed. *The Discovery of America 1492–1584*, 184–204. Cambridge: Cambridge University Press, 1917. 212 pp.

909. Allen, Elsa G. "Some Sixteenth Century Paintings of American Birds." *Auk*, n.s. 53 (1936): 17–21. Describes three albums of John White drawings in the British Museum.

910. ———. "The History of American Ornithology before Audubon." *Transactions of the American Philosophical Society*, n.s. 41 (1951): 386–591. Discusses John White, Jacques Le Moyne, Edward Topsell, and their drawings of American birds.

911. Alther, Lisa. "Into the Melting Pot." *Mankind* 5 (1976): 8–10, 48–51. Describes the Melungeons of eastern Tennessee and southwest Virginia, who are said to be descendants of the Lost Colonists.

912. Andersen, Jorgen. "Kunstner og Kolonisator. John Whites Tegninger fra Virginia." *Bogvennen* 10 (1955): 94–113. Discusses White's role as governor and artist at Roanoke.

913. Anderson, R. C. "The Sixteenth-Century *Tiger*." *Mariner's Mirror* 51 (1965): 194 and 2 plates. Argues that White's 1585 painting of the *Tiger*, Grenville's flagship on the Roanoke

voyage, is so different from a 1580 painting of the *Tiger* that the name must have been transferred in the interim.

914. Andrews, Charles McLean. "Raleigh's Place in American Colonization." *Proceedings of the State Literary and Historical Association of North Carolina* 25 (1918): 55–76. Notes that Ralegh was the first to demonstrate the practicability of transporting English men and women overseas to find new homes.

915. _____. *The Colonial Period of American History*. 4 vols. 1:23–26. New Haven, Conn.: Yale University Press, 1934. Describes Ralegh's colony at Roanoke.

916. Andrews, Kenneth R. *Elizabethan Privateering: English Privateering during the Spanish War, 1585–1603*, 191–96. Cambridge: Cambridge University Press, 1964. 297 pp. Ranks Ralegh among the greatest promoters of privateering, and considers the role it played in the Roanoke colonization.

917. _____. *Drake's Voyages: A Re-Assessment of Their Place in Elizabethan Maritime Expansion*. London: Weidenfeld and Nicolson, 1967. 190 pp. Discusses Drake's 1586 visit to the Roanoke colony.

918. _____, ed. *English Privateering Voyages to the West Indies 1588–1595*. Cambridge: Hakluyt Society, 1959. 421 pp. Edits accounts of voyages by John Watts in 1588 and others, originally published by Hakluyt.

919. Arciniegas, Germán. "El dorado, principio y fin del siglo de oro." In *Biografía del Caribe*, 191–212. Buenos Aires: Editorial Sudamericana, 1945. [11]- 531 pp. Had reached 10th edition by 1973.

920. Ashe, Samuel A'Court. "Raleigh's Explorations and Colonies." In *History of North Carolina*. 2 vols. 1:1–49. Greensboro, N.C.: Van Noppen, 1908.

921. Bacon, Edwin M. *English Voyages of Adventure and Discovery, Retold from Hakluyt*, 308–88. New York: Scribner, 1908. 401 pp. Considers Ralegh's voyages to America and the Roanoke Colony.

922. Bancroft, Edward. *An Essay on the Natural History of Guiana, in South America*. London: Becket, DeHondt, 1769. 402 pp. Discusses traditions of Ralegh in Guiana.

923. Bancroft, George. *History of the United States, from the Discovery of the American Continent*. 10 vols. 1:91–111.

Boston: Little, Brown, 1834–75. Portrays Ralegh's role in colonizing America as most important.

924. Bandelier, A. F. *The Gilded Man*. New York: Appleton, 1893. 302 pp.

925. Barlowe [or Barlow], Arthur. *The First voyage to Roanoke, 1584. The first voyage made to the coasts of America, with two barks, wherein were Captains M. Philip Amadas, and M. Arthur Barlowe . . . Written by one of the said Captaines, and sent to Sir Walter Ralegh . . . .* Boston: Directors of the Old South Work, 1898. 20 pp. Reprints Barlowe's report, which first appeared in Hakluyt's *Voyages*.

926. Barrow, John. "Sir Walter Raleigh's First Voyage to Guiana" and "Sir Walter Raleigh's Last Voyage to Guiana." In *A Collection of Authentic, Useful, and Entertaining Voyages and Discoveries, digested in a chronological series*. 3 vols. 1:184–99. London: J. Knox, 1765.

927. Barton, Lewis Randolph. *The Most Ironic Story in American History: An Authoritative, Documented History of the Lumbee Indians of North Carolina*. Charlotte, N.C.: Associated Printing, 1967. 142 pp. Asserts that the Lumbee Indians are descendants of the Lost Colonists and notes the similarity of some Lumbee and colonists' names.

928. Baxter, James Phinney. "Raleigh's Lost Colony." *New England Magazine* 11 (1895): 565–87. Gives considerable attention to the Croatan Indians of North Carolina.

929. Bayle, Constantino, S. J. "Los dorados ingleses." In *El Dorado Fantasma*, 328–47. Madrid: Editorial Razón y fé, [1930]. 488 pp. 2d ed. Madrid: Consejo de la Hispanidad, 1943.

930. _____. "Un 'dorado' inglés en la cárcel de la villa de Madrid." *Revista de Indias* 4 (1943): 167–76. Quotes from statement by "Captain Francisco Sparri, inglés," companion of Ralegh in the search for El Dorado.

931. Bayo, Ciro. "Walter Raleigh." In *Los caballeros del dorado*, 207–26. Madrid: Imp. Clásica Española, 1915. 244 pp.

932. Bell, Albert Q. *Actors in the Colony, Sixteenth Century*. n.p., c. 1946. 50 pp. Contains sketches of the Roanoke colonists and two poems: "The Versatile Sir Walter," 13–19, and "Fantasy: Queen Elizabeth and Sir Walter Raleigh," 20–22.

933. Berkhofer, Robert F., Jr. *The White Man's Indian*. New York:

Knopf, 1978. 261 pp. Discusses Roanoke colonists' reactions to Indians.

934. Berry, Brewton. *Almost White*. London and New York: Macmillan, 1963. 212 pp. Discusses the Lumbee Indians and the tradition that they are descendants of the Lost Colonists.

935. Bettex, Albert. "Sir Walter Raleigh Searches for Manoa." In *The Discovery of the World*, 149–52. New York: Simon & Schuster, 1960. 379 pp.

936. Betts, Robert E. "Raleigh's Lost Colony." *Cornhill Magazine* 158 (1938): 50–67. Includes theories about its fate and accounts of the White Doe legend.

937. Bevan, Bryan. *The Great Seamen of Elizabeth I*. London: Robert Hale, 1971. 319 pp. Devotes two chapters to Ralegh's role in Virginia and Guiana.

938. [Bigges, Walter]. *A summarie and true discourse of Sir Frances Drakes West Indian Voyage: Wherein were taken the townes of Sant Iago, Sancto Domingo, Cartagena, and Saint Augustine*. London: Richard Field; Roger Ward, 1589. 52 pp. Also published in Latin, French, and German, and in Hakluyt's *Principal Navigations*, this account includes a description of Drake's visit to Roanoke Island and his removal of the Lane colony in 1586. The author was killed at Cartagena, and his journal was completed by Lieutenant Croftes or Cripps.

939. Binyon, R. Laurence. *Catalogue of Drawings by British Artists and Artists of Foreign Origin Working in Great Britain, Preserved in the Department of Prints and Drawings in the British Museum*. 4 vols. 4:326–37. London: Printed by Order of the Trustees, 1898–1907. Describes an album of 75 water-color drawings by John White, and another book of drawings attributed to White, containing 130 studies but obviously the work of a copyist.

940. ———. "Governor John White, Painter and Virginian Pioneer." *Putnam's Magazine* 2 (1907): 400–411. Discusses White's career and praises his skill and sensitivity as a painter.

941. ———. "The Drawings of John White, Governor of Raleigh's Virginia Colony." In *Thirteenth Volume of the Walpole Society, 1924–1925*, 19–24. Oxford: Oxford University Press, 1925. 84 pp. Describes the volume of White's drawings acquired by the British Museum in 1866.

942. Boden, S. M. "Raleigh's Map of Guiana." *Times Literary Supplement*, 29 July 1960, 481. Questions how a map of Guiana that Ralegh wished kept secret came into the hands of the Spanish government.

943. Borst, E. B. "The First Anglo-American. The Tragic Story of Roanoke Island." *Four-Track News*, October 1904, 233–34. Praises Ralegh and the Roanoke settlers.

944. Bourne, Henry R. F. "Sir Walter Raleigh's Virginia." In *English Seamen under the Tudors*. 2 vols. 1:200–244 and passim. London: Bentley, 1868.

945. Bradley, A. G. "The First Colonists of Virginia." *Captain John Smith*, 41–61. London: Macmillan, 1905. 226 pp. Describes Ralegh's Roanoke enterprise.

946. Brereton, M. John. *A Briefe and True Relation of the Discouerie of the North Part of Virginia; being a most pleasant, fruitfull and commodious soile; made this present yeere 1602, by Captaine B. Gosnolde, Captaine Bartholowmew Gilbert, and diuers other gentlemen, their associats, by the permission of the honourable knight, Sir W. Ralegh*. London: Geor. Bishop, 1602. 24 pp. A second impression with some additions was issued in the same year. Reprint. New York: Dodd, Mead, *c.* 1903. Contains an account of Samuel Mace's voyage to Virginia in 1602 to locate the Lost Colony.

947. *A Brief Account of Ralegh's Roanoke Colony of 1585; Being a Guide to an Exhibition Commemorating the Three Hundred and Fiftieth Anniversary . . . .* Ann Arbor, Mich.: [Ann Arbor Press], 1935. 18 pp. Comments on the books, maps, and engravings displayed for the occasion by the William Clements Library.

948. Brown, Alexander. *The Genesis of the United States.* 2 vols. 1:13–21. Boston and New York: Houghton Mifflin, 1890. Describes Ralegh's Roanoke colony.

949. Bruce, Edward C. "Loungings In The Footprints Of The Pioneers II." *Harper's New Monthly Magazine* 20 (1860): 721–36. Describes a visit to Fort Raleigh on Roanoke Island.

950. Brushfield, T. N. "Raleigh in America." *Notes and Queries*, 9th ser. 12 (1903): 250–51. Traces the legend that Raleigh personally discovered Virginia to John Shirley's *Life of Raleigh* (1677), which was quoted by John Prince in 1701 and Lewis

Theobald in 1719 but denied by William Oldys in 1736.

951. Bry, Theodore de. *Americae*. [Often called the *Great and Small Voyages*]. Frankfurt am Main: Oppenheim, 1590–1634. Multiple volumes. Includes Hariot's *Brief and true Report of Virginia*, with engravings based on John White's drawings, as Part 1 and Ralegh's *Discovery of Guiana* as Part 8 of the *Great Voyages*. De Bry's intention, only partly achieved, was to publish in Latin, German, French, and English. The complicated publishing history is discussed in Joseph Sabin's *Dictionary of Books Relating to America* (1870), 3:20–63, and in George Watson Cole's *Catalogue of Books [from] the E. D. Church Library* (1907), 316–580.

952. Burrage, Henry Sweetser, ed. *Early English and French Voyages, Chiefly from Hakluyt, 1534–1608*. New York: Scribner, 1906. 451 pp. Reprint. New York: Barnes & Noble, 1959.

953. Burtnett, Jane. "Raleigh's Unique Discovery." *St. Nicholas* 50 (1922): 208–9. Describes Pitch Lake, a great asphalt deposit in Guiana, which Ralegh saw.

954. Busbee, Jacques. "Art as a Handmaiden of History." *North Carolina Booklet* 10 (1910): 4–11. Describes how the White pictures illustrate the Ralegh colonies.

955. ————. "Elizabethan Settlements in North Carolina." *Mentor* 14 (1928): 21–22.

956. Bushnell, David I., Jr. "John White—The First English Artist to Visit America, 1585." *Virginia Magazine of History and Biography* 35 (1927): 419–30; 36 (1928): 17–26, 124–34. Includes 18 black-and-white photographs of the White drawings in the British Museum.

957. Bushnell, George Herbert. *Sir Richard Grenville: The Turbulent Life and Career of the Hero of the Little "Revenge."* London: Harrap, 1936. 341 pp. Treats in detail Grenville's role in the Roanoke enterprise.

958. Canton, Francisco Janvier Sanchez. *Don Diego Sarmiento de Acuña, Conde de Gondomar (1567–1626)*, 31–34. Madrid, n.p. 1935. Describes how the Spanish ambassador at James's court used diplomacy and bribery to insure Ralegh's doom.

959. Carrington, C. E. *The British Overseas, Part I: Making of the Empire*, 2d ed., 19–21. Cambridge: Cambridge University Press, 1968. 543 pp. Considers Ralegh's American expeditions.

960. Carrington, Dorothy. *The Traveller's Eye*, 277–87. New York: Pilot, 1947. 381 pp. Describes Ralegh's efforts at colonization in America.

961. Carse, Robert. *The Age of Piracy: A History*, 133–45. New York: Rinehart, 1957. 276 pp. Describes Ralegh's final voyage.

962. *Catalogue of the Exhibition of Water-color Reproductions of John White's Drawings on Loan from the University of North Carolina at Chapel Hill Exhibited as a Part of the Fifth Annual John White Art Show August 18, 19 and 20, 1967, by the Roanoke Island Historical Assn. in the Lost Colony Building, Fort Raleigh National Historic Site, Roanoke Island, Manteo, North Carolina.* [Manteo, N.C.]: Roanoke Island Historical Association, [1967]. 6 pp. Describes 46 of White's drawings.

963. Caulín, Fray Antonio. *Historia coro-gráphica, natural, y evangélica de la Nueva Andalucía, provincias de Cumaná, Guyana y vertientes del Rio Orinoco.* 185–93. Madrid: Juan de San Martín, 1779. 482 pp. 6th ed., edited by Pablo Ojer, S. J. Caracas: Fuentes para la Historia Colonial de Venezuela, 1966. Discusses Ralegh's incursion into Guiana.

964. Chandler, J. A. C., and T. B. Thames. "The Lost Colony of Roanoke Island." In *Colonial Virginia*, 1–15. Richmond, Va.: Times-Dispatch, 1907. 388 pp.

965. Channing, Edward. "The English Seamen." In *History of the United States*. 7 vols. 1:115–42. New York: Macmillan, 1918.

966. Chapman, Walker [Robert Silverberg]. "Raleigh and the Gold of Manoa." In *The Golden Dream: Seekers of El Dorado*, 307–51. Indianapolis: Bobbs-Merrill, 1967. 437 pp. Discusses Ralegh's first expedition to Guiana, drawing on his *Discovery of Guiana*.

967. Chatterton, E. Keble. *English Seamen and the Colonization of America.* London: Arrowsmith, 1930. 326 pp. Provides a narrative, based on Hakluyt, of the efforts to establish a settlement in Virginia.

968. Cheshire, Joseph Blount. "Baptism of Virginia Dare." *North Carolina Booklet* 10 (1911): 167–75. Prints an address delivered on Roanoke Island praising the English settlers there.

969. Chorley, E. Clowes. "The Planting of the Church in Virginia." *William and Mary Quarterly*, 2d. ser. 10 (1930): 191–213. Considers Ralegh's role in the church.

970. Christy, Bayard H. "Topsell's 'Fowles of Heaven.'" *Auk*, n.s. 50 (1933) 275–83. Describes a pre-1614 manuscript about birds, naming 17 American kinds known to the author, the Rev. Edward Topsell.

971. Clapp, Henry. *With Raleigh to British Guiana.* London: Muller, 1965. 142 pp.

972. Clark, Walter. *On Roanoke Island.* Goldsboro, N.C.: Nash, 1902. 9 pp. Reprinted as "The Cradle of American Civilization." In *North Carolina Historical Commission Literary and Historical Activities in North Carolina 1900–1905* (1907). Reprinted as "Roanoke Island." In *North Carolina Booklet* (1911). Prints a 1902 address by Judge Clark at Manteo, celebrating the westward movement of the Anglo-Saxon people to Roanoke Island in the 1580s.

973. Clift, Jane M. "First Evidences of Masonry in Virginia." *Virginia Masonic Herald* 33 (1938): 13–15. Describes the excavation of an Indian mound in Burke County, N.C., which might be the grave of Roanoke Island colonists.

974. Coke, Roger. *A Detection of the Court and State of England during the last four reigns, and the inter-regnum.* 2 vols. London: n.p., 1694. 2d ed. London, n.p., 1696. 3d ed. London: Printed for Andr. Bell, 1697. 4th ed. London: Brotherton & Meadows, 1719. Includes comments on Ralegh's last Guiana voyage.

975. *A Collection of Voyages and Discoveries, by the most celebrated navigators, viz. Columbus, Cortes, Drake, Raleigh . . . ,* 401–48. Glasgow: James Turner, 1792. 531 pp.

976. Colliber, Samuel. "Sir Walter Raleigh's Expedition to Guiana." In *A Critical History of the English Sea-affairs.* London: Robinson, 1727. 312 pp.

977. Collier, J. Payne. "On Richard Hakluyt and American Discoveries." *Archaeologia* 33 (1849): 283–92. Describes *Divers Voyages* and reprints two letters by Hakluyt.

978. Connor, Robert D. W. *The Beginnings of English America: Sir Walter Raleigh's Settlements on Roanoke Island, 1584–1587.* Raleigh: North Carolina Historical Commission, 1907. 39 pp.

979. _____. "North Carolina's Patron Saints." *American Monthly Magazine* 40 (1912): 209–13. Summarizes the roles of Ralegh, Drake and Grenville in the Roanoke enterprise.

980. _____. "Sir Walter Raleigh and His Associates." *North Carolina Booklet* 11 (1912): 135–57. Prints an address by Connor in 1911 to the Roanoke Island Colony Association.

981. _____. *The Colonial and Revolutionary Periods 1584–1783*, 1–20. Volume 1 of *History of North Carolina*, 6 vols. Chicago and New York: Lewis, 1919.

982. _____, ed. "Anglo-American Relations in Commemoration of the Tercentenary of Sir Walter Raleigh." *Publications of the State Literary and Historical Association of North Carolina* 25 (1918): 23–146.

983. Corbitt, David Leroy, ed. *Explorations, Descriptions and Attempted Settlements of Carolina, 1584–1590*. Raleigh: North Carolina State Department of Archives and History, 1948. 136 pp. Another ed. 1953. Reprints Hakluyt's accounts of the Roanoke voyages.

984. Cotten, Sallie Southall, and Florence S. Tucker. *The Women of North Carolina To the Women of America*. [Raleigh]: Virginia Dare Association, [c. 1893]. 7 pp. Calls for the establishment in Raleigh of a national manual training school for girls in honor of Ralegh and Virginia Dare.

985. Craven, Wesley Frank. "Roanoke Island." In *The Southern Colonies in the Seventeenth Century 1607–1689*. Baton Rouge: Louisiana State University Press, 1949. 451 pp. Discusses the Roanoke expeditions, blaming Ralegh for abandoning the 1587 settlers.

986. Crawford, H. D. "British America's Birthplace." *American Forests* 72 (1966): 14–17, 38–39. Describes Roanoke Island and Ralegh's enterprise there.

987. Crittenden, C. C. "The Fort Raleigh Restoration." *Daughters of the American Revolution Magazine* 70 (1936): 923. Describes the erection on the site of Fort Raleigh of log buildings with thatched roofs, designed by Frank Stick.

988. Croft-Murray, Edward, and Paul Hulton. *Catalogue of British Drawings, Volume One: XVI & XVII Centuries*. 2 vols. London: Trustees of the British Museum, 1960. Describes John White's career (1:28ff.) and reproduces his drawings (2: plates 1–8, 17–64).

989. Cronau, Rodolfo. "Sir Walter Raleigh en Virginia y Guyana." In *América: Historia de su descubrimiento desde los tiempos primitivos hasta los más modernos*. 3 vols. 3:207–21.

Barcelona: Montaner y Simón, 1892. Discusses Ralegh's Roanoke enterprise but gives more attention to his Guiana ventures.

990. Cumming, William Patterson. "The Identity of John White, Governor of Roanoke, and John White, the Artist." *North Carolina Historical Review* 15 (1938): 197–203. Demonstrates that John White was both governor and artist.

991. _____. "Our Earliest Known Map." *State* 25 (1958): 10–11, 22. Describes a crude map of the North Carolina coast made by the Lane colonists in 1585, found in the British Public Record Office, and noted by D. B. Quinn in 1955.

992. Cumming, William Patterson, R. A. Skelton, and David B. Quinn. *The Discovery of North America.* New York: American Heritage Press, 1971. 304 pp. Describes the discoveries, with 370 plates, including some of John White's drawings, De Bry's engravings, and contemporary maps.

993. Daniell, David Scott. "The Lost Colony." *Geographical Magazine* 13 (1941): 288–94.

994. Dart, A. Denison. "Historic Roanoke Island." *New Age* 6 (1907): 47–48.

995. _____. "Raleigh's Lost Colony." *Southern Workman* 42 (1913): 445–46. Claims that the Croatans are the descendants of the Lost Colonists.

996. Daves, Edward Graham. "Raleigh's 'New Fort in Virginia'— 1585." *Magazine of American History* 29 (1893): 459–70. Reprint. New York: Little, 1893. Surveys Ralegh's Roanoke enterprise and proposes that the ruins of the fort be purchased and preserved as a symbol of the English heritage in America.

997. _____. "Raleigh's 'New Fort in Virginia'—1585." *Trinity Archive* 9 (1896): 193–206, 257–70. Reprinted in *Trinity College Historical Society Annual Publications* (1897). Describes the efforts to settle Roanoke Island.

998. _____. "Virginia Dare." *North Carolina Booklet* 1 (1901): 3–16. Cites a tradition that Eleanor Dare was known as "The White Doe" and her daughter Virginia as "The White Fawn."

999. Davies, K. G. *The North Atlantic World in the Seventeenth Century*, 23–24. Minneapolis: University of Minnesota Press, 1974. 366 pp. Describes Ralegh's search for Eldorado and mentions him *passim*.

1000. Davis, John D. "What Inlet Did Amadas and Barlow Enter in

1584?" *University of North Carolina Magazine*, n.s. 12 (1893): 243–57; 13 (1893): 124–28. Claims that it was not Ocracoke Inlet as historians have stated but rather some inlet a short distance west of Cape Lookout lighthouse, and that the large island visited by these explorers was not Roanoke but Cedar Island.

1001. Davis, N. Darnell. "Sir Walter Ralegh's Search for El Dorado." *Blackwood's Edinburgh Magazine* 194 (1913): 771–80. Describes Ralegh's two Guiana expeditions.

De Bry, Theodore. *See* Bry, Theodore de.

1002. "De Bry Collection des Grands et Petits Voyages." *Molinismo* 71, 1971, 33–56. Contains 16 colored illustrations with text and the map of Virginia from De Bry's *Grands Voyages*.

1003. "De Commissione Speciali Directa Waltero Rawley Militi Concernente Voiagium Guianianum." In *Foedera*, compiled by Thomas Rymer. 17 vols. 16:789. London: Churchill, 1704–17. Reproduces the license, dated 26 August 1616, for Ralegh to sail to Guiana.

1004. Detweiler, Robert. "Was Richard Hakluyt a Negative Influence in the Colonization of Virginia?" *North Carolina Historical Review* 48 (1971): 359–69. Says that Ralegh chose Hakluyt as the spokesman for the venture but Hakluyt may have encouraged treasure-seeking adventurers rather than hard-working artisans and farmers to emigrate and thereby contributed to the Roanoke Colony's failure.

1005. Dial, Adolph L., and David K. Eliades. *The Only Land I Know: A History of the Lumbee Indians.* San Francisco: Indian Press, [1975]. 188 pp. Concludes that the Lumbees are descendants of the Lost Colonists and of the Hatteras and other Eastern Sioux Indians.

1006. Dolan, Robert, and Kenton Bosserman. "Shoreline Erosion and the Lost Colony." *Annals of the Association of American Geographers* 62 (1972): 424–26. Suggests that the repeated failure of archaeologists to locate the site of the Lost Colony on Roanoke Island may be caused by shoreline erosion.

1007. Doran, Joseph Ingersoll. "Sir W. Raleigh, Chief Governor of Virginia and Founder of Roanoke Colony, 1585." *Pennsylvania Society of Colonial Governors* 1 (1916): 52–72.

1008. Doyle, J. A. *English Colonies in America: Virginia, Maryland,*

and the Carolinas, 56–74. New York: Holt, 1882. 420 pp. Describes Ralegh's Roanoke enterprise.

1009. Drake, E. C. "The Voyages of Sir Walter Raleigh and Others." In *A New Universal Collection of Authentic Voyages and Travels From the Earliest Accounts to the Present Time*, 285–302. London: Cooke, 1768. 706 pp. Deals especially with Ralegh's first voyage to Guiana.

1010. Dromgoole, W. A. "The Malungeons." *Arena* 3 (1891): 470–79. Describes these supposed descendants of the Lost Colonists.

1011. Dunbar, Gary S. "The Hatteras Indians of North Carolina." *Ethnohistory* 7 (1960): 410–18. Dismisses as implausible the theory that the Croatans are descendants of the Lost Colonists by way of the Hatteras Indians.

1012. Durant, David N. *Ralegh's Lost Colony*. New York: Atheneum; London: Weidenfeld and Nicolson, 1981. 188 pp. Makes extensive use of the documents and offers new findings.

1013. Dyke, Gwenyth. "Thomas Cavendish and the Roanoke Voyage, 1585: Notes on Some Recently Discovered Documents." *Suffolk Review* 1 (1956): 33–36. Shows that Cavendish mortgaged five manors in 1585, probably to outfit a ship to sail to Roanoke, and cites a list of rules for governing a fort, indicating that he was to be second-in-command of the Ralegh expedition.

1014. ———. "The Finance of a Sixteenth-Century Navigator, Thomas Cavendish of Trimley in Suffolk." *Mariner's Mirror* 44 (1958): 108–15. Describes Cavendish's financing of three voyages, including the 1585 voyage to Roanoke under Grenville, on which he served as Grand Marshal, and how he redeemed his five mortgaged manors after the voyage.

1015. Eggleston, Edward. "The Beginning of a Nation," and "The Aborigines and the Colonists." *Century Illustrated Monthly Magazine*, n.s. 3 (1882): 61–83; 4 (1883): 96–114. Describes English ideas of America at the time of Ralegh's attempted settlement there, discusses it, and provides illustrations from White's drawings.

1016. ———. "John White's Drawings." *Nation* 52 (1891): 340–41. Compares the White drawings in the Grenville collection with those in the British Museum and concludes that Grenville's were used by De Bry in making his engravings.

1017. Eifert, Virginia L. S. "Land of the Sassafras Tree." In *Tall Trees and Far Horizons: Adventures and Discoveries of Early Botanists in America*, 1–22. New York: Dodd, Mead, 1965. 301 pp. Account of Hariot and the Ralegh colonies.

1018. Emerson, Everett. "Thomas Hariot, John White, and Ould Virginia." In *Essays in Early Virginia Literature Honoring Richard Beale Davis*, edited by Joseph A. Leo Lemay, 1–12. New York: Burt Franklin, 1977. 282 pp. Claims that Hariot is a poor propagandist for Old Virginia but a humane analyzer of Indians, and that White's drawings should be seen with Hariot's captions from De Bry.

1019. Entick, John. *A New Naval History*, 238–95. London: Printed for Manby, et al., 1757. approx. 880 pp. Mentions Ralegh's voyages to Virginia and Guiana passim.

1020. Esler, A. J. "Influences of Social and Cultural Developments and of Traditional Geography on Elizabethan Concepts of the Nature of the American Indian." Master's thesis, Duke University, 1958. 179 pp.

1021. Etheridge, B. R. "Fort Raleigh—Its History." *Trinity Archive* 13 (1899): 18–30.

1022. Ewen, Cecil H. L'Estrange. *Raleigh's Last Adventure: Bailie's Allegation of Piratical Intent Refuted by Unpublished Depositions*. London: Privately printed, 1938. 16 pp. Reproduces High Court of Admiralty records in Public Record Office.

1023. ———. "Raleigh's Last Voyage." *Notes and Queries* 174 (1938): 254–56. Discusses Ralegh's voyage to Guiana in 1617.

1024. Farrar, Frederick William. *Sir Walter Raleigh and America*. London: Anglo-American Times Press, 1882. 21 pp. Reprinted in *Social and Present Day Questions*. Boston: Bradley & Woodruff, 1891. Extract in *Our Continent* (1882). Discusses the Raleigh Window in St. Margaret's Church, Westminster, a gift from Americans.

1025. Febres Cordero, Julio G. "Los Dorados del Parime." In *Acta Americana* 4 (1946): 26–44. Discusses Ralegh's contribution to the El Dorado myth.

1026. *The First English on Roanoke Island, 1584–1587: A Fact Book with a Preface by W. O. Saunders*. Manteo, N.C.: Roanoke Colony Memorial Association, c. 1937. 38 pp. Gives accounts of the Roanoke voyages derived from Hakluyt.

1027. *The First English Settlements in America.* Manteo, N.C.:
Roanoke Island Historical Association, 1937. 20 pp.

1028. Fiske, John. *Old Virginia and Her Neighbours.* 2 vols. 1:28–
32, 52–55, 197–201. Boston and New York: Houghton
Mifflin, 1900. Describes Ralegh's voyages to Virginia and
Guiana.

1029. Fitch, William Edward. *The First Founders in America, With
Facts to Prove that Sir Walter Raleigh's Lost Colony Was Not
Lost.* New York: New York Society of the Order of the
Founders and Patriots of America, 1913. 40 pp. Claims that the
Croatan Indians are descendants of the Lost Colonists.

1030. Fletcher, Inglis. "The Elizabethan Background of North
Carolina." *Daughters of the American Revolution Magazine* 86
(1962): 274–78.

1031. Floyd, Dolores Boisfeuillet. "The Legend of Sir Walter Raleigh
at Savannah." *Georgia Historical Quarterly* 23 (1939): 103–
21. Holds that an interview between Ralegh and an Indian chief
took place where Savannah now stands; General Oglethorpe
later used the legend to strengthen England's claim to the
Georgia region.

1032. Ford, Alexander Hume. "The Finding of Raleigh's Lost
Colony." *Appleton's Magazine* 10 (1907): 22–31. Claims that
the Croatans are descendants of the Lost Colonists.

1033. "Fort Diggings May Solve Mystery of Lost Colony." *Science
News Letter* 51 (1947): 328. Reports discovery of man-made
objects on site of Fort Raleigh on Roanoke Island.

1034. Foss, Michael. *Undreamed Shores: England's Wasted Empire
in America.* New York: Scribner; London: Harrap, [1974]. 186
pp. Attributes the failure of colonizing attempts by Ralegh and
others to the rashness and greed of the colonizers.

1035. Foster, C. Le Neve. "A Journey Upon the Orinoco to the
Caratal Gold Fields—Raleigh's 'El Dorado.' " In *Illustrated
Travels: A Record of Discovery, Geography, and Adventure,*
edited by H. W. Bates. 6 vols. 1: 257–63, 297–302, 335–38,
375–78. London: Cassell, Petter & Galpin, [1869–75].

1036. Franklin, Wayne. *Discoverers, Explorers, Settlers: The Diligent
Writers of Early America.* Chicago and London: University of
Chicago Press, 1979. 252 pp. Analyzes early narratives about
America, including those relating to Ralegh.

1037. Friederchsen, L. "Sir Walter Ralegh's Karte von Guayana um

1595." In *Hamburgische Festschrift zur Erinnerung an die Entdeckung Amerikas.* 2 vols. 2:1–9 (paged separately at end). Hamburg: Friederchsen, 1892. Reprinted in *Acta Cartographica.* Amsterdam: Theatrum Orbis Terrarum, 1969. Reproduces and discusses Ralegh's map of Guiana in 1595.

1038. Frost, Thomas. "Sir W. Ralegh's Explorations and Adventures in Guiana." In *Half-hours with the Early Explorers,* 192–208. London: Cassell, 1873. 238 pp.

1039. G., S. [S. Gibson]. "The 350th Anniversary of the First English Settlement in America." *Bodleian Quarterly Record* 7 (1934): 424–26. Describes books displayed for this occasion.

1040. Galinsky, Hans. "Frühkoloniales Amerika in dreifacher europäischer Sicht: Pedro de Castañeda, Samuel de Champlain, Thomas Hariot." In *Beiträge zur vergleichenden Literaturgeschichte: Festschrift für Kurt Wais zum 65. Geburtstag,* 19–52. Tübingen: Niemeyer, 1972. 406 pp.

1041. ———. "Exploring the 'Exploration Report' and Its Image of the Overseas World: Spanish, French, and English Variants of a Common Form Type in Early American Literature." *Early American Literature* 12 (1977): 5–24. Sees the exploration report as a distinctive genre, exemplified by Hariot's *Brief and True Report.*

1042. Gardiner, Samuel Rawson. "Letter of the Council to Sir Thomas Lake, Relating to the Proceedings of Sir Edward Coke at Oatlands; and, Documents Relating to Sir Walter Raleigh's last Voyage." In *Camden Miscellany* 87 (1864): 7–13. Contains transcripts from the Proceedings of the Privy Council in 1618.

1043. ———. "The Case Against Sir Walter Raleigh." *Fortnightly Review,* n.s. 1 (1867): 602–14; subsumed in Gardiner's *History of England* (1883), 3:108–55. Introduces some new documents and discusses Raleigh's contact with the French before his voyage to Guiana in 1617, denies that James I betrayed Ralegh, and argues that Ralegh was guilty as charged.

1044. Geer, Curtis Manning. *English Colonization Ideas in the Reign of Elizabeth.* Danvers, Mass.: Danvers Mirror Press, 1895. 47 pp. Considers that the motives for colonization were patriotic, philanthropic, and acquisitive.

1045. Glasgow, Tom. "Ferdinando." *State* 30 (1962): 9. Sketches the life of Simon Fernandes and his role in the Roanoke voyage.

1046. _____. "*H.M.S. Tiger.*" *North Carolina Historical Review* 43 (1966): 115–21. Describes Grenville's flagship in the fleet which carried the Lane colonists to Roanoke.

1047. "A Golden Legend (Ralegh's Search for Manoa)." *Household Words* 18 (1858): 561–65.

1048. González Brum, Guillermo. "Sir Walter Raleigh y su expedición al Orinoco." *Boletín de Historia y Antigüedades* 17 (1929): 468–73.

1049. Goodman, Edward J. *The Explorers of South America.* New York: Macmillan; London: Collier-Macmillan, [1972]. 408 pp. Mentions Ralegh's activities in Guiana.

1050. Goodrich, Frank B. *Ocean's Story; or, Triumphs of Thirty Centuries; A Graphic Description of Maritime Adventures, Achievements, Explorations, Discoveries and Inventions; and of the Rise and Progress Of Ship-Building And Ocean Navigation From The Ark To The Iron Steamships.* Fond du Lac, Wis.: Benjamin; Philadelphia and Boston: Hubbard, 1873. 712 pp. Includes a chapter on Ralegh's Guiana ventures.

1051. H., V. T. [V. T. Harlow]. "Sir Walter Ralegh's Voyage to Guiana (1617–18)." *Bodleian Quarterly Record* 6 (1929): 78. Reports the recent acquisition of a volume (MS Eng. hist. d. 138) comprising contemporary transcripts of Ralegh's "Letter to Prince Henry [concerning] the modell of a Shipp," "Letter . . . before he undertooke his Voyage" to Sir Ralph Winwood, "Apology for his Voyage," and "Letter to King James at his returne from Guiana."

1052. Hakluyt, Richard. *Voyages of the Elizabethan Seamen to America: Select Narratives from the 'Principal Navigations' of Hakluyt,* edited by Edward John Payne. Oxford: Clarendon Press, 1900. 298 pp. Includes Ralegh's *Discovery of Guiana* and Amadas and Barlow's account of their 1584 voyage to Roanoke.

1053. _____. *Hakluyt's Voyages and Discoveries,* edited by Jack Breeching. Harmondsworth: Penguin Books, 1972. 444 pp.

1054. Hale, Edward Everett, ed. "Original Documents from the State-Paper Office, London, and the British Museum; Illustrating the History of Sir Walter Raleigh's First American Colony, and the Colony at Jamestown . . . with an appendix containing a memoir of Sr. Ralph Lane." *Archaeologia*

Americana, Transactions and Collections of the American Antiquarian Society 4 (1860): 61–65, 317–44.

1055. Hale, John R. *Age of Exploration.* New York: Time, 1966. 192 pp. Contains references to Ralegh and reproduces 16 watercolors by John White.

1056. Hamilton, P. J. "Raleigh Founds Virginia." In *The Colonization of the South*, 43–54. Philadelphia: Barrie, 1904. 494 pp.

1057. Hannay, David. "El Dorado." *Blackwood's Magazine* 193 (1913): 400–411. Describes Ralegh's and other expeditions to Guiana.

1058. _____. "Ralegh's Orders." *Mariner's Mirror* 3 (1913): 212–15. Claims that Ralegh's orders to his squadron as it prepared to sail for Guiana in 1617 helped to form naval law.

1059. Harcourt, Robert. *A Relation of a Voyage to Guiana. Describing the Climat, Scituation, fertilitie, provisions and commodities of that Country, containing seven Provinces, and other Signiories within that Territory: Together, with the manners, customes, behaviors, and dispositions of the people. Performed by Robert Harcourt, of Stanton Harcourt Esquire. The Patent for the Plantation of which Country, his Majesty hath granted to the said Robert Harcourt, under the Great Seal.* London: Printed by John Beale for W. Welby, 1613. 88 pp. 2d ed. 1626. Published in *Purchas his Pilgrimes* (1625), through which Harcourt's work reached the continent. Reprinted in *Harleian Miscellany* (1809 and 1810); a long abstract in J. Harris, *Collection of Voyages* (1705); in *Hakluyt Society Publications* (1928), edited by Sir C. Alexander Harris. Describes the Guiana voyages of Ralegh in 1595 and of Harcourt in 1608.

1060. Harlow, V. T. *Colonising Expeditions to the West Indies and Guiana, 1623–1667.* London: Hakluyt Society, 1925. 262 pp. Includes an account of Ralegh's activities in Guiana and Trinidad.

1061. _____. *Ralegh's Last Voyage. Being an Account Drawn Out of Contemporary Letters and Relations, Both Spanish and English, of which the Most Part Are Now for the First Time Made Public, Concerning the Voyage of Sir Walter Ralegh, Knight, to Guiana in the Year 1617 and the Fatal Consequences of the Same.* London: Argonaut Press, 1932. 379 pp. Reprint. Amsterdam: N. Israel; New York: Da Capo, 1971. Using documentary evidence, argues in a 99-page "Interpretation" that events and the characters of King James and Ralegh ensured his destruction.

1062. _____, ed. *Voyages of Great Pioneers.* London: Oxford University Press, 1929. 380 pp. Includes Ralegh's *Discoverie of Guiana.*

1063. Harrington, J. C. "Archaeological Explorations at Fort Raleigh National Historic Site." *North Carolina Historical Review* 26 (1949): 127–49. Reports recent excavations which show that Ralph Lane's 1585 fort was on the site.

1064. _____. "The Finding of Fort Raleigh." *Southern Indian Studies* 1 (1949): 18–19. Describes the fort's remains as an earth embankment surrounded by a dry moat.

1065. _____. "Historic Relic Found: An Old Iron Sickle from Fort Raleigh, North Carolina." *Iron Worker* 15 (1951): 12–15. Declares that the sickle, apparently a relic of the Ralegh settlement, is probably the oldest iron object of English origin yet found in the United States.

1066. _____. "Fort Raleigh, 1585." *Journal of the Society of Architectural Historians* 13 (1954): 27–28.

1067. _____. "Evidence of Manual Reckoning in the Cittie of Ralegh." *North Carolina Historical Review* 33 (1956): 1–11. Reports the discovery in 1950 at Fort Raleigh of three metal casting counters or jettons manufactured by Hans Schultes of Nuremberg (fl. 1550–74).

1068. _____. *Search for the Cittie of Ralegh: Archaeological Excavations at Fort Raleigh National Historic Site.* Washington, D.C.: National Park Service, U. S. Department of the Interior, 1962. 63 pp. Describes the excavations carried on from 1947 to 1953 at Fort Raleigh, its reconstruction, and the objects of Indian and European origin uncovered there.

1069. _____. *An Outwork at Fort Raleigh: Further Archaeological Excavations at Fort Raleigh National Historic Site, North Carolina.* Philadelphia: Eastern National Park and Monument Association, 1966. 66 pp. Describes recent excavations following the discovery of brick and other items.

1070. _____. "The Manufacture and Use of Bricks at the Raleigh

Settlement on Roanoke Island." *North Carolina Historical Review* 44 (1967): 1–17. Concludes that bricks were made by the Ralegh colonists, but for what buildings remains unknown.

1071. _____. *Archaeology and the Enigma of Fort Raleigh*. Raleigh, N.C.: America's Four Hundredth Anniversary Committee, North Carolina Department of Cultural Resources, 1984. 36 pp. Traces the history of archaeological research at Fort Raleigh and describes in detail the outwork and bricks discovered at the site in the late 1950s.

1072. Harrison, Thomas Perrin, ed. *John White and Edward Topsell: The First Water Colors of North American Birds*. Austin: University of Texas Press, 1964. 59 pp. Reproduces in pairs colored sketches of Virginian birds from Topsell's "Fowles of Heaven" and their apparent originals drawn by John White.

1073. Hawke, David. *The Colonial Experience*, 34–37. New York and Indianapolis: Bobbs-Merrill, 1966. 774 pp. Describes Ralegh's Roanoke enterprise.

1074. Hawks, Francis L. *History of North Carolina*. 2 vols. Fayetteville, N.C.: Hale, 1857. Spartanburg, S.C.: Reprint, 1961. Devotes volume 1 to the Roanoke Colonies and reprints important documents.

1075. Hearnshaw, F. J. C. "Sir Walter Raleigh: A Great Englishman." *Overseas* 3 (1918): 41–43.

1076. Heat Moon, William Least [William Trogdon]. *Blue Highways: A Journey into America*, 55–65. Boston and Toronto: Little, Brown, 1982. 421 pp. Considers Ralegh, Hariot, and the Lost Colony from the author's perspective as an American Indian.

1077. Hemming, John. *The Search for El Dorado*. London: Michael Joseph, 1978; New York: Dutton, 1979. 223 pp. In the last chapter, tells of Ralegh's two expeditions up the Orinoco.

1078. Henderson, Archibald. "The Roanoke Island Colony 1584–87." In *North Carolina, the Old North State and the New*. 5 vols. 1:1–24. Chicago: Lewis, 1941.

1079. Henry, William Wirt. "Sir Walter Ralegh; The settlements at Roanoke and voyages to Guiana (with a critical essay on the sources of information)." In *Narrative and Critical History of America*, edited by Justin Winsor. 8 vols. 3:105–26. Boston and New York: Houghton Mifflin, 1884–89.

1080. Higinbotham, Betty Wilson. "Sassafras Shaped History." *Natural History* 56 (1947): 159–64. Claims that Ralegh tried to control the importation from Virginia into England of sassafras, which was regarded as medicinal, in order to keep up the price.

1081. Hind, Arthur Mayger. *Engraving in England in the Sixteenth and Seventeenth Centuries: A Descriptive Catalogue With Introductions.* 3 vols. Cambridge: Cambridge University Press, 1952–64. Provides an account of De Bry's engravings of Virginia from John White's drawings (*Part I: The Tudor Period,* 124–137) and discusses the engravings of Ralegh which appear as the frontispiece to his *History of the World* (*Part II: The Reign of James I,* 266–67, 333–34).

1082. *An Historical Account of the Voyages and Adventures of Sir Walter Raleigh. With the Discoveries and Conquests He made for the Crown of England. Also a particular Account of his several attempts for the Discovery of the Gold Mines in Guiana, and the Reason for the Miscarriage, shewing that it is not from any Defect in the Scheme he had laid, or in the Reality of the Thing it self, but in a treacherous Discovery of his Design, and of the strength he had with him, to the Spaniards. To which is added, An Account how that rich Country might now be with Ease, Possess'd, Planted, and Secur'd to the British Nation, and what Immense Wealth and Encrease of Commerce might be rais'd from thence. Humbly proposed to the South-Sea Company.* London: Printed and Sold by W. Boreham, 1719. 55 pp. Written by some relation of Philip Ralegh, according to Oldys' *Life of Ralegh,* 51.

1083. Holland, W. J. "The First Picture of an American Butterfly." *Scientific Monthly* 29 (1929): 44–48. Speculates about how John White's drawing of the male Tiger Swallowtail butterfly came to be used in the *Insectorum Theatrum* published in 1634.

1084. Honour, Hugh. *The New Golden Land: European Images of America from the Discoveries to the Present Time.* New York: Pantheon Books, 1975. 299 pp. Contains a few quotes from Ralegh and mentions him passim.

1085. Howard, Sir Esme. *Address. Virginia Dare Day: Annual Celebration by the Roanoke Colony Memorial Association. Old*

Fort Raleigh, Roanoke Island, North Carolina, August 18,
1926. Raleigh: Edwards & Broughton, 1926. 16 pp. Compares
Ralegh with Cecil Rhodes as great empire builders.

1086. Howe, Charles Kent. *Solving the Riddle of the Lost Colony.*
Beaufort, N.C.: Skarren, 1947. 45 pp. Publishes a diary
allegedly written by Virginia Dare.

1087. Hulton, Paul Hope. "John White, Artist." *North Carolina*
Museum of Art Bulletin 5 (1965): 3–43. Discusses White's life,
with numerous reproductions of his pictures.

1088. _____. "Images of the New World: Jacques Le Moyne de
Morgues and John White." In *The Westward Enterprise:*
English Activities in Ireland, the Atlantic, and America 1480–
1650, edited by K. R. Andrews, N. P. Canny, and P. E. H. Hair,
195–214. Liverpool: Liverpool University Press, 1978. 326 pp.
Speculates about the artists' indebtedness to each other.

1089. _____. *America 1585: The Complete Drawings of John*
White. Chapel Hill: University of North Carolina Press and
British Museum Publications, 1984. 213 pp.

1090. Hulton, Paul Hope, and David B. Quinn. *The American*
Drawings of John White, 1577–1590. 2 vols. London: Trustees
of the British Museum; Chapel Hill: University of North
Carolina Press, 1964.

1091. Humber, John Leslie. "Backgrounds of the Roanoke Voyages,
1584–1590." Master's thesis, University of North Carolina at
Chapel Hill, 1962. 194 pp. Provides evidence that Ralegh and
his associates in the enterprise profited from resultant
privateering.

1092. _____. *Backgrounds and Preparations for the Roanoke*
Voyages, 1584–1590. Raleigh: America's Four Hundredth
Anniversary Committee, North Carolina Department of
Cultural Resources, 1986. 108 pp. Utilizes the preceding item,
supplemented by numerous drawings.

1093. Innes, Arthur D. *The Maritime and Colonial Expansion of*
England under the Stuarts, 32–35. London: Sampson, Low,
Marston, 1932. 376 pp. Considers Ralegh's hopes for
transatlantic settlements.

1094. Jaffe, Bernard. "Thomas Harriot (1560–1621): Bringing the
Seeds of Science to America." In *Men of Science in America:*
The Role of Science in the Growth of Our Country, 1–22. New
York: Simon & Schuster, 1944. 600 pp. Another ed. titled *Men*

of Science in America: The Story of American Science Told Through the Lives and Achievements of Twenty Outstanding Men from Earliest Colonial Time to the Present Day. New York: Simon & Schuster, 1958. Discusses Ralegh as patron of Hariot, Ralegh's enthusiasm about corn and tobacco, and his efforts at colonization.

1095. Jeffery, Reginald W. *The History of the Thirteen Colonies of North America 1497–1763*, 15–18, 20–23. London: Methuen, 1908. 308 pp. Considers Ralegh's colonizing enterprise.

1096. Jeudwine, J. W. "Raleigh and El Dorado." In *Studies in Empire and Trade*, 228–32. London: Longmans, 1923. 399 pp.

1097. Johnson, Guy B. "Personality in a White-Indian-Negro Community." *American Sociological Review* 4 (1939): 516–23. Discusses the naming of the Indians of Robeson County. In 1885 they were given the name Croatan by the North Carolina legislature, in recognition of the legend that they descended from the Lost Colonists. But the name was sneeringly shortened to "Cro" by whites and blacks, and in 1913 the legislature changed their legal name to "Cherokee Indians of Robeson County."

1098. Jones, Evan D. "An Account Book of Sir Thomas Myddelton for the Years 1583–1603." *National Library of Wales Journal* 1 (1939): 83–88. Notes Middleton's loans to Ralegh for his ventures.

1099. Jones, Joseph Seawell. *Memorials of North Carolina*, 7–23. New York: Scatcherd & Adams, 1838. 87 pp. Provides an account of the Amadas and Barlowe voyage of 1584, drawn from Hakluyt.

1100. Jones, Samuel. "Sir Walter Raleigh's Last Voyage." *Notes and Queries*, 2d ser. 11 (1861): 5–7. Reprinted in J. Spedding, *Life of Lord Bacon* (1872) and V. T. Harlow, *Ralegh's Last Voyage* (1932). Provides an unfriendly account of the 1617 voyage to Guiana by the chaplain on one of Ralegh's ships.

1101. Keeler, Mary Frear. "The Boazio Maps of 1585–86." *Terrae Incognitae* 10 (1978): 71–80. Establishes that Boazio was on Drake's West Indian voyage of 1585–86; reproduces his maps and some of John White's drawings.

1102. Keymis, Lawrence. *A Relation of the Second Voyage to Guiana. Performed and written in the yeere 1596.* London: Imprinted by Thomas Dawson, 1596. 32 leaves. Published as

follows (generally with Ralegh's account): in Hakluyt's *Voyages*,
1598–1600, and in all other complete editions of Hakluyt; in
Dutch, by Claesz, 1598 and 1605; in Latin and German, by De
Bry, 1599; in Dutch by Colijn, 1617; in German and Latin, by
De Bry, 1624 and 1625; in Dutch, by Commelin, 1644; in
French by Coreal, 1722 and 1738; in German, by Schwabe,
1747; in Cayley's *Life of Ralegh*, 1805. Keymis committed
suicide during the Guiana expedition of 1617.

1103. Kidder, Frederick. "Roanoke Island, The Site of the First
English Colony in America." *Continental Monthly* 1 (1862):
541–52. Gives the history of the island from Ralegh's colonies
to the battle there in 1862.

1104. Konetzke, Richard. "Sir Walter Raleigh und der englisch-
spanische Kampf um Amerika." *Ibero-Amerikanisches Archiv* 8
(1934): 133–52. Analyzes Ralegh's aims and achievements in
the campaigns against Spain.

1105. ———. "Sir Walter Raleigh und die geistesgeschichtlichen
Grundlagen des englischen Imperialismus." *Neuphilologische
Monatsschrift* 2 (1936): 61–74. Considers Ralegh's imperialistic
ideas in the context of his time.

1106. Kupperman, Karen Ordahl. "English Perceptions of Treachery,
1583–1640: The Case of the American 'Savages.'" *Historical
Journal* 20 (1977): 263–88. Argues that the Indians' use of
treachery was regarded by the colonists as "a mark of
competence, even of civilization."

1107. ———. *Settling with the Indians: The Meeting of English and
Indian Cultures in America, 1580–1640*. Totowa, N.J.:
Rowman and Littlefield, 1980. 224 pp. Shows that the early
colonists did not regard the Indians as inferior and to be
dominated.

1108. ———. *Roanoke: The Abandoned Colony*. Totowa, N.J.:
Rowman & Allanheld, 1984. 192 pp. Draws on colonists'
narratives and stresses the effect of Indians on their lives.

1109. Lane, Ralph. *Raleigh's First Roanoke Colony*. Boston:
Directors of the Old South Work, 1902. 24 pp.

1110. Latham, Agnes M. C. "Sir Walter Ralegh's Gold Mine: New
Light on the Last Guiana Voyage." *Essays and Studies*, n.s. 4
(1951): 94–111. Reproduces newly discovered documents to
prove that by attacking the Spaniards and not searching for
Eldorado, Keymis ruined his commander Ralegh in 1617.

1111. Lee, Sidney. "Sir Walter Ralegh." In *Great Englishmen of the Sixteenth Century*, 116–54. London: Constable; New York: Scribner, 1904. 337 pp. Revised ed. London: Constable, 1907. Other eds. London and New York: Nelson, [1907?]; London: Harrap, [1925]; Freeport, N.Y.: Books for Libraries Press, 1970; Port Washington, N.Y.: Kennikat Press, 1972. Focuses on Ralegh's Roanoke Island and Guiana ventures.

1112. ———. "Raleigh's Discovery of Guiana." *United Empire: The Royal Colonial Institute Journal*, n.s. 10 (1919): 23–26.

1113. ———. *Elizabethan And Other Essays*, edited by Frederick S. Boas. Oxford: Clarendon Press, 1929. 344 pp. Reprint. Freeport, N.Y.: Books for Libraries Press, 1968. Frequently discusses Ralegh between pages 225 and 319, in this reprint of the four essays headed "The Call of the West: America and Elizabethan England," which appeared in *Scribner's* in 1907.

1114. Lefler, Hugh T., ed. *North Carolina History Told by Contemporaries*, 3–9. Chapel Hill, N. C.: University of North Carolina Press, 1934. 502 pp. 2d ed. 1948. Considers Ralegh's Roanoke enterprise.

1115. Lefler, Hugh T., and Albert Ray Newsome. *North Carolina: The History of a Southern State*, 5–7. Chapel Hill: University of North Carolina Press, 1954. 676 pp. Rev. ed. 1963. Describes the Amadas-Barlowe expedition and the Roanoke enterprise.

1116. Lemert, Ben Franklin. "Geographic Influences in the History of North Carolina." *North Carolina Historical Review* 12 (1935): 297–319. Concludes that the Ralegh settlements would not have thrived because the region could not have supported a host of immigrants.

1117. Lemonnier, León. "Découverte de la Virginie (juillet, 1584)." *Revue Anglo-Américaine* 8 (1930): 52–54. Describes the arrival of the first Roanoke expedition.

1118. ———. "Le Mirage de la Cité d'Or: Variété inédite." *Oeuvres Libres*, no. 114 (1930): 241–78. Depicts Ralegh's long obsession with Eldorado.

1119. Lewis, Norman. "English Missionary Interest in the Indians of North America, 1578–1700." Ph.D. diss., University of Washington, 1968. 503 pp. Discusses what Hariot told Ralegh.

1120. Lindquist, Gustavus Elmer Emanuel. "The Lost Colony of Roanoke Today." *Southern Workman* 57 (1928): 442–44.

1121. Lorant, Stefan, ed. *The New World: The First Pictures of*

America Made by John White and Jacques Le Moyne. New York: Duell, Sloan, and Pearce, 1946, 1965. 292 pp. London: Theodore Brun, 1954. Includes contemporary pictures and narratives about the Roanoke colonies.

1122. Lorimer, Joyce. "English Trade and Exploration in Trinidad and Guiana, 1569–1648." Ph.D. diss., University of Liverpool, 1973. 423 pp.

1123. _____. "Ralegh's First Reconnaissance of Guiana? An English Survey of the Orinoco in 1587." *Terrae Incognitae* 9 (1977): 7–21. Reports from newly found Spanish sources that Ralegh may have sent out a party to reconnoitre the Orinoco region as early as 1587.

1124. _____. "The English Contraband Tobacco Trade in Trindad and Guiana 1590–1617." In *The Westward Enterprise: English Activities in Ireland, the Atlantic, and America 1480–1650*, edited by K. R. Andrews, N. P. Canny, and P. E. H. Hair, 124–50. Liverpool: Liverpool University Press, 1978. 326 pp. Shows Ralegh's involvement with this trade.

1125. Lowrey, Clarence E. *The Lumbee Indians of North Carolina*. Lumberton, N.C.: n.p., 1960. 64 pp. Expresses the belief that the Lumbee Indians are descendants of the Roanoke colonists and that the grave of Virginia Dare is near Red Springs, N.C.

1126. Lowry, D. F. "No Mystery." *State* 20 (1952): 24. Claims that the Lowry family is linked with the Roanoke colonists through marriage with Lumbee Indians.

1127. Lyon, Francis Hamilton. "Raleigh's Last Voyage." In *Diego de Sarmiento de Acuña Conde de Gondomar*, 62–75. Oxford: Blackwell, 1910. 118 pp.

1128. McAtee, W. L. "The North American Birds of Virginia Chroniclers, 1588–1686." *Journal of the Society for the Bibliography of Natural History* 3 (1955): 92–101 (pt. 2). Says that from Hariot's *Briefe and True Report* only the turkey, partridge or bobwhite, and parrot or Carolina parakeet can be firmly identified.

1129. McIntyre, Ruth A. "William Sanderson: Elizabethan Financier of Discovery." *William and Mary Quarterly*, 3d ser. 13 (1956): 184–201. Shows that merchant Sanderson provided cash and credit for Ralegh's efforts to explore and colonize.

1130. McKay, Arnold A. "Nobody Knows Anything about the Croatans." *State* 1 (1934): 1–2. Considers the possible descent of the Croatan Indians from the Lost Colonists, Huguenots, Spanish, or Portuguese.

1131. McMillan, Hamilton. *Sir Walter Raleigh's Lost Colony.* Wilson, N.C.: Advance Press, 1888. 27 pp. Raleigh: Edwards & Broughton, c. 1907. Sketches the attempts to establish the Roanoke colony and claims that Croatan Indians are descendants of the Lost Colonists.

1132. _____. "The Croatans." *North Carolina Booklet* 10 (1911): 115–21. Mingles fact and fiction about the Croatan Indians and reasserts that they are descendants of the Lost Colonists.

1133. McMillan, Hamilton, and Rev. J. J. Blanks. *The Lost Colony Found. An Historical Sketch of the Discovery of the Croatan Indians. . . . Their Advance Movement. Condition Before and After the War. Progress in Civilization and Religion.* Lumberton, N.C.: Robesonian Job Print, [c. 1898?]. 35 pp. and 3 following unnumbered.

1134. McPherson, O. M., ed. "Indians of North Carolina." *Senate Documents.* 63d Cong., 3d sess., 1915. Vol. 4. no. 677. 252 pp. Examines the question of whether the Croatan Indians are descendants of Ralegh's Lost Colonists.

1135. Mangum, O. R. "The Lost Colony Found." *Wake Forest Student* 25 (1906): 517–25. Claims the Croatans are descendants of the Lost Colonists.

1136. Manso, J. A. [John A. Zahm]. "Quest of El Dorado, Part V: The Expedition of Sir Walter Ralegh." *Bulletin of the Pan-American Union* 34 (1912): 607–21. Describes Ralegh's two expeditions to Guiana.

1137. Marsh, Thad Norton. "English Voyages to America, 1496–1603, and the Idea of Primitive Society." D. Phil. thesis, Oxford University, 1956. 455 pp.

1138. Martínez-Mendoza, Jerónimo. *La leyenda de El Dorado: Su historia e influencia en la Venezuela antigua.* Caracas: Academia Nacional de la Historia, 1967. 66 pp. Discusses Ralegh among those involved in the legend of Eldorado.

1139. Melton, Frances Jones. "Croatans: The Lost Colony Of America." *Mid-Continent Magazine* 6 (1885): 195–202. Maintains that the Croatan Indians are descendants of the Lost Colonists.

1140. Miller, Helen Hill. *Passage to America: Ralegh's Colonists Take Ship for Roanoke.* Raleigh: America's Four Hundredth

Anniversary Committee, North Carolina Department of
Cultural Resources, 1983. 84 pp. Describes the Roanoke
voyages, as well as Elizabethan ships, navigation, and
shipboard life.

1141. Montague, Leopold A. D. "A Ralegh Document." *Devon and
Cornwall Notes and Queries* 15 (1929): 259–66. Reprints the
commission dated 23 March 1616 and signed by Ralegh for
John Chudleigh to captain one of Ralegh's ships that sailed to
Guiana in 1617.

1142. Mook, Maurice Allison. "Algonkian Ethnohistory of the
Carolina Sound." *Journal of the Washington Academy of
Sciences* 34 (1944): 181–97, 213–28. Reprinted together as
Algonkian Ethnohistory of the Carolina Sound. Philadelphia:
University of Pennsylvania, 1944. Discusses the Indian tribes
encountered by the Ralegh colonists.

1143. Morales Lezcano, Victor. "Sir Walter Raleigh y los
archipiélagos del atlántico ibérico." *Anuario de Estudios
Atlánticos* 13 (1967): 339–64. Discusses Ralegh's expeditions
against Spain's transatlantic possessions.

1144. Morgan, Edmund Seares. "John White and the Sarsaparilla."
William and Mary Quarterly, 3d ser. 14 (1957): 414–17. Notes
that White gave John Gerard a description of sarsaparilla,
which is printed in his *Herball* of 1597 on pages 709–10;
Gerard calls White "an excellent painter who caried very many
people into Virginia."

1145. Morris, Charles. "Sir Walter Raleigh, The Prince of
Colonizers." In *Heroes of Discovery in America*, 166–75.
Philadelphia and London: Lippincott, 1906. 344 pp. 2d ed.,
revised, 1919.

1146. Morton, Richard L. *Colonial Virginia*. 2 vols. 1:2–4. Chapel
Hill: University of North Carolina Press, 1960. Considers
Ralegh's Roanoke enterprise.

1147. N., T. "Was Raleigh in Virginia?" *Notes and Queries* 4 (1851):
448–52. Reprinted in *American Bibliopolist* (1870). Shows that
Ralegh never visited that region, contrary to the claim made by
his early biographers Shirley and Theobald but denied by Oldys
in 1736.

1148. Naipaul, V. S. *The Loss of El Dorado: A History*. London:
André Deutsch, 1969. 334 pp. Revised ed. Harmondsworth:

Penguin, 1973. Translated into Swedish as *Det forlorado Eldorado* (1974). Links Ralegh's quest for El Dorado with the later English dream of making Port of Spain in Trinidad a great British trading post for an independent South America.

1149. Nash, Gary B. "The Image of the Indian in the Southern Colonial Mind." *William and Mary Quarterly*, 3d ser. 29 (1972): 197–230. Describes Ralegh's notions of the North American Indians.

1150. *Newes of Sr. Walter Rauleigh. With the True Description of Guiana: As also a Relation of the Excellent Gouerment, and much hope of the prosperity of the Voyage. Sent from a Gentleman of his Fleet, to a most especiall Friend of his in London. From the riuer of Caliana, on the coast of Guiana, Nouemb. 17, 1617.* London: Printed for H. G., 1618. 45 pp. Reprinted in *Photostat Americana*, 2d ser., no. 112. Boston: Massachusetts Historical Society, 1940. Describes various voyages to Guiana, including Ralegh's in 1617.

1151. Newson, Linda A. *Aboriginal and Spanish Colonial Trinidad: A Study in Culture Contact.* London: Academic Press, 1976. 344 pp. Includes discussion of Trinidad's use as a military base for the search for Eldorado.

1152. "The New World: New Book Shows How America Looked in 16th Century." *Life* 22 (1947): 80–85. Reproduces from Stefan Lorant's *New World* some of John White's watercolors and Le Moyne's engravings from De Bry.

1153. Noe, Thomas P., ed. *Pilgrimage to Old Fort Raleigh on Roanoke Island, North Carolina, Aug. 20, 1587–May 20, 1908.* New Bern, N.C.: Owen G. Dunn, 1908. 41 pp. Describes services and addresses given at Fort Raleigh.

1154. Norman, Charles. *Discoverers of America*, 157–251. New York: Crowell, [1968]. 322 pp. Discusses Ralegh's Roanoke enterprise.

1155. "North Carolina's Patron Saints." *American Monthly Magazine* 40 (1912): 209–13. Discusses the Ralegh colony, drawing on an address given on Roanoke Island by R. D. W. Connor.

1156. Oakeshott, Walter Fraser. *Founded Upon the Seas: A Narrative of Some English Maritime and Overseas Enterprises During the Period 1550 to 1616.* London: Macmillan; Cambridge:

Cambridge University Press, 1942. 200 pp. Gives considerable attention to Ralegh's role in the Roanoke colonies and the Guiana voyages.

1157. Ojer, Pablo, S.J. *Don Antonio de Berrio, gobernador del Dorado*. Caracas: Universidad Católico "Andrés Bello," 1960. 210 pp. Discusses Berrio's involvement with Ralegh in "Tragedia en el ocaso" (pages 109–31), unfavorably to Ralegh.

1158. ———. "Guayana entre la rivalidad de las vecinas gobernaciones y la amenaza inglesa." In *La formación del oriente venezolano*, 514–82. Caracas: Universidad Católica "Andrés Bello," 1966. 618 pp. Describes Ralegh's ventures to Guiana.

1159. Oramas, Luis R. *En pos del dorado (Odisea de Sir Walter Ralegh: El gran imperio de oro de la Guayana venezolana)*. Caracas: Tip. Garrido, 1947. 365 pp. Provides a Latin-American perspective on Ralegh's involvement with Guiana.

1160. Osborne, Thomas, ed. "Guiana." In *A Collection of Voyages and Travels, consisting of authentic writers in our own tongue, which have not before been collected in English, or have only been abridged in other collections. And continued with others of note, that have published histories, voyages, travels, journals, or discoveries in other nations and languages, relating to any part of the continent of Asia, Africa, America, Europe, or the islands thereof, from the earliest account to the present time*. 2 vols. 2:749–55. London: T. Osborne, 1745.

1161. Outhwaite, Leonard. "Sir Walter Raleigh." In *Unrolling the Map: The Story of Exploration*, 167–70. New York: Reynal & Hitchcock, 1935. 351 pp.

1162. Page, Evelyn. "The Meeting Point Between Savagery and Civilization." In *American Genesis: Pre-colonial Writing in the North*, 100–113. Boston: Gambit, 1973. 286 pp. Discusses the writings of Barlowe, Lane, Hariot, and White concerning the Roanoke Colony and the theme of utopianism in Ralegh's writings.

1163. Painter, Floyd. "The Ancient Indian Town of Chesapeake on the Peninsula of Great Neck (A Brief History)." *Chesopia* 17 (1979): 65–75. Describes a site in Tidewater Virginia, relates it to John White's map, and concludes that whether the Chesapeakes figured in the disappearance of the Lost Colony will never be known.

1164. Parsons, Elsie Clews. "Folk-Lore of the Cherokee of Robeson County, North Carolina." *Journal of American Folklore* 32 (1919): 384–93. Claims that the theory of the Lumbee Indians' descent from the Lost Colonists is becoming a national legend.

1165. Pearce, Haywood Jefferson, Jr. "New Light on the Roanoke Colony: A Preliminary Examination of a Stone Found in Chowan County, North Carolina." *Journal of Southern History* 4 (1938): 148–63. Describes a quartz stone found by the Chowan River with an inscription signed EWD (Eleanor White Dare?), purporting to tell the fate of the Lost Colony.

1166. _____. "The Dare Stones." *Brenau College Bulletin* 30 (1939): 1–8; 31 (November 1940): 1–14.

1167. Peele, W. J. "The First English Settlement in America—A Study in Location." *North Carolina Booklet* 4 (1904): 3–23. Reprinted in *Literary and Historical Activities in North Carolina, 1900–1905.* Raleigh: North Carolina Historical Commission, 1907. Asserts that the inlet through which Amadas and Barlowe sailed into the Carolina sound was located about twenty miles northeast of Roanoke Island and was called Trinity Harbor. It was badly damaged in the great storm of 1896 and subsequently closed.

1168. _____. "The White Pictures." *North Carolina Booklet* 6 (1907): 243–50. Describes John White's and modern paintings of the Roanoke colony.

1169. _____. "Sir Walter Raleigh and His Colonies." *Publications of the North Carolina Historical Commission* 1 (1907): 251–66.

1170. Pennington, Edgar Legare. "Raleigh's Narrative of Guiana." *South Atlantic Quarterly* 21 (1923): 352–59.

1171. Pennington, Loren E. "The Amerindian in English Promotional Literature 1575–1625." In The *Westward Enterprise: English Activities in Ireland, the Atlantic, and America 1480–1650,* edited by K. R. Andrews, N. P. Canny, and P. E. H. Hair, 175–94. Liverpool: Liverpool University Press, 1978. 326 pp. Sees Ralegh as the initiator of the anti-Spanish and pro-Indian narrative of exploration.

1172. Penrose, Boies. "The Quest for El Dorado." In *Travel and Discovery in the Renaissance 1420–1620,* 112–19. Cambridge, Mass.: Harvard University Press, 1952. 369 pp. Rev. ed. 1955.

1173. Perdue, Theda. *Native Carolinians: The Indians of North Carolina.* Raleigh: Division of Archives and History, North

Carolina Department of Cultural Resources, 1985. 73 pp.

1174. Phelps, David Sutton. *Archeological Studies in the Northern Coastal Zone of North Carolina.* Raleigh: North Carolina Archeological Council and Archeology Branch, Division of Archives and History, North Carolina Department of Cultural Resources, 1978. 100 pp. Contains three reports relating to Roanoke Island.

1175. Phillips, P. Lee. *Virginia Cartography: A Bibliographical Description.* Washington: Smithsonian Institution, 1896. 85 pp. Questions whether John White the artist and the governor of the Lost Colony were the same person.

1176. Pierce, Nancy J. "Croatoan: The Myth and Mysteries of the Lost Colony." *Tar Heel* 10 (1981): 52–55. Discusses different theories about the fate of the Lost Colony, such as the "Dare stones," Beechland, and the Chesapeake "massacre."

1177. Pinkerton, John, ed. "The voyages and navigations of the English nation to Virginia, and the several discoveries thereof; chiefly at the charges of the Honourable Sir Walter Ralegh." In *A General Collection of the best and most interesting voyages and travels.* 17 vols. 12:560–628. London: Longman, Hurst, Rees, and Orme, 1808–14. Also contains numerous references to Ralegh passim.

1178. Poe, Clarence. "The Tercentenary of Sir Walter Raleigh's Death." *South Atlantic Quarterly* 18 (1919): 1–5. Praises Ralegh for bringing Anglo-Saxon ideals to America.

1179. Porter, Charles W., III. "Fort Raleigh National Historic Site, North Carolina: Part of the Settlement Sites of Sir Walter Raleigh's Colonies of 1585–1586 and 1587." *North Carolina Historical Review* 20 (1943): 22–42. Describes the history of the Ralegh settlements and how the site became a National Historic Site.

1180. _____. *Fort Raleigh National Historic Site, North Carolina.* Washington, D.C.: National Park Service, 1952. 39 pp. Describes efforts to establish a colony on Roanoke Island and the present site.

1181. _____. "What Became of the Lost Colonists?" *American Heritage,* n.s. 4 (1953): 53. Cites some theories but concludes that nobody knows the answer.

1182. _____. *Adventures to a New World: the Roanoke Colony,*

1585–87. Washington: National Park Service, United States Department of the Interior, 1972. 56 pp. Reproduces 12 of the John White paintings.

1183. Porter, H. C. *The Inconstant Savage: England and the North American Indian 1500–1660.* London: Duckworth, 1979. 588 pp. Discusses Ralegh's colonization efforts in the 1580s.

1184. Powell, William Stevens. "Sir Walter Raleigh" and "Roanoke from Tribulation to Tragedy." *American Heritage,* n.s. 4 (1953): 46–49, 50–52. Describes Ralegh's interest in the New World and the Roanoke settlements.

1185. _____. "Roanoke Colonists and Explorers: An Attempt at Identification." *North Carolina Historical Review* 34 (1957): 202–26. Establishes, from research in England, that most of the nearly 280 people who came to Roanoke Island were from London or from Devon and Cornwall.

1186. _____. *Paradise Preserved.* Chapel Hill: University of North Carolina Press, 1965. 259 pp. Provides a history of the Roanoke Island Historical Association and its forerunners, their efforts to restore Fort Ralegh, and the development of Paul Green's drama *The Lost Colony.*

1187. Price, Edward T. "A Geographic Analysis of White-Negro-Indian Racial Mixtures in Eastern United States." *Annals of the Association of American Geographers* 43 (1953): 138–55. Notes that the most frequent Croatan surnames, Locklear and Oxendine, do not appear among those of the Lost Colonists, and concludes that it is difficult to tell whether the tradition that the Lost Colonists were absorbed into the Croatan Indians is an ancient one among them or developed in the nineteenth century as a device for gaining status.

1188. Quinn, David Beers. *Raleigh and the British Empire.* London: Hodder and Stoughton, 1947. 284 pp. Other eds.: N.Y.: Macmillan, 1949; N.Y.: Collier; London: English Universities Press, 1962; Harmondsworth: Penguin Books, 1973. Considers Ralegh's activities in Ireland, Guiana, and Virginia and his leadership in developing England's empire.

1189. _____. "The Failure of Raleigh's American Colonies." In *Essays in British and Irish History in Honour of James Eadie Todd,* edited by H. A. Croone, T. W. Moody, and D. B. Quinn, 61–85. London: Frederick Muller, 1949. 336 pp. Argues that

Ralegh's colonists failed because they set out with inadequate information, were too far from home, were on too small a scale, and were precariously financed.

1190. ———. "Preparations for the 1585 Virginia Voyage." *William and Mary Quarterly*, 3d ser. 6 (1949): 208–36. Discusses three recently uncovered documents concerning the Grenville-Lane expedition of 1585.

1191. ———. "Some Spanish Reactions to Elizabethan Colonial Enterprises." *Transactions of the Royal Historical Society*, 5th ser. 1 (1951): 1–23. Reprinted in Quinn, *England and the Discovery of America* (1974). Describes the Spanish efforts to gain information about the Roanoke settlement, which they feared could be used to destroy their treasure fleets.

1192. ———. "Edward Hayes, Liverpool Colonial Pioneer." *Transactions of the Historical Society of Lancashire and Cheshire* 109 (1960): 25–45. Reprinted in Quinn, *England and the Discovery of America* (1974). Shows that while Hayes generally promoted English enterprise in North America, he avoided associating himself with Ralegh's Roanoke venture because his principal patron, Lord Burghley, opposed these "southern" schemes for fear they might lead to war with Spain, although many years later Hayes unsuccessfully sought to associate himself with Ralegh in his Guiana venture.

1193. ———. "Simão Fernandes, A Portuguese Pilot in the English Service, circa 1573–88." *Actas* 3 (1961): 449–66. Reprinted in Quinn, *England and the Discovery of America* (1974). Discusses the career of the mariner Simon Fernandes and his significant part in the Roanoke voyages.

1194. ———. "Elizabethan Birdman." *Times Literary Supplement*, 1 April 1965, 260. Supports the reviewer of *The First Water Colors of North American Birds*, edited by Thomas P. Harrison (*Times Literary Supplement*, 11 March 1965) for asking certain questions about White's drawings.

1195. ———. *The New Found Land: The English Contribution to the Discovery of North America. An Address Delivered at the Annual Meeting of the Associates of the John Carter Brown Library, May 14, 1964, Together with a Catalogue of the Exhibition Opened on that Occasion.* Providence: Associates of the John Carter Brown Library, 1965. 45 pp. Surveys English

activity in North America from possible pre-Columbian
discovery to the settlement of Jamestown and assesses the chief
contributions of the Ralegh colonies as Hariot's *Briefe and True
Report*, John White's drawings, and initiating a tradition of
settlement.

1196. ———. "The Road to Jamestown." In *Shakespeare
Celebrated: Anniversary Lectures Delivered at the Folger
Library*, edited by Louis B. Wright, 31–60. Ithaca, N.Y.:
Published for the Folger Shakespeare Library by Cornell
University Press, 1966. 176 pp. Reprinted in Quinn, *England
and the Discovery of America* (1974). Sees the Roanoke
settlements as temporary laboratories which failed mainly
because they were too small.

1197. ———. "Thomas Hariot and the Virginia Voyages of 1602."
William and Mary Quarterly, 3d ser. 27 (1970): 268–81.
Reprinted in Quinn, *England and the Discovery of America*
(1974). Describes the voyage of Samuel Mace to the area below
Cape Lookout in 1602, where he was supposed to conduct a
search for the Lost Colony but failed to do so.

1198. ———. " 'Virginians' on the Thames in 1603." *Terrae
Incognitae* 2 (1970): 7–14. Reprinted in Quinn, *England and
the Discovery of America*. Reproduces a document that shows
payment to American Indians for demonstrating canoe
paddling on the Thames in September, 1603, a time when
Ralegh's interest in North American ventures was reviving.

1199. ———. *North American Discovery, circa 1000–1612*. New
York: Harper & Row; Columbia: University of South Carolina
Press, 1971. 324 pp. Presents documents that illustrate the
gradual discovery by Europeans of the Atlantic seaboard of
North America, including a section entitled "The Roanoke
Voyages and the First English Settlements" (pages 184–209).

1200. ———. *England and the Discovery of America, 1481–1620.
From the Bristol Voyages of the Fifteenth Century to the
Pilgrim Settlement at Plymouth: The Exploration,
Exploitation, and Trial-and-Error Colonization of North
America, by the English*. New York: Knopf; London: Allen and
Unwin, 1974. 497 pp. Collects Quinn's published and three
hitherto unpublished essays, including "The Lost Colony in
Myth and Reality, 1586–1625," which hypothesizes that the

Lost Colonists moved in among the Chesapeake Indians and were killed by Powhatan's men when Captain Newport's fleet arrived.

1201. _____. "Renaissance Influences in English Colonization." *Transactions of the Royal Historical Society*, 5th ser. 26 (1976): 76–93. Maintains that while many English exponents of colonization looked back to the precedents of Rome or to Machiavelli or other Renaissance theorists, once the notion of planting American colonies took hold between 1576 and 1578 the discussion became almost wholly pragmatic.

1202. _____. *North America from Earliest Discovery to First Settlements: The Norse Voyages to 1612.* New York: Harper and Row, 1977. 621 pp.

1203. _____. *The Lost Colonists: Their Fortune and Probable Fate.* Raleigh: America's Four Hundredth Anniversary Committee, North Carolina Department of Cultural Resources, 1984. 53 pp. Conjectures that most of the Lost Colonists settled in the Chesapeake Bay area, and that they may have been annihilated in the massacre of the Chesapeakes.

1204. _____, ed. *The Voyages and Colonizing Enterprises of Sir Humphrey Gilbert.* 2 vols. London: Hakluyt Society, 1940. Contains documents relating to Gilbert's activities and his influence on Ralegh, his half-brother.

1205. _____, ed. *The Roanoke Voyages 1584–1590. Documents to Illustrate the English Voyages to North America under the Patent Granted to Walter Raleigh in 1584.* 2 vols. London: Hakluyt Society, 1955. Photolithographic reprint in 1 vol. Nendel, Liechtenstein: Kraus, 1967. Contains most of the extant documents regarding the Roanoke colonies, an extended introduction, and copious explanatory footnotes.

1206. Quinn, David Beers, and Paul H. Hulton. "John White and the English Naturalists." *History Today* 13 (1963): 310–20. Discusses White's abortive plan to publish with Hariot a great illustrated record of Virginia and its natural history.

1207. Quinn, David Beers, and Alison M. Quinn, eds. *Virginia Voyages from Hakluyt.* London: Oxford University Press, 1973. 195 pp. Contains fifteen items from Hakluyt's works concerning Ralegh's efforts to establish a settlement on Roanoke Island, with substantial apparatus by the editors.

1208. Quinn, David Beers, A. M. Quinn, and S. Hillier, eds. *New*

American World: A Documentary History of North America to
1612. 5 vols. New York: Arno Press and Hector Bye, 1979.
3:265–339. Contains "The Roanoke Voyages, 1584–1590," a
collection of documents relating to the Ralegh enterprise.

1209. Quinn, David Beers, and Alison M. Quinn, eds. *The First
Colonists: Documents on the Planting of the First English
Settlements in North America, 1584–90*. Raleigh, N.C.:
Division of History and Archives, North Carolina Department
of Cultural Resources, 1982. 199 pp. Reprints fifteen important
documents and narratives connected with Ralegh's Roanoke
enterprise.

1210. Rabb, Theodore K. *Enterprise and Empire: Merchant and
Gentry Investment in the Expansion of England, 1575–1630*.
Cambridge, Mass.: Harvard University Press, 1967. 420 pp.
Concludes that about 150 investors put "at most £50,000" into
the Roanoke voyages; Ralegh was one of the few gentry who
contributed more than money to such ventures.

1211. "Ralegh's Role in Settling Virginia." *Gentleman's Magazine* 25
(1755): 291, 458–61.

1212. Raleigh, Sir Walter Alexander. *The English Voyages of the
Sixteenth Century*. Glasgow: MacLehose, 1906. 204 pp. Part of
the MacLehose edition of Hakluyt.

1213. "Raleigh's Exploration of the Orinoco in 1595." *Bulletin of
the Pan American Union*, English ed., 69 (1935): 196–204;
Spanish ed., 69 (1935): 239–44; Portuguese ed., 37 (1935):
225–30.

1214. Ramos Pérez, Demetrio. *El mito del dorado: Su genesis y
proceso con el "Discovery" de Walter Raleigh (traducción de
Betty Moore) y otros papeles doradistas*. Caracas: Academia
Nacional de la Historia, 1973. 718 pp. Traces the development
of the myth of Eldorado and reprints related documents,
including Ralegh's *Discovery of Guiana* translated into Spanish.

1215. ———. "Walter Ralegh y la hispanificación de sus ideas, como
motivo de su decisión sobre la Guayana." *Archivo Hispanense*,
2d ser. 56 (1973): 237–55. Argues that Ralegh's anti-Spanish
attitude led to his dream of becoming another Hernando
Cortez, as can be seen in his *Discovery of Guiana*, in which he
interpolated the records of Domingo de Veras' 1593 expedition
to Guiana.

1216. Ramsay, Raymond H. *No Longer on the Map: Discovering*

Places that Never Were. New York: Viking Press, [1972]. 276 pp. Devotes the first chapter to Eldorado and to Ralegh's role in helping to establish its legend.

1217. Raven, Charles Earle. *English Naturalists from Neckam to Ray: A Study of the Making of the Modern World*. Cambridge: Cambridge University Press, 1947. 379 pp. Notes that from his observations at Roanoke, John White contributed to Thomas Moffet's *Theatrum Insectorum* descriptions of the gadfly, the cicada, and the glowworm.

1218. Reuter, Edward Byron. *The Mulatto in the United States, Including a Study of the Role of Mixed-blood Races throughout the World*. Boston: Badger, 1918. 417 pp. Maintains that the Croatans are a mixture of runaway slaves, renegade whites, and Indians, and that the theory that they are descendants of the Lost Colonists is baseless.

1219. Reynell-Upham, W. U. "Ralegh and Exeter (Proposed Tercentenary Celebration)." *Devon and Cornwall Notes and Queries* 10 (1918): 41–42.

1220. _____. "Raleigh's Boyhood." *Times Literary Supplement*, 21 March 1918, 142. Claims that Ralegh grew up in Exeter after moving there with his family at the age of two.

1221. Riddell, Justice. "The Last Days of Sir Walter Raleigh." *Dalhousie Review*, n.s. 10 (1930): 181–87. Draws upon recently published *Acts of the Privy Council (Colonial Series)* to describe its actions during and after Ralegh's voyage to Guiana in 1617.

1222. Rights, Douglas LeTell. "The Lost Colony Legend." *Archaeological Society of North Carolina Bulletin* 1 (1934): 3–7. Concludes that the mystery remains unsolved.

1223. _____. "The Indians Meet the English." In *The American Indian in North Carolina*, 11–27. Durham: Duke University Press, 1947. 296 pp. Reprint. Winston-Salem, N.C.: Blair, 1957. Deals with the relationship of the Indians with the Roanoke colonists.

1224. Roanoke [*sic*]. "A Critical Inquiry About Sir Walter Raleigh." *Magazine of American History* 17 (1887): 77–79. Rebukes those writers, including historians, who claim that Ralegh personally came to Virginia.

1225. Roberts, Henry. *The Sea-man's Triumph*. [London?]: R. B[lore] for W. Barley, 1592. 19 pp. Exults over the 1592 capture of the great carrack, *Madre de Dios*.

1226. Roberts, John. "The Younger Sir John Gilbert (c. 1575–1608)." *Report and Transactions of the Devonshire Association for the Advancement of Science, Literature, and Art* 100 (1968): 205–17.

1227. Robinson, Melvin. *Riddle of the Lost Colony*. New Bern, N.C.: Owen G. Dunn, 1946. 64 pp. Claims that the Lost Colony was established not on Roanoke Island but on Cedar Island and that descendants of the colonists survive as the Indians of Robeson County.

1228. Rondthaler, Howard E. "Extracts from Remarks Delivered at Roanoke Island Celebration, August, 1914." *North Carolina Booklet* 14 (1914): 65–73. Celebrates the Ralegh colonies.

1229. Rosenberg, Eleanor. "Giacopo Castelvetro: Italian Publisher in Elizabethan London and his Patrons." *Huntington Library Quarterly* 6 (1943): 119–48. Declares that Castelvetro dedicated his edition of Stella's epic on Columbus, the *Columbeidos*, to Ralegh as part of a publicity campaign for the Virginia project and that this act was probably instigated by Hakluyt.

1230. Rosenberger, Francis Coleman, ed. *Virginia Reader: A Treasury of Writings from the First Voyages to the Present*. New York: Dutton, 1948. 576 pp. Includes narratives by Barlowe, Lane, and Hariot.

1231. Rossi, Franca. "Le prime relazioni inglesi sulla Virginia." *Studi Americani* 11 (1965): 7–41. Surveys English exploration narratives, starting with those about the Roanoke voyages.

1232. Rowse, A. L. "Ralegh and Virginia." In *Sir Richard Grenville of the Revenge, an Elizabethan Hero*, 193–204. London: Cape, 1937. 365 pp.

1233. _____. *The Expansion of Elizabethan England*. London: Macmillan; New York: St. Martin's Press, 1955. 449 pp. Another ed. New York: Harper, Row, 1965.

1234. _____. "Sir Richard Grenville's Place in English History: The Raleigh Lecture on History." *Proceedings of the British Academy* 43 (1957): 79–95. Printed separately. London: Oxford University Press, 1957. Emphasizes Grenville's role in the Virginia voyages.

1235. ———. "The 'Delicious Land.'" *American Heritage* 11 (1959): 46–59. Discusses the ways America appears in Elizabethan literature.

1236. ———. *The Elizabethans and America*. New York: Harper, 1959. 221 pp.

1237. ———. "Of Raleigh and the First Plantation." *American Heritage* 10 (1959): 4–19, 105–11. Reprinted in *Treasury of American Heritage*. New York: Simon and Schuster, 1960. Discusses Ralegh's energizing effect on the Roanoke enterprise.

1238. Ruíz, Helena. "La Búsqueda de Eldorado por Guyana." *Anuario de Estudios Americanos* 16 (1959): 1–166. Considers the quest for Eldorado, in which Ralegh is presented as a Don Quixote.

1239. Sams, Conway Whittle. *The Conquest of Virginia. The Forest Primeval: An Account, Based on Original Documents, of the Indians in that Portion of the Continent in Which Was Established the First English Colony in America*. New York and London: Putnam, 1916. 432 pp. Shows Ralegh's efforts to thwart the colonial ambitions of Spain.

1240. ———. *The Conquest of Virginia. The First Attempt: Being an Account of Sir Walter Raleigh's Colony on Roanoke Island. Based on Original Records, and Incidents in the Life of Raleigh, 1584–1602*. Norfolk, Va.: Keyser-Doherty, 1924. 547 pp.

1241. ———. *The Conquest of Virginia. The Second Attempt. An Account, Based on Original Documents, of the Attempt, Under the King's Form of Government, to Found Virginia at Jamestown. 1606–1610*. Norfolk, Va.: Keyser-Doherty, 1929. 916 pp. Includes references to the Lost Colony and the search for it.

1242. ———. *The Conquest of Virginia. The Third Attempt 1610–1624. Virginia Founded under the Charters of 1609 and 1612. An Account Based on Original Documents of the Establishment of the Colony, by the Virginia Company of London*. New York: Putnam, 1939. 824 pp. Refers intermittently to Ralegh.

1243. Sauer, Carl Ortwin. *Sixteenth-Century North America: The Land and the People as Seen by the European*. Berkeley: University of California Press, 1971. 319 pp. Includes a chapter entitled "The Roanoke Colony (1584–1590)."

1244. Saunders, W. O., ed. *The First English Settlement in America.* Elizabeth City, N.C.: Roanoke Island Historical Association, c. 1932. 53 pp. Describes the Roanoke colonies.

1245. _____, ed. *Two Historic Shrines: The Wright Memorial and Fort Raleigh on Roanoke Island,* 26–30. Elizabeth City, N.C.: Saunders, 1937. 30 pp.

1246. Seelye, John. *Prophetic Waters: The River in Early American Life and Literature.* New York: Oxford University Press, 1977. 423 pp. Views Ralegh's American enterprises as characteristically self-dramatizing.

1247. Sellman, R. R. *The Elizabethan Seamen,* 31–34, 61–62. London: Methuen, 1957. 70 pp. Considers Ralegh's voyages to the Americas.

1248. Serrano y Sánz, Manuel. "Las piraterías de Walter Raleigh en la Guayana (documentos inéditos) 1616–1619." *Revista de Archivos, Bibliotecas y Museos* 6 (1902): 209–21. Reports on some Spanish documents about Ralegh's last voyage.

1249. Shammas, Carole. "The Elizabethan Gentleman Adventurers and Western Planting." Ph.D. diss., Johns Hopkins University, 1971. 244 pp. Says that Stucley, Grenville, Frobisher, and Ralegh not only initiated most of the colonizing projects, but played the primary role in planning, organizing, and financing them.

1250. _____. "English Commercial Development and American Colonization 1560–1620." In *The Westward Enterprise: English Activities in Ireland, the Atlantic, and America 1480–1650,* edited by K. R. Andrews, N. P. Canny, and P. E. H. Hair, 161–74. Liverpool: Liverpool University Press, 1978. 326 pp. Claims that Ralegh and his ilk came to America seeking rewards in revenues, tributes, rents, and offices for their followers.

1251. Shirley, John W. "George Percy at Jamestown, 1607–1612." *Virginia Magazine of History and Biography* 57 (1949): 227–43. Discusses how contacts between the "Wizard Earl's" brother and Ralegh and Hariot may have caused Percy to go out to Virginia, where he served as President, 1609–10.

1252. _____. "Sir Walter Raleigh's Guiana Finances." *Huntington Library Quarterly* 13 (1949): 55–69. Shows that William Sanderson raised or stood bond for the money used to finance Ralegh's Guiana voyage of 1595, and that then Ralegh used forged documents to sue Sanderson, a relative, when it seemed he might gain thereby.

1253. _____. *Sir Walter Ralegh and the New World*. Raleigh, N.C.: America's Four Hundredth Anniversary Committee, North Carolina Department of Cultural Resources, 1985. 129 pp. Discusses Ralegh's life and personality, concentrating on his colonization efforts at Roanoke and in Guiana.

1254. "A Short Account of British Plantation in America." *London Magazine* 24 (1755): 307.

1255. Simkins, Francis Butler. *Virginia: History, Government, Geography*, 38–46. New York: Scribner, 1957. 599 pp.

1256. Simón, Pedro. *Noticias historiales de las conquistas de tierra firme en las indias occidentales*, edited by Manuel José Forero. 9 vols. Bogotá: M. Rivas, 1882, Autores Colombianos, 1953. Provides information about Ralegh's expedition to Guiana, from a Spanish work first published in part in 1626.

1257. "Sir Walter Ralegh and Virginia." *Historical Magazine* 2 (1858): 290–93.

1258. "Sir Walter Ralegh's Map of Guiana." *Geographical Journal* 1 (1893): 167–68. Describes the facsimile of the map recently published by L. von Friederichsen.

1259. "Sir Walter Raleigh and Virginia." *Historical Magazine* 6 (1862): 188. Reiterates a note by D. M. Stevens.

1260. *Sir Walter Raleigh Day, December 3, 1954*. Raleigh: State Superintendent of Public Instruction, 1954. 16 pp. Appeals for funds to erect a memorial to Ralegh.

1261. Sisco, Louis Dow. "Discovery of the Chesapeake Bay 1525–1573." *Maryland Historical Magazine* 40 (1945): 277–86. Says that De Bry's 1590 publication of White's chart, which placed the Chesapeake Bay's entrance in the right position but incorrectly represented its outline, publicized the bay's existence.

1262. _____. "Voyage of Vincente Gonzalez in 1588." *Maryland Historical Magazine* 42 (1947): 95–100. Describes the voyage of Gonzalez northward along the coast from St. Augustine, during which he was told of an English settlement not far to the north.

1263. Smith, Alan, ed. *Virginia 1584–1607: The First English Settlement in North America: A Brief History with a Selection of Contemporary Narratives*. London: Brun, 1957. 112 pp.

1264. Smith, Bradford. *Captain John Smith: His Life and Legend*, 78–89. Philadelphia: Lippincott, 1953. 375 pp. Summarizes Ralegh's colonization efforts.

1265. Snell, Tee Loftin. "Bloody Florida Lost Roanoke." In *The Wild Shores: America's Beginnings*, 43–60. Washington, D.C.: National Geographic Society, [1974]. 204 pp. Describes the Roanoke voyages, with photographs by W. M. Edwards.

1266. Sparkes, Boyden. "Writ on Rocke, Has America's First Murder Mystery Been Solved?" *Saturday Evening Post* 213 (1941): 9–11, 118–28. Offers evidence that the inscribed "Dare stones" found in 1937 are fakes.

1267. Sparrey, Francis. "The Description of the Ile of Trinidad, the rich Countrie of Guiana, and the mightie Riuer of Orenoco. Written by Francis Sparrey, left there by Sir Walter Raleigh, 1595, and in the end taken by the Spaniards and sent prisoner into Spaine, and after long captiuitie got into England by great sute, 1602." In *Purchas his Pilgrimes*. 4 vols. 4:1247–50. London: Fetherstone, 1625.

1268. Spearman, Walter. "The Lost Colony of Roanoke Island." *American History Illustrated* 4 (1969): 22–30. Discusses theories about the colonists' fate.

1269. Spielmann, Percy E. "Who Discovered the Trinidad Asphalt Lake?" *Science Progress* 33 (1938): 52–62. Denies that Ralegh was the discoverer.

1270. Squires, W. H. T. *The Days of Yester-Year in Colony and Commonwealth: A Sketch Book of Virginia*, 2–8. Portsmouth, Va.: Printcraft Press, 1928. 301 pp. Considers Ralegh's colonial expeditions.

1271. _____. *Through Centuries Three: A Short History of the People of Virginia*, 21–41. Portsmouth, Va.: Printcraft Press, 1929. 605 pp.

1272. Stanard, Mary Newton. "Raleigh's Colony." In *The Story of Virginia's First Century*, 16–22. Philadelphia and London: Lippincott, 1928. 322 pp.

1273. Stern, Virginia F. "A Second Set of John White Drawings?" *Renaissance Quarterly* 21 (1968): 24–32. Suggests that the 24 Indian pictures on the White staircase in Scadbury Manor in Kent, listed in 1727, may be the lost De Bry set of John White drawings.

1274. Stevens, D. M. "Sir Walter Raleigh and Virginia." *Notes and*

Queries, 3d ser. 1 (1862): 147–48. Says that the misconception that Ralegh personally discovered Virginia is traceable to De Bry's translation of Hariot's sentence "the actions of those who have been by Sir Walter Raleigh therein employed" into Latin as "Qui generosum D. Walterum Raleigh in eam regionem *comitati sunt.*"

1275. Stevens, Henry. "The Raleigh volume of drawings." *Massachusetts Historical Society, Proceedings* 20 (1884): 58–60. Describes 76 John White drawings in the Grenville Library, British Museum, no. 6837.

1276. ———. *Thomas Hariot, the Mathematician, the Philosopher, and the Scholar, Developed Chiefly from Dormant Materials, with Notices of His Associates, Including Biographical and Bibliographical Disquisitions Upon the Materials of the History of "Ould Virginia."* London: Chiswick Press, 1900. 213 pp. Frequently refers to Ralegh.

1277. Stick, David. *Fabulous Dare: The Story of Dare County, Past and Present.* Kitty Hawk, N.C.: Dare Press, 1949. 71 pp.

1278. ———. *Roanoke Island: The Beginnings of English America.* Chapel Hill: University of North Carolina Press, 1983. 266 pp. Focuses on what can be documented about the Roanoke colonists and how they prepared the way for the Jamestown settlement.

1279. Strachey, William. *The Historie of Travaile into Virginia Britannia,* edited by R. H. Major. London: Hakluyt Society, 1849. 203 pp. New ed., edited by Louis B. Wright and Virginia Freund. London: Hakluyt Society, 1953. Contains information about the Lost Colony learned from the Indians by the Majestown settlers and recorded 1612–16.

1280. Strathmann, Ernest A. "The New World and Sir Walter Raleigh." *American Quarterly* 1 (1949): 83–91. Observes that when writing about the New World, Ralegh interprets the new in terms of the familiar.

1281. ———. "Ralegh Plans His Last Voyage." *Mariner's Mirror* 50 (1964): 261–70. Reprints from the papers of Sir Ralph Winwood, the Secretary of State, a hitherto unknown proposal by Ralegh to the king to lead an expedition to Guiana costing £9593.

1282. Stringfield, Mary Love. "The Lost Colony of Sir Walter Raleigh: Mystery Surrounding the Fate of the Unhappy

Colonists Perhaps Solved." *American Monthly Magazine*, June 1900, 1159–63. Claims that the Lost Colonists joined the Croatan Indians, and that their descendants live in North Carolina.

1283. Sturcken, H. Tracy. "Raleigh and El Dorado of Guiana." *Américas* 19 (1967): 15–21. Declares that Ralegh's quest cost him his life but immortalized him in legend.

1284. Sturtevant, William C. "Ethnographic Details in the American Drawings of John White, 1557–1590." *Ethnohistory* 12 (1965): 54–63. Notes 23 plates containing ethnographic material in Hulton and Quinn's volume of White's drawings and points out differences between the reproductions and the originals.

1285. Swan, Michael. *The Marches of El Dorado: British Guiana, Brazil, Venezuela*, 277–81. London: Jonathan Cape; Toronto: Clarke, Irwin; Boston: Beacon Press, 1958. 304 pp. Harmondsworth: Penguin Books, 1961. States that Ralegh's account of Guiana was surprisingly accurate, apart from his credulity over Eldorado and Amazon women.

1286. Swanton, J. R. "Probable Identity of the Croatan Indians." *Senate Reports*, 73d Cong., 2d Sess., 1934. no. 204.

1287. Tarbox, Increase Niles, ed. *Sir Walter Raleigh and His Colony in America. Including the Charter of Queen Elizabeth in his Favor, March 25, 1584, with letters, discourses, and narratives of the voyages made to America at his charges, and descriptions of the country, commodities, and inhabitants*. Boston: Prince Society, 1884. 329 pp. Reprint. New York: Burt Franklin, 1966.

1288. Taylor, Eva G. R. "Hariot's Instructions for Ralegh's Voyage to Guiana, 1595." *Journal of the Institute of Navigation* 5 (1952): 345–50.

1289. Terry, G. Cunningham. "Sir Walter Raleigh's Lost Colony of Roanoke." *Blackwood's Magazine* 194 (1913): 320–28. Contains demonstrably inaccurate comments.

1290. Trevelyan, George Macaulay. *England under the Stuarts*, 91–92, 94–95. London: Methuen, 1904. 566 pp. Revised eds. 1925, 1946. Discusses Ralegh's 1617 expeditions to Guiana.

1291. Turner, Frederick. *Beyond Geography: The Western Spirit Against the Wilderness*. New York: Viking Press, 1980. 329 pp. Devotes a chapter (pages 171–99) to the Lost Colony.

1292. Turton, Godfrey. *Builders of England's Glory*, 261–76. Garden

City, N.Y.: Doubleday, 1969. 303 pp. British ed. *The Dragon's Breed: The Story of the Tudors from Earliest Times to 1603.* London: Peter Davies, 1970. Describes the Roanoke settlement.

1293. Tyler, Lyon Gardiner. "Gilbert and Raleigh Colonies (1583–1602)." In *England in America 1580–1652*, 18–33. New York: Harper, 1904. 355 pp.

1294. Vance, Zebulon Baird. *1584–1884: Three Hundred Years Ago. Memorial to Sir Walter Raleigh. Speech of Senator Z. B. Vance, in the Senate of the United States, May 13, 1884.* Washington, D.C.: Government Printing Office, 1884. 7 pp. Urges support for a joint resolution to appropriate $30,000 to erect a monument on Roanoke Island to commemorate the Amadas and Barlowe expedition.

1295. Van Heuvel, Jacob Adrien. *El Dorado: being a Narrative of the circumstances which gave rise to Reports, in the sixteenth century, of the existence of a Rich and Splendid City in South America, to which that name was given, and which led to many enterprises in search of it; including a Defence of Sir Walter Raleigh, in regard to the relations made by him respecting it, and a Nation of Female Warriors, in the vicinity of the Amazon, in the Narration of his Expedition to the Oronoke in 1595.* New York: Winchester, 1844. 166 pp. Also includes a memoir of Ralegh and transcripts of his letter to Prince Henry and of Ralegh's *Instructions to his Son.*

1296. Van Noppen, Ina W., ed. *The South: A Documentary History*, 11–15. Princeton and New York: Van Nostrand, 1958. 564 pp. Relates Ralegh's efforts to plant a colony and includes many quotes from Hakluyt.

1297. Verne, Jules. "Travels of Ralegh." In *The Exploration of the World*, translated from the French by D. Leigh, pt. 1. London: Low, Marston, Searle & Rivington, 1882. 432 pp.

1297ª. Villa-Urrutia, Wenceslao Ramírez de. *La Embajada del Conde de Gondomar à Inglaterra en 1613*, 40–44. Madrid: Jaime Ratés Martín, 1913. 119 pp. Describes how Gondomar in 1618 secured a written note from James's minister Buckingham declaring that Ralegh would be tried for attacking the Spanish in Guiana.

1298. Villiers, J. A. J. de. "Famous Maps in the British Museum." *Geographical Journal* 44 (1914): 168–88. Describes the c. 1595 map of Guiana drawn by or for Ralegh.

1299. "Virginia Dare Celebration." *World Review* 4 (1927): 270–71.

1300. *Virginia Dare Day: Annual Celebration by the Roanoke Colony Memorial Association, Old Fort Raleigh, Roanoke Island, North Carolina, August 18, 1926.* Raleigh: Edwards & Broughton, 1926. 16 pp. Contains addresses by Congressman Lindsay Warren and the English Ambassador to the United States, Sir Esme Howard.

1301. Virginia Dare Memorial Association. "In Memory of Virginia Dare." *North Carolina Teacher* 10 (1892): 97–101.

1302. Von Hagen, Victor Wolfegang. "The Search for the Gilded Man." *Natural History* 61 (1952): 312–21, 335–36. Tells the history of the Eldorado legend.

1303. ———. *The Golden Man: A Quest for El Dorado.* Farnborough, Hants.: Saxon House, 1974. 338 pp.

1304. *Voyages and Adventures of Sir Walter Raleigh. With the Voyage of Captain Cowley,* 1–36. London: Printed by T. Maiden for Ann Lemoine and J. Roe, 1806. 46 pp. Part of vol. 1 of *The Pocket Navigator.* Another ed. 1820.

1305. *Voyages en Virginie et en Floride, traduits du latin par L. Ningler et confrontés avec les textes anglais, français ou allemands.* Paris: Duchartre and Van Buggenhoudt, 1927. 311 pp. Includes a translation into French of Hariot's *Brief and True Report.*

1306. Wallace, Mary. "The Teller at the Outer Banks." *Saturday Review* 51 (1968): 56–58. Suggests that the coast still looks as it must have to the Roanoke colonists.

1307. Warren, Lindsay Carter. *The Memorial to Virginia Dare: Speech in the House of Representatives, Monday, May 17, 1926.* Washington, D.C.: Government Printing Office, 1926. 8 pp.

1308. *The Watercolor Drawings of John White from the British Museum.* Washington, D.C.: National Gallery of Art; Raleigh: North Carolina Museum of Art; New York: Pierpont Morgan Library, 1965. 53 pp. Includes Paul Hulton's essay "John White's Drawings in the British Museum" and an illustrated catalogue of the 113 White items in this exhibition.

1309. Weeks, Stephen Beauregard. "Lane and White, the Governors of Roanoke." *North Carolina University Magazine,* n.s. 9 (1890): 225–36. Discusses Ralegh's two governors on Roanoke Island.

1310. ———. "The Lost Colony of Roanoke: Its Fate and Survival." *Papers of the American Historical Association*, 5 (1891):439–80. Printed separately. New York: Knickerbocker Press, 1891. Summarized in *Annual Report of the American Historical Association for 1890*. Discusses the history of the Lost Colony and argues that its descendants are the Croatan Indians of Robeson County, North Carolina, as shown by their family names, traditions, language, and character.

1311. ———. "Raleigh's Settlements on Roanoke Island: An Historical Survival." *Magazine of American History* 25 (1891): 127–39. Reiterates the claim that the Croatans are descended from the Lost Colonists.

1312. Weitenkampf, Frank. "Early Pictures of North American Indians: A Question of Ethnology." *Bulletin of the New York Public Library* 53 (1949): 591–614. Says White and Le Moyne invested Indians with European qualities and gave them conventional artistic poses.

1313. Welch, William Lewis. *An Account of the Cutting Through of Hatteras Inlet, North Carolina, Sept. 7, 1846. Also, through which inlet did the English adventurers of 1584 enter the sounds of North Carolina and some changes in the coast line since their time.* Salem: Salem Press, 1885. 13 pp. Reprinted from *Bulletin of the Essex Institute* (1885). Concludes that Amadas and Barlowe entered Pamlico Sound at Caffey Inlet.

1314. Wernham, R. B., ed. *The New Cambridge Modern History.* 13 vols. 3:508–28. Cambridge: Cambridge University Press, 1969. Discusses Ralegh's Roanoke ventures and expeditions to Guiana.

1315. Whitbourne, Sir Richard. *A discouse and discovery of New-fovnd-land, with many reasons to prooue how worthy and beneficiall a plantation may there be made, after a far better manner than now it is. Together with the laying open of certaine enormities and abuses committed by some that trade to that countrey, and the meanes laide downe for reformation thereof.* London: F. Kyngston for W. Barret, 1620. 9 pp. Tells of deserters from Ralegh's Guiana fleet; cited in D. W. Prowse, *History of Newfoundland* (1895).

1316. White, John. "Portraits to the Life and Manners of the Inhabitants, of that Province in America, called Virginia." In

Graphic Sketches from Old and Authentic Works Illustrating the Costume, Habits and Character of the Aborigines of America. New York: Langley, 1841. 15 pp. and 24 plates.

1317. White-Thomson, Sir R. T. "The Activities of the National Society of Colonial Dames of America, More Particularly with Reference to Certain Devonians." *Report and Transactions of the Devonshire Association for the Advancement of Science, Literature, and Art* 46 (1914): 308–25. Considers Ralegh's Roanoke expedition.

1318. Williams, Neville. *The Sea Dogs: Privateers, Plunder and Piracy in the Elizabethan Age.* London: Weidenfeld and Nicolson, 1975. 278 pp. Discusses Ralegh's ventures at Roanoke and Guiana.

1319. Williams, Talcott. "The Surroundings and Site of Raleigh's Colony." In *Annual Report of the American Historical Association for 1895,* 1896, 47–61. Discusses the topography of the region and excavations at the fort site.

1320. Williamson, Hugh. "Sir Walter Raleigh Attempts to Settle a Colony in North Carolina." In *The History of North Carolina.* 2 vols. 1:26–66. Philadelphia: Dobson, 1812. Reprint. Spartanburg, S.C.: Reprint. 1973.

1321. Williamson, James A. *The English Colonies in Guiana and on the Amazon, 1604–1668,* 21–23. 74–79. Oxford: Clarendon Press, 1923. 191 pp. Describes Ralegh's Guiana voyage of 1617–18.

1322. ———. *The Age of Drake,* 224–52, 358–70. London: Adam and Charles Black, 1938. 400 pp. 2d ed., 1946. 3d ed., 1952. 4th ed., 1960. 5th ed., 1965. Discusses Ralegh's role in colonizing America and his Guiana efforts.

1323. ———. *The Ocean in English History: Being the Ford Lectures.* Oxford: Oxford University Press, 1941, 1948. 208 pp. Reprint. Westport, Conn.: Greenwood Press, 1979. Discusses Ralegh's role as propagandist for colonization.

1324. ———. *The Tudor Age,* 354–56. New York and London: Longmans, Green, 1953. 468 pp. Considers Ralegh's colonization attempts.

1325. Willson, David Harris. "Ralegh's Last Voyage." In *King James VI and I,* 357–77. New York: Holt; London: Jonathan Cape, 1956. 480 pp. Reprint. London: Jonathan Cape, 1963.

1326. Wilson, E. Y. "The Lost Colony of Roanoke." *Canadian Magazine* 4 (1895): 500–504.

1327. Wood, Eric. *Famous Voyages of the Great Discoverers,* 210–19, 257–63. London: Harrap, 1928. 270 pp. Includes accounts of Ralegh's American settlements and his search for Eldorado.

1328. Wood, William, *Elizabethan Sea-Dogs: A Chronicle of Drake and His Companions,* 205–22. New Haven: Yale University Press, 1921. 252 pp. Calls Ralegh chief of the prospectors because he sought to establish an English nation in America.

1329. Wright, Louis B. "The Elizabethan Dream of Wealth." In *The Colonial Search for a Southern Eden: Three Lectures on the Dancy Foundation, Alabama College, April 29, 30 and May 1, 1951,* 1–19. [University, Ala.]: University of Alabama Press, 1953. 64 pp. Treats Ralegh's efforts, motivated largely by dreams of wealth and power through conquest of the Spanish Empire.

1330. ———. "Elizabethan Politics and Colonial Enterprise." *North Carolina Historical Review* 32 (1955): 254–69.

1331. ———. *The Dream of Prosperity in Colonial America.* New York: New York University Press, 1965. 96 pp. Discusses Ralegh's search for Eldorado.

1332. ———. "Competition for El Dorado." In *Gold, Glory, and the Gospel: The Adventurous Lives and Times of the Renaissance Explorers,* 257–86. New York: Atheneum, 1970. 362 pp. Details Ralegh's activities in Guiana.

1333. ———, ed. *The Elizabethans' America; A Collection of Early Reports by Englishmen on the New World.* Cambridge, Mass.: Harvard University Press; London: Arnold, 1965. 295 pp. Contains 42 accounts, including selections by Barlowe, Lane, White, and Hariot on the Roanoke settlement.

1334. Wright, Louis B., and Elaine W. Fowler, eds. *West and by North: North America Seen Through the Eyes of Its Seafaring Discoverers,* 214–46. New York: Delacorte Press, [1971]. 389 pp. Describes Ralegh's Roanoke enterprise and reprints some documents.

1335. Yardley, J. H. R. *Before the Mayflower.* London: Heinemann, 1931. 408 pp. Begins by describing Ralegh's Roanoke enterprise.

1336. Zahm, John Augustine. *The Quest of El Dorado: The Most*

Romantic Episode in the History of South American Conquest, 140–89. New York and London: Appleton, 1917. 260 pp. Includes an account of Ralegh's exploits in Guiana, first published in 1912 in the *Pan American Bulletin* under the pseudonym of J. A. Manso.

Chapter 5.

RALEGH IN LITERARY HISTORY

AND CRITICISM

1337. Abraham, Gerald. "A Lost Poem by Queen Elizabeth I." *Times Literary Supplement*, 30 May 1968, 553. Suggests that Ralegh's poem "Fortune hath taken away my love" may have given rise to the ballad "Fortune My Foe."

1338. Acheson, Arthur. *Shakespeare and the Rival Poet*, 76–99. London and New York: John Lane, 1903. 360 pp. Claims that Ralegh and his group are satirized in *Love's Labour's Lost*.

1339. Adams, Percy G. "The Discovery of America and European Renaissance Literature." *Comparative Literature Studies* 13 (June 1976): 100–115. Maintains that the exploration of America affected such themes as the noble savage, the earthly paradise, and Spanish cruelty.

1340. _____. *Travel Literature and the Evolution of the Novel*, 254–55, passim. Lexington: University Press of Kentucky, 1983. 368 pp. Claims that Ralegh's writings about Guiana contributed to the development of the novel.

1341. Akrigg, D. P. V. "Webster and Raleigh." *Notes and Queries* 193 (1948): 427–28. Points out that a passage in Webster's *The White Devil* criticizes James's seizure of Ralegh's estate at Sherborne.

1342. Akrigg, G. P. V. *Shakespeare and the Earl of Southampton*, 207–19. Cambridge, Mass.: Harvard University Press, 1968. 280 pp. Identifies Ralegh as Don Armado in *Love's Labour's Lost*.

1343. Allen, Morse Shepard. *The Satire of John Marston*, 32. Columbus, Ohio: Heer, 1920. 187 pp. Suggests that Ralegh may be Puntarvolo in *Every Man Out of His Humour*.

1343ᵃ. Allen, Sally Geraghty. "Hermetic Influences in Ralegh's *History of the World*." Master's thesis, University of Manitoba, 1972. 131 pp.

1344. Anderson, Judith H. " 'In living colours and right hew': The Queen of Spenser's Central Books." In *Poetic Traditions of the English Renaissance*, edited by Maynard Mack and George deForest Lord. New Haven and London: Yale University Press, 1982. 319 pp. Claims that in Book 4 of *The Faerie Queene* the problems of Amoret signify the trials of Elizabeth Throckmorton after her marriage to Ralegh.

1345. Appleton, William W. *Beaumont and Fletcher: A Critical Study*, 56, 63, 88, 99. London: Allen, 1956. 131 pp. Says that Ralegh is Archas in Fletcher's *The Loyal Subject*.

1346. Arms, G. W., J. P. Kirby, L. G. Locke, and R. W. Whidden. "Ralegh's 'The Lie.' " *Explicator* 3 (1945): item 50. Sees the poem as warning against the rashness of denying worldly values, and cites Hadrian's *Anima vagula blandula* as a possible source.

1347. Arnold, Matthew. "On the Modern Element in Literature." In *Macmillan's Magazine* 19 (1869): 304–14. Contains a disparaging comparison of Ralegh to Thucydides.

1348. Aryanpur-Kashani, Manoochehr. "Sir Walter Raleigh's *Historie of the World* and Persia." Ph.D. diss., University of Colorado, 1958. 160 pp. Praises Ralegh's description of the history of Persia in his *History* as comparatively reliable but considers his emphasis on divine providence a flaw.

1349. Askew, Melvin W. "Ralegh's 'The Pilgrimage.' " *Explicator* 13 (1954): item 9. Sees the poem's unity as deriving from the image of blood in line 7.

1350. Atkins, Sidney H. " 'Fortunio' and 'Raymundus.' " *Times Literary Supplement*, 3 October 1935, 612. Identifies Keymis as Fortunio and Ralegh as Raymundus in Joseph Hall's *Virgdemiarum*.

1351. Ault, Norman. "Ralegh's Last Poem?" *Times Literary Supplement*, 27 October 1932, 789. Denies that Ralegh wrote the final stanza of "Nature, that washed her hands in milk" as his own epitaph.

1352. Barnes, Richard Gordon. "The Effect of the New World on English Poetry 1600–1625." Ph.D. diss., Claremont, 1960. 281 pp. Considers responses to the New World reflected in the poetry of Ralegh, Donne, Alexander, and Drayton.

1353. Battenhouse, Roy W. "Ralegh's Religion." In *Marlowe's*

Tamburlaine: A Study in Renaissance Moral Philosophy, 50–68. Nashville, Tenn.: Vanderbilt University Press, 1941. 266 pp. Reprint. 1964. Denies that Ralegh was an atheist and asserts that he was persecuted because of his bold social criticism and his association with men of science and philosophy.

1354. Bednarz, James P. "Ralegh in Spenser's Historical Allegory." *Spenser Studies: A Renaissance Poetry Annual* 4 (1984): 49–70. Describes Spenser's relationships with Ralegh and with the queen and notes that the Timias and Belphoebe episode can be interpreted as either a vindication or a condemnation of Ralegh.

1355. Bennett, Josephine Waters. "Early Texts of Two of Ralegh's Poems from a Huntington Library Manuscript." *Huntington Library Quarterly* 4 (1941): 469–75. Discusses the appearance of "The Lie" and "Walsingham" in Huntington MS 198.

1356. ———. *The Evolution of The Faerie Queene*, passim. Chicago: University of Chicago Press, 1942. 299 pp. Argues that Spenser and Ralegh did not meet before 1589 and sees some early parts of *The Faerie Queene* as attempts by Spenser to gain Ralegh's patronage.

1357. Bennett, R. E. "John Donne and the Earl of Essex." *Modern Language Quarterly* 3 (1942): 603–4. Conjectures that Donne was aboard one of the ships that followed Ralegh on the Azores expedition and that Donne wrote the first letter in the Burley Manuscript.

1358. Bennett, Robert B. "John Webster's Strange Dedication: An Inquiry into Literary Patronage and Jacobean Court Intrigue." *English Literary Renaissance* 7 (1977): 352–67. Describes Ralegh's ill-will toward Robert Carr, James's favorite, who persuaded the King to confiscate Ralegh's estate at Sherborne and give it to him.

1359. Bibas, H. "Ralegh's Last Poem." *Times Literary Supplement*, 13 October 1932, 734. Notes "Even such is time" in a manuscript in the Bibliothèque Nationale.

1360. Bishop, Carolyn J. "Ralegh Satirized by Harington and Davies." *Review of English Studies*, n.s. 23 (1972): 52–56. Suggests that Harington's epigrams, in which he is thought to satirize Ralegh as Paulus, are a clue that Sir John Davies is also satirizing Ralegh in his six-line poem "In Paulum."

1361. Black, L. G. "A Lost Poem by Queen Elizabeth I." *Times*

Literary Supplement, 23 May 1968, 535. Suggests that
Elizabeth's poem beginning "Ah silly pugge wert thou so sore
afraid" was an answer to Ralegh's "Fortune hath taken thee
away my love."

1362. Blackwood, Robert J. "Coriolanus: In Shakespeare and the
Historians." Ph.D. diss., Loyola University of Chicago, 1973.
292 pp. Discusses, in chapter 7, Ralegh as one of seventeen
historians who contributed to Shakespeare's depiction of
Coriolanus.

1363. Blondell, Jacques. "Milton et l'Eden." In *Le Paradis Perdu
1667–1967*, 60–62. Paris: Minard, 1967. 280 pp. Glances at
Ralegh's view of Eden in his *History of the World*.

1364. Böker, Uwe. "Sir Walter Ralegh, Daniel Defoe und die
Namengebung in Aphra Behns *Oroonoko*." *Anglia* 90 (1972):
92–104. Says that Mrs. Behn derived her hero's name from
Ralegh's *Discovery of Guiana*.

1365. Bradbrook, Muriel C. *The School of Night: A Study in the
Literary Relationships of Sir Walter Raleigh*. Cambridge:
Cambridge University Press, 1936. 189 pp. Elaborates on the
theory that in the "School of Night" in *Love's Labour's Lost*
Shakespeare was satirizing a group of intellectuals, including
Chapman, Marlowe, Hariot, Ralegh, and the "Wizard" Earl of
Northumberland, whose skepticism and interest in the occult
and new knowledge frequently caused them to be accused of
atheism; Shakespeare's satire is said to be directed at their
obsession with the contemplative life and at Ralegh in the
character Don Armado.

1366. _____. "Yeats and Elizabethan Love Poetry." *Dublin
Magazine* 4 (1965): 40–55. Suggests that Ralegh influenced
Yeats in his phase of "love for a new kind of phoenix—a young
child."

1367. Braden, Gordon. " 'Vivamus, mea Lesbia' in the English
Renaissance." *English Literary Renaissance* 9 (1979): 199–224.
Praises Ralegh's "Now Serena, be not coy" for its defense of
sexuality and sees the poem as inaugurating seventeenth-
century seduction poetry.

1368. Brink, J. R. "The Masque of the Nine Muses: Sir John Davies's
Unpublished *Epithalamion* and the 'Belephoebe-Ruby' Episode
in *The Faerie Queene*." *Review of English Studies* 23 (1972):
445–47. Suggests that the "Belephoebe-Ruby" episode may

allude to Arthur Throckmorton's plan, possibly instigated by his brother-in-law, Ralegh, to present a heart-shaped ruby to Queen Elizabeth during a masque, probably Davies's *Epithalamion.*

1369. Brooke, C. F. Tucker. "Sir Walter Ralegh as Poet and Philosopher." *ELH: A Journal of English Literary History* 5 (1938): 93–112. Reprinted in *Essays on Shakespeare and Other Elizabethans.* New Haven: Yale University Press, 1948. Surveys Ralegh's poetry and prose, and concludes that his poetry reveals his mind while his prose reveals his heart; calls Ralegh the last Elizabethan romanticist.

1370. ———. "The Renaissance." In *A Literary History of England,* edited by Albert C. Baugh, 624–25. New York: Appleton-Century Crofts, 1948. 1673 pp.

1371. Brown, Harry M., and John Milstead, eds. *Patterns in Poetry,* 52–53. Glenview, Ill.: Scott, Foresman, 1968. 432 pp. Analyzes "The Nymph's Reply."

1372. Brushfield, T. N., "Sir Walter Ralegh's 'Cynthia.' " *Western Antiquary* 5 (1886): 182. Comments on Gosse's article in the *Athenaeum,* arguing that Edwards knew the true nature of the fragment but Hannah did not.

1373. ———. "Memorable Copies of Sir W. Ralegh's *History of the World.*" *Western Antiquary* 7 (1887): 154–56. Describes four copies of Ralegh's *History.*

1374. ———. "Sir Walter Ralegh and His *History of the World.*" *Report and Transactions of the Devonshire Association for the Advancement of Science, Literature, and Art* 19 (1887): 389–418. Discusses the composition of the *History,* the literary assistance Ralegh received, its attempted suppression, and the alleged burning of the manuscript continuation.

1375. ———. "Note on 'An Elegy Upon S(ir) W(alter) R(alegh).' " *Devon Notes and Queries* 1 (1900): 150–51.

1376. ———. "Sir Walter Ralegh and 'The Art of War by Sea': A Lost Treatise." *Devon Notes and Queries* 4 (1906–7): 237–41. Reproduces the only extant fragment of a treatise entitled "The Art of War by Sea," begun by Ralegh for Prince Henry but discontinued after the prince died.

1377. Buchan, Alexander M. "Ralegh's *Cynthia*—Facts or Legend." *Modern Language Quarterly* 1 (1940): 461–74. Contends that

The Ocean to Cynthia was written in 1589, the year of Ralegh's alienation from the Queen because of his feud with Essex and argues that the poem is not part of a larger epic.

1378–1387. No entries.

1388. _____. "The Political Allegory of Book 4 of *The Faerie Queene.*" *Journal of English Literary History* 11 (1944): 237–48. Argues that Spenser felt England's anti-Spanish policy depended on Essex and Ralegh working together and that the theme of Book 4 is the establishment of harmony between these two leaders.

1389. Buchan, John. "Shakespeare and Raleigh." In *Comments and Characters*, 203–8. London: Nelson, 1940. 422 pp. Reviews Professor Raleigh's *Shakespeare* and adds reflections on Sir Walter Ralegh.

1390. Buff, Adolf, of Augsburg. "Who is the Author of the Tract entitled: *Some Observations touching Trade and Commerce with the Hollander and other Nations,* commonly ascribed to Sir Walter Ralegh?" *Englische Studien* 1 (1877): 187–212. Maintains that John Keymer wrote the *Observations* in 1613.

1391. _____. "Über drei Ralegh'sche Schriften." *Englische Studien* 2 (1879): 392–416. Contends that Ralegh's *Observations on the Causes of the Magnificencie and Opulencie of Cities, The Cabinet-Council,* and *The Prince or Maxims of State* were respectively derived from Botero's *Tre libri delle causa della Grandezza . . . delle città,* Venetia, 1589; *Les six livres de la République,* de Jean Bodin Angevin, Paris, 1577; and two of Machiavelli's works.

1392. Bühler, Curt F. "Four Elizabethan Poems." In *Joseph Quincy Adams Memorial Studies,* edited by James G. McManaway, Giles E. Dawson, and Edwin E. Willoughby, 695–706. Washington, D.C.: Folger Shakespeare Library, 1948. 808 pp. Discusses versions of Ralegh's reply to Marlowe's "Passionate Shepherd," found in a seventeenth-century manuscript in the Pierpont Morgan Library.

1393. Bush, Douglas. *Mythology and the Renaissance Tradition in English Poetry,* 271–78. Minneapolis: University of Minnesota Press, 1932. 360 pp. Reprint. New York: Norton, 1963. Suggests that Ralegh influenced Milton concerning the origins of pagan deities.

1394. _____. *English Literature in the Earlier Seventeenth Century,*
    1600–1660, 100, 223–25. Oxford: Clarendon Press, 1945. 621
    pp. Revised ed. 1962. Praises Ralegh's skill in historiography
    and admires his later poems.

1395. Buxton, John. *Sir Philip Sidney and the English Renaissance,*
    219–23. London: Macmillan, 1954. 283 pp. Considers
    Ralegh's relationship with Sidney and theirs with Spenser.

1396. "C." "The 'Faerie Queene' Unveiled." *Notes and Queries,* 3d
    ser. 4 (1863): 21–22, 65–66, 101–3. Sees Ralegh portrayed as
    both Timias and Scudamour and says the three tales of
    Amoretta, Belphoebe, and Florimell attest to Spenser's esteem
    for Ralegh and Ralegh's high position at court.

1397. Cain, Thomas H. *Praise in "The Faerie Queene,"* 91–101.
    Lincoln: University of Nebraska Press, 1978. 229 pp. Argues
    that Ralegh strongly influenced the scenes of the Bower of Bliss
    and the Cave of Mammon in Book 2 of *The Faerie Queene.*

1398. Caldwell, George S. *Is Sir Walter Raleigh the Author of*
    Shakespere's [sic] Plays and Sonnets? Melbourne: Stillwell and
    Knight, 1877. 32 pp. Maintains that Ralegh wrote
    Shakespeare's works, citing internal evidence and apparent
    correspondence between the dates of the plays and the dates of
    events in Ralegh's life.

1399. Campbell, Lily B. *Shakespeare's "Histories": Mirrors of*
    Elizabethan Policy, 79–84. San Marino, Calif: Huntington
    Library, 1947. 346 pp. Reprint, 1958. Discusses the preface to
    Ralegh's *History.*

1400. Canning, Albert S. G. *Literary Influence in British History.*
    London: Allen, 1889, 1904. 280 pp. Devotes chapter 5 to the
    relationship between Spenser and Ralegh.

1401. Carey, John. *John Donne: Life, Mind, and Art*, 94–95, 198,
    246–47. New York: Oxford University Press, 1981. 303 pp.
    Sees a relationship between passages from Ralegh's *History of*
    the World and Donne's "Death, be not proud" and his *Second*
    Anniversary, and compares both authors' descriptions of the
    battle at Cadiz.

1402. Carré, Meyrick H. *Phases of Thought in England*, 196–217.
    Oxford: Clarendon Press, 1949. 392 pp. Examines hermetic
    and cabalistic ideas in Ralegh's works.

1403. Carter, H. G. " 'Even Such Is Time.' " *Times Literary*

Supplement, 2 November 1951, 693. Notes that the poem appears on a 1677 tomb in Sanderstead Church, Surrey.

1404. Casper, Leonard. "Ralegh's 'Revenge'; Great Victories in Words." *Renaissance News* 13 (1960): 129–133. Points out that Ralegh's *Report of the Truth* is a defense of Grenville and of the capabilities of the English fleet when properly supported.

1405. Cawley, Robert Ralston. "Drayton and the Voyagers." *Publications of the Modern Language Association* 38 (1923): 530–56. Notes that in Drayton's *Polyolbion* his tribute to Ralegh is a rare instance of Drayton escaping his adherence to Hakluyt and permitting his imagination full rein.

1406. _____. *The Voyagers and Elizabethan Drama*, 318–38, passim. Boston: Heath; London: Oxford University Press, 1938. 428 pp. Attributes to Ralegh's writings many references to the world's regions found in plays and other Elizabethan literature.

1407. _____. *Unpathed Waters: Studies in the Influence of the Voyagers on Elizabethan Literature*, 23, 157. Princeton: Princeton University Press, 1940. 285 pp. Reprint. New York: Octagon Books, 1967. Discusses the Elizabethan background to Ralegh's description of Paradise in *The History of the World* and notes allusions to Ralegh by Joseph Hall and Thomas Middleton.

1408. Chambers, E. K. "The Disenchantment of the Elizabethans." In *Sir Thomas Wyatt and Some Collected Studies*, 181–204. London: Sidgwick & Jackson, 1933. 227 pp. Reprint. New York: Russell and Russell, 1965. Sees the disenchantment of the late Elizabethans reflected in Ralegh's poems.

1409. Chang, H. C. "Timias the Squire and Sir Walter Ralegh." In *Allegory and Courtesy in Spenser: A Chinese View*, 152–68. Edinburgh: Edinburgh University Press, 1955. 227 pp. Argues that Spenser's Timias-Belphoebe episode in *The Faerie Queene* is an allegory of Ralegh's problems with Queen Elizabeth, and suggests that Spenser may have intended the episode as constructive criticism for Ralegh.

1410. Cheney, Donald. "Spenser's Fortieth Birthday and Related Fictions." *Spenser Studies: A Renaissance Poetry Annual* 4 (1984): 3–31. Questions Spenser's assertions of friendship with Ralegh, citing apparent allusions in Spenser's *Amoretti* 74 to the disgrace of Ralegh's secret marriage, and suggests that in *Colin Clout* and *The Faerie Queene* Ralegh functions as a foil to Spenser.

1411. Churchill, R. C. *Shakespeare and His Betters: A History and a Criticism of the Attempts Which Have Been Made to Prove That Shakespeare's Works Were Written by Others*, 96, 109, 185–86. London: Max Reinhardt, 1958. 255 pp. Denies that Ralegh wrote Shakespeare's works.

1412. _____. "The Noble Candidates: A Study in Ermine." In *Jahrbuch der Deutschen Shakespeare—Gesellschaft West Jahrbuch*, edited by Herman Heuer with Ernst Theodore Schist and Rudolf Stomm, 149–60. Heidelberg: Quelle & Meyer, [1965]. 526 pp. Includes Ralegh among those nobles or persons highly placed at court for whom authorship of Shakespeare's works has been claimed.

1413. Clanton, Stacy Merl. "Ages and Tymes: A Study of Sir Walter Ralegh's 'Book of the Ocean to Cynthia.' " Ph.D. diss., University of Arkansas, 1979. 278 pp.

1414. Clark, Eleanor Grace. *Elizabethan Fustian: A Study in the Social and Political Backgrounds of the Drama, with Particular Reference to Christopher Marlowe*, 112–25. New York: Oxford University Press, 1937. 223 pp. Discusses allusions to Ralegh in Marlowe's plays.

1415. _____. *Ralegh and Marlowe: A Study in Elizabethan Fustian.* New York: Fordham University Press, 1941. 488 pp. Includes material from the above item and further examines Marlowe's allusions to Ralegh and his circle.

1416. Collier, J. Payne. *Bibliographical Account of Early English Literature.* 4 vols. 3:268–78. New York: Scribner, 1866. Contains comments on Ralegh's *Discoverie of Guiana* and his poems, and a letter from Ralegh to Robert Carr in 1608.

1417. Cooper, Kenneth S. "Walter Raleigh and the Truth of the World's Story." *Peabody Journal of Education* 44 (July 1966): 8–12. Sees the value of Ralegh's *History of the World* as giving the modern world an understanding of the process of historical thinking and compares Ralegh with Gibbon and Hume.

1418. "A Court Poet of the Sixteenth Century." *Chambers's Journal* 16 (1851): 252–55. Reprinted in *Eclectic Magazine* (1852). Points out echoes of Ralegh in Shakespeare's works.

1419. Cousins, A. D. "The Coming of Mannerism: The Later Ralegh and the Early Donne." *English Literary Renaissance* 9 (1979): 86–107. Cites Ralegh's later poetry as preparing the way for the mannerist style of Donne's early work.

1420. _____. "Ralegh's 'A Vision upon this Conceipt of *The Faery Queene*.'" *Explicator* 41 (1983): 14–16. Calls Ralegh's sonnet an example of "political Petrarchism," and praises Ralegh for his criticism of Spenser and his understanding of the queen.

1421. Covington, Nina Holland. "Sir Walter Raleigh as a Poet." *North Carolina Booklet* 14 (1915): 155–62. Reviews Ralegh's poetry and some theories about its provenance.

1422. Cuvelier, Eliane. *Thomas Lodge, témoin de son temps*. Paris: Etudes Anglaises Didier, 1984. Argues that Lodge satirizes Ralegh in *A Looking-Glass for London and England* (1594).

1423. Danchin, F. C. "Etudes critiques sur Christopher Marlowe: Quelques documents concernant les dramaturges Thomas Kyd et Christopher Marlowe et Sir Walter Raleigh et son entourage." *Revue Germanique* 9 (1913): 566–87.

1424. Davenport, Arnold. " 'Raymundus' and Ralegh." *Times Literary Supplement*, 1 January 1938, 12. Claims that Raymundus in Joseph Hall's *Virgidemiarum* represents the alchemist Raymond Lully, not Ralegh.

1425. _____, ed. *The Collected Poems of Joseph Hall, Bishop of Exeter and Norwich*, 210. Liverpool: Liverpool University Press, 1949. 309 pp. Repeats that Ralegh is not Raymundus.

1426. David, Richard, ed. "Introduction." In *Love's Labour's Lost*, by William Shakespeare, xliv–li. Cambridge, Mass.: Harvard University Press, 1951. 196 pp. Argues that Shakespeare's satiric treatment of the academy of Navarre was an attack on Ralegh and his associates, written for Essex and his faction.

1427. Davie, Donald. "A Reading of 'The Ocean's Love to Cynthia.'" In *Elizabethan Poetry*, edited by John Russell Brown and Bernard Harris, 71–89. London: Edward Arnold, 1960. 224 pp. Dates the poem after 1592 and questions the claims of modern critics about its modernity.

1428. Dean, Leonard F. "Tudor Theories of History Writing." *University of Michigan Contributions in Modern Philology*, no. 1, 1947, 24 pp. Examines Ralegh's concept of providential justice in *The History of the World*.

1429. "Diary of William Oldys, Esq." *Notes and Queries*, 2d ser. 11 (1861): 141–42. Discusses Ralegh's "Steele Glass" stanzas.

1430. "Did Ralegh Write Shakespeare's Sonnets?" *Devonian Year Book*, 1917, 71.

1431. Dobell, Bertram. "Poems by Sir Thomas Heneage and Sir Walter Raleigh." *Athenaeum*, 14 September 1901, 349. Says that Ralegh wrote "Farewell, false love" in answer to a poem by Heneage, citing as evidence a superscription in a manuscript volume.

1432. Dodson, Daniel B. "King James and *The Phoenix*—Again." *Notes and Queries* 10 (1958): 434–37. Identifies Phoenix as King James and the conspirator Proditor as Ralegh in Middleton's play, arguing that Middleton was seeking to curry favor with James by depicting him as the ideal sovereign.

1433. Donno, Elizabeth Story. "Sir Walter Ralegh." In *A Milton Encyclopedia*. 8 vols. 7:89–90. Lewisburg: Bucknell University Press; London: Associated University Press, [1978–1980]. Discusses Ralegh's influence on Milton, particularly through his *History of the World* and his poetry.

1434. Drummond, William. *Notes of Ben Jonson's conversations with William Drummond of Hawthornden, January, 1619*, edited by D. Laing. London: Shakespeare Society, 1842. 51 pp. Reprint. London: John Lane, 1923. First published in Folio edition of Drummond's *Works* in 1711, and often included in Jonson's works. Reports Jonson's claim that he wrote part of the Punick War section for Ralegh's *History of the World*.

1435. Duffy, Maureen. *The Erotic World of Faery*, 137–59. London: Hodder and Stoughton, 1972. 352, [24] pp. Argues that Ralegh is satirized as Bottom in *A Midsummer Night's Dream*.

1436. Dukes, W. B. "Ralegh's *History of the World*." *Times Literary Supplement*, 25 January 1934, 60. Remarks that the motto "Data Fata Sequutus" was erased above the coat of arms on the title page of the *History*.

1437. Duncan, Ronald. "Religio." *Agenda* 4 (1965): 56. Suggests that Ralegh's "wholeness of vision" is comparable to Ezra Pound's.

1438. Duncan-Jones, Katherine. "Ralegh's 'Walsingham': A Faux-naif Ballad." *Critical Survey* 4 (1969): 90–92. Attributes the poem to Ralegh because it employs his characteristic iteration in groups of twos or threes and argues that the ambiguities and obscurities in the last two stanzas were intended by him.

1439. ———. "The Date of Ralegh's '21th: [sic] and Last Booke of the Ocean to Scinthia.'" *Review of English Studies*, n.s. 21 (1970): 143–58. Argues that Ralegh wrote the poem while in the Tower after 1603.

1440. Dunn, Esther Cloudman. "Ralegh and the 'New' Poetry." In *The Literature of Shakespeare's England*, 140–63. New York: Scribner, 1936. 326 pp. Criticizes Ralegh's poetry as ambiguous, but finds its revelation of his character interesting and calls his poetry "new" in that it deals with personal feeling and experience.

1441. Eccles, Mark. "Sir George Buc, Master of the Revels." In *Thomas Lodge and Other Elizabethans*, edited by Charles J. Sisson, 409–506. Cambridge, Mass.: Harvard University Press, 1933. 526 pp. Notes a description by Buc which suggests that Ralegh's elegy on Sidney derives from Sidney's epitaph.

1442. Edwards, Philip W. *Sir Walter Ralegh*. London: Longmans, Green, 1953. 184 pp. Studies Ralegh as a literary figure.

1443. ———. "Who Wrote *The Passionate Man's Pilgrimage?*" *English Literary Renaissance* 4 (1974): 83–97. Concludes the author was probably a Catholic and certainly not Ralegh.

1444. Edwards, Thomas R. *Imagination and Power: A Study of Poetry on Public Themes*, 47–63. New York: Oxford University Press, 1971. 232 pp. Compares the situation of Ralegh, as the Shepherd of the Ocean, with the love affair of the rivers Bregog and Mulla in Spenser's *Colin Clout's Come Home Again*.

1445. Emperor, John Bernard. *The Catullian Influence in English Lyric Poetry, Circa 1600–1650*, 29. Columbia: University of Missouri Press, 1928. 133 pp. Sees Ralegh's translation of part of Catullus's "Vivamus, mea Lesbia" in *The History of the World* as the only trace of Catullus in his works.

1446. English, H. M., Jr. "Spenser's Accommodation of Allegory to History in the Story of Timias and Belphoebe." *Journal of English and Germanic Philology* 59 (1960): 417–29. Discusses the relationship of allegory to history in the story of Timias and Belphoebe, and suggests that the Ralegh-Throckmorton affair compelled Spenser to continue the story in Book 4 of *The Faerie Queene*.

1447. Evans, Berger, ed. "The Last Fight of the Revenge." In *Fifty Essays*, 3–11. Boston: Little, Brown, 1938. 363 pp. Based on Ralegh's *Report of the Truth*.

1448. Evans, J. M. "Microcosmic Adam." *Medium Aevum* 35 (1966): 38–42. Cites *The Book of Secrets of Enoch* as a source for Ralegh's depiction of man's microcosmic nature in *The History of the World*.

1449. Evans, Oswald Hardey. "Raleigh and North." *Times Literary Supplement*, 14 November 1929, 926. Says that the verse legend on the frontispiece of Ralegh's *History of the World* comes from North's Plutarch.

1450. Ewen, Cecil Henry L'Estrange. *Sir Walter Ralegh's Interpretation of the Lex Mercatoria*. London: Printed for the author, 1938. 7 pp.

1451. Fink, Lila Ruth. "Times Trans-shifting: Classical Conventions of Time in Renaissance Lyric Poetry." Ph.D. diss., University of Southern California, 1976. Considers classical conventions of time in the lyric poetry of Spenser, Ralegh, and others.

1452. Firth, Sir Charles Harding. "Sir Walter Raleigh's *History of the World*." *Proceedings of the British Academy* 8 (1918): 427–46. Reprinted separately. 1919. Also reprinted in *Essays, Historical and Literary*. Oxford: Clarendon Press, 1938. Examines how the *History* came to be written, its plan, Ralegh's research assistants and sources, his method of handling material, and the book's reception and impact upon other writers and British leaders.

1453. Forster, Leonard. "The Political Petrarchism of the Virgin Queen." In *The Icy Fire: Studies in European Petrarchism*, 122–47. Cambridge: Cambridge University Press, 1969. 204 pp. Notes that the depiction of Queen Elizabeth in Renaissance literature bears a close resemblance to the descriptions of the ideal lady of Petrarchan convention, citing Ralegh's Cynthia poems as evidence.

1454. Forsythe, R. S. " 'The Passionate Shepherd' and English Poetry." *Publications of the Modern Language Association* 40 (1925): 692–742. Cites Ralegh's "Nymph's Reply" as among the first of many works to be influenced by Marlowe's "Passionate Shepherd."

1455. Fowler, Alastair. *Spenser and the Numbers of Time*, 244n. London: Routledge and Kegan Paul, 1964. 314 pp. Notes evidence of numerical composition in four of Ralegh's poems, and considers the effect of the last couplet on line total in "The Passionate Man's Pilgrimage."

1456. Fraser, John. "Raleigh." In *Chaucer to Longfellow . . . Lectures on English Literature*, 263–85. Chicago: Crum, 1891. 656 pp. Includes a biography, with some criticism and a few selections.

1457. Frye, Roland Mushat. "Shakespeare's 'Second Best Bed' and a Contemporary Parallel." *Notes and Queries*, n.s. 1 (1954): 468–69. Notes how Shakespeare evidently and Ralegh explicitly were against leaving one's widow the marital bed and suggests the practice may have been common in their era.

1458. Fulton, Thomas Wemyss. *The Sovereignty of the Sea*, 127–28. Edinburgh: Blackwood, 1911. 799 pp. Attributes *Observations Touching Trade and Commerce with the Hollander* to John Keymer.

1459. Fussner, F. Smith. "Sir Walter Ralegh and Universal History." In *The Historical Revolution: English Historical Writing and Thought 1580–1640*, 191–210. New York: Columbia University Press; London: Routledge and Kegan Paul, 1962. 343 pp.

1460. Gardner, J. "Sir Walter Raleigh, a Study, with Special Reference to *The History of the World*." Ph.D. diss., Cambridge University, 1955.

1461. Garrod, H. W. "Walter Raleigh." In *The Profession of Poetry and Other Lectures*, 266–70. Oxford: Clarendon Press, 1929. 270 pp.

1462. Gasquet, Emile. *Le Courant machiavelien dans la pensée et la littérature anglaises du XVIe siècle*, 371–90. Montreal, Paris, and Brussels: Didier, 1974. Discusses the influence of Machiavelli on Ralegh.

1463. Gilbert, Allan H. "Belphoebe's Misdeeming of Timias." *Publications of the Modern Language Association* 62 (1947): 622–43. Considers that whether or not Timias represents Ralegh, Timias is akin to the Lancelot of chivalric romance.

1464. Giles, Phyllis M. "A Handlist of the Bradfer-Lawrence Manuscripts Deposited on Loan at the Fitzwilliam Museum." *Transactions of the Cambridge Bibliographical Society*, 6, Part 2 (1943), 86–99. Describes a manuscript containing several of Ralegh's essays and letters.

1465. Gillett, Charles Ripley. *Burned Books: Neglected Chapters in*

British History and Literature. 2 vols. 1:113. New York: Columbia University Press, 1932.

1466. Gilson, J. P. "Sir Walter Ralegh's *Cynthia*." *Review of English Studies* 4 (1928): 340. Claims that "21th" is the Elizabethan manner of writing twenty-first, repudiating Latham's claim that the numbers "21th" and "22" in the Hatfield manuscript of Ralegh's *Ocean to Cynthia* should be read as "11th" and "12."

1467. Godshalk, William Leigh. "Daniel's *History*." *Journal of English and Germanic Philology* 63 (1964): 45–57. Attributes the *History of England* to Samuel Daniel rather than to Ralegh.

1468. Goldberg, Jonathan. *Endless Worke: Spenser and the Structures of Discourse,* 50–52. Baltimore: Johns Hopkins University Press, 1981. 177 pp. Discusses the Timias-Belphoebe episode and notes echoes of Ralegh's poems in *The Faerie Queene.*

1469. Gordon, Ian A. *The Movement of English Prose,* 105–8. London: Longman, 1966. 182 pp. Classifies Ralegh's prose style as Ciceronian.

1470. Gosse, Sir Edmund. "Sir Walter Raleigh's 'Cynthia.'" *Athenaeum* 1 (1886): 32–33, 66–67. Identifies the "Continuation of Cynthia" as a fragment of "Cynthia" itself and claims that the Hatfield manuscript is not in Ralegh's hand but that of his wife.

1471. Gottfried, Rudolf B. "The Authorship of *A Breviary of the History of England*." *Studies in Philology* 53 (1956): 172–90. Compares the manuscripts of the *Breviary* and concludes that Samuel Daniel is the author, not Ralegh.

1472. ———. "Autobiography and Art: An Elizabethan Borderland." In *Literary Criticism and Historical Understanding: Selected Papers from the English Institute, 1966,* edited by Phillip Damon, 109–34. New York: Columbia University Press, 1967. 190 pp. Considers how Ralegh's *Ocean to Cynthia* could be autobiographical and how Spenser's *Colin Clout's Come Home Again* may reflect his relations with Ralegh.

1473. Greaves, Margaret. *The Blazon of Honour: A Study in Renaissance Magnanimity,* 125–26. New York: Barnes and Noble, 1964. 142 pp. Claims that Don Armado in *Love's Labour's Lost* represents Ralegh.

1474. Grove, Robin. "Ralegh's Courteous Art." *Melbourne Critical*

Review, no. 7 (1964): 104–13. Focuses on "My body in the walls captived," "The Nymph's Reply," "Now Serena, be not coy," and "On the Life of Man," and praises Ralegh's individuality and elegance.

1475. Gullans, Charles B. "Ralegh and Ayton: The Disputed Authorship of 'Wrong Not Sweete Empress of My Heart.'" *Studies in Bibliography* 13 (1960): 191–98. Argues that the six-line preliminary stanza is by Ralegh but the rest of the poem is by Sir Robert Ayton.

1476. ———, ed. *The English and Latin Poems of Sir Robert Ayton,* 197–98, 318–26. Edinburgh and London: Scottish Text Society, 1963. 385 pp. Discusses the authorship of "Wrong not Sweete Empress of My Heart."

1477. Hannah, John. "Elizabethan Sacred Poetry." *British Critic* 31 (1842): 344–49. Maintains that Ralegh wrote "Go Soul, the Bodies Guest" earlier than the night before his execution.

1478. ———. "Raleigh's Poetry and Life." *Quarterly Review* 168 (1889): 483–501. Surveys his poetry.

1479. Harlow, V. T. "Harington's Epigrams." *Times Literary Supplement,* 14 July 1927, 488. Maintains that Ralegh is Paulus in Harington's epigrams.

1480. Harman, Edward George. *Edmund Spenser and the Impersonations of Francis Bacon,* 367–94. London: Constable, 1914. 608 pp. Claims that Bacon, not Ralegh, wrote the sonnets prefixed to *The Faerie Queene.*

1481. ———. *The "Impersonality" of Shakespeare,* 140–59, 274–326. London: Cecil Palmer, 1925. 330 pp. Argues that *Othello* is an analogy for the fall of Ralegh and asserts—unconventionally—that Timias represents Essex and Scudamour represents Ralegh in *The Faerie Queene.*

1482. Harrison, G. B. *Elizabethan Plays and Players,* 75–78, 127–28. London: Routledge, 1940. 306 pp. Considers Ralegh, Greene, and the "School of Night."

1483. Hart, E. F. "The Answer-Poem of the Early Seventeenth Century." *Review of English Studies,* n.s. 7 (1956): 19–29. Considers Ralegh's reply to Marlowe's "Come live with me and be my love" as an early example of the seventeenth-century answer-poem.

1484. Helgerson, Richard. *The Elizabethan Prodigals,* 16–43.

Berkeley: University of California Press, 1976. 178 pp. Argues that Ralegh's *Instructions to His Son* derives as much from literature as from experience.

1485. Heltzel, Virgil B. "Ralegh's 'Even Such Is Time.' " *Huntington Library Bulletin* no. 10 (1936): 185–88. Claims that Ralegh adapted the last stanza of "Nature, that washed her hands in milk" the night before his death.

1486. Heninger, S. K., Jr. "The Passionate Shepherd and the Philosophical Nymph." In *Renaissance Papers 1962*, edited by George Walton Williams, 63–70. Durham, N.C.: Southeastern Renaissance Conference, 1963. 70 pp. Notes how each poem clarifies themes in the other.

1487. Hepler, Dianne Koortz. "The Poetry of Sir Walter Ralegh: Its Relationships to the Elizabethan and Metaphysical Traditions." Master's thesis, East Carolina University, 1968. 67 pp.

1488. Herendeen, W. H. "The Rhetoric of Rivers: The River and the Pursuit of Knowledge." *Studies in Philology* 78 (1981): 107–27. Examines Ralegh's use of the river as a metaphor for reason and for writing and his comparisons of history with geography and topology.

1489. Hersey, Frank Wilson Cheney. "Sir Walter Ralegh as a Man of Letters." *Proceedings of the State Literary and Historical Association of North Carolina* 25 (1918): 42–54. Maintains that Ralegh's writings reflect his experiences and feelings.

1490. Heseltine, G. C. " 'Even Such Is Time . . . .' " *Times Literary Supplement*, 26 October 1951, 677. Notes the inclusion of this poem in William Graham's *Collection of Epitaphs and Monumental Inscriptions* (1821).

1491. Hexter, Jack H. "The Storm Over the Gentry." In *Reappraisals in History*, 117–62. London: Longmans, 1961. Evanston, Ill.: Northwestern University Press, 1962. Quotes extensively from Ralegh.

1492. Himelick, Raymond. "Walter Ralegh and Thomas More: The Uses of Decapitation." *Moreana* 11 (1974): 59–64. Notes the influence of More's *Dialogue of Comfort Against Tribulation* (1534) on Ralegh's "Passionate Man's Pilgrimage."

1493. Hobsbaum, Philip. "Elizabethan Poetry." *Poetry Review* 56 (1965): 80–97. While finding much Elizabethan poetry dull, considers Ralegh a major poet and praises his poetic realism.

1494. Höltgen, Karl Josef. "Richard Latewar: Elizabethan Poet and Divine." *Anglia* 89 (1971): 417–38. Identifies Latewar, an Anglican divine who served with Mountjoy on the Irish expedition, as author of one of the answer-poems to "The Lie" by Ralegh.

1495. Horner, Joyce. "The Large Landscape: A Study of Certain Images in Ralegh." *Essays In Criticism* 5 (1955): 197–213. Notes a lack of sea imagery in Ralegh's poetry, even in *The Ocean to Cynthia*, but significant use of earth and seasonal imagery.

1496. Howarth, Herbert. "Shakespeare's Flattery in *Measure for Measure*." *Shakespeare Quarterly* 16 (1965): 29–37. Speculates that the theme of clemency in Shakespeare's play may be connected with the Countess of Pembroke's pleas in November 1603 on behalf of the condemned Ralegh.

1497. Howell, Demont H. "Ralegh and 'The Ocean to Cynthia.' " Ph.D. diss., University of Utah, 1972. 111 pp. Examines the poem and provides an annotated edition in modern English.

1498. Hudson, Hoyt Hopewell. "Notes on the Ralegh Canon." *Modern Language Notes* 46 (1931): 386–89. Attributes to Ralegh the poems "Would I were changed into that golden shower" and "Sweet are the thoughts where Hope persuadeth Hap."

1499. ———. "The Transition in Poetry." *Huntington Library Quarterly* 5 (1942): 188–90. Describes Ralegh as a forerunner of Donne.

1500. ———. *The Epigram in the English Renaissance*, 163–64. Princeton: Princeton University Press, 1947. 178 pp. Discusses the epigrammatic features in the lyric "Her face, her tongue, her wit," attributed to Ralegh.

1501. Hughey, Ruth. "The Harington Manuscript at Arundel Castle and Related Documents." *Library*, 4th ser. 15 (1935): 388–444. Attributes to Ralegh the epitaph on Sidney.

1502. ———, ed. *The Arundel Harington Manuscript of Tudor Poetry*. 2 vols. 1:190, 194, 225, 235. Columbus: Ohio State University Press, 1960. Includes four poems attributed to Ralegh.

1503. Hulbert, Viola Blackburn. "A New Interpretation of Spenser's 'Muiopotmos.' " *Studies in Philology* 25 (1928): 128–48. Sees

"Muiopotmos" as allegorizing the Sidney-Oxford quarrel
rather than the Ralegh-Essex one.

1504. Humphreys, John A. "Sir Walter Raleigh's Interpretation of
Ancient History." Ph.D. diss., Yale University, 1942.

1505. Inglis, Fred. *The Elizabethan Poets: The Making of English
Poetry from Wyatt to Ben Jonson*, 46–64. London: Evans,
1969. 168 pp. Classifies Ralegh, Gascoigne, and Nashe as
"plain blunt men."

1506. Jacquot, Jean. "L'Elément platonicien dans 'L'Histoire du
monde,' de Sir Walter Ralegh." In *Mélanges d'histoire littéraire
de la renaissance offerts à Henri Chamond*, 347–53. Paris:
Librairie Nizet, 1951. 357 pp.

1507. ———. "Ralegh's 'Hellish Verses' and the *Tragical Raigne of
Selimus*." *Modern Language Review* 48 (1953): 1–9. Discusses
an atheistical poem attributed to Ralegh in a manuscript dated
1603 and shows it to be an adaptation of lines in an
anonymous tragedy of 1594, though the ideas are not inimical
to Ralegh's.

1508. ———. "Lyrisme et sentiment tragique dans les madrigaux
d'Orlando Gibbons." *Colloques Internationaux du Centre
National de la Recherche Scientifique: Sciences Humaines* 5
(1954): 139–51. Considers Gibbons's setting of "What is our
Life."

1509. Jaggard, William. "Books Written in Prison." *Notes and
Queries* 184 (1943): 23–24. Terms Ralegh's *History of the
World* probably the most learned work ever written in prison.

1510. Jaggard, William, A. J. H., E. G. B., and M. "Sir Walter
Ralegh: *History of the World*, 1621." *Notes and Queries* 171
(1936): 394–95. Notes that the allegorical frontispiece of the
first edition, dated 1614, was used in each edition through that
of 1634, but that the true date of publication of each edition is
given in the colophon.

1511. Jayne, Sears. "Ficino and the Platonism of the English
Renaissance." *Comparative Literature* 4 (1952): 214–38. Notes
that in his *History of the World* Ralegh often refers to Ficino
but as an authority on various subjects rather than as a
Platonist.

1512. Jennings, John Melville. "The Literary Remains of Sir Walter
Raleigh." *Virginia Magazine of History and Biography* 60

(1952): 367–71. Surveys Ralegh's works, especially *The History of the World*, and sees Machiavelli's influence in Ralegh's prose.

1513. Johnson, Arnold. "The Letter of Advice by Burghley, Raleigh and Sidney." Master's thesis, University of Nebraska, 1966.

1514. Johnson, Michael L. "Some Problems of Unity in Sir Walter Ralegh's *The Ocean's Love to Cynthia*." *Studies in English Literature* 14 (1974): 18–30. Criticizes the structure of the poem, praises its continuity of tone, and classifies it as a winter pastoral.

1515. Johnson, William C. *Milton Criticism: A Subject Index*, 340. Folkestone, Kent: Dawson, 1978. 450 pp. Includes 69 entries which deal with Ralegh's influence on Milton.

1516. Jones, Susanne Stephens. "The Poetry of Sir Walter Ralegh: A Critical Consideration." Ph.D. diss., University of Colorado, 1974. 154 pp. Labels Ralegh a skillful amateur in poetry, who at first followed the plain-style school of Gascoigne but developed a more elaborate prosody.

1517. Jorgensen, Paul A. "Views of War in Elizabethan England." *Journal of the History of Ideas* 13 (1952): 469–81. Considers Ralegh's views on war.

1518. Jusserand, J. J. *A Literary History of the English People*. 3 vols. 2:390–93. London: Unwin, 1906.

1519. Kabat, Lillian Trena Gonan. "*The History of the World*: Reason in the Historiography of Sir Walter Raleigh." Ph.D. diss., University of Southern California, 1968. 184 pp.

1520. Kelliker, Hilton, and Katherine Duncan-Jones. "A Manuscript of Poems by Robert Sidney: Some Early Impressions." *British Library Journal* 1 (1975): 107–44. Reports on a rediscovered collection of manuscript poems by Robert Sidney, Earl of Leicester, whose wife was Ralegh's first cousin, and says that the influence of Ralegh on the poems is very evident.

1521. Kempner, Nadja. *Raleghs staatstheoretische Schriften: Die Einführung des Machiavellismus in England*. Leipzig: Tauchnitz, 1928. 138 pp. Discusses the influence of Machiavelli, Bodin, and Aristotle on Ralegh's political writings.

1522. Kirkconnell, Watson. *The Celestial Cycle*, 599. Toronto: University of Toronto, 1952. 701 pp. Considers Ralegh's *History of the World* as an analogue to *Paradise Lost*.

1523. Kistner, Arthur Leroy. "Despair in Some Elizabethan Tragedy."

Ph.D. diss., University of Illinois, 1963. 181 pp. Surveys the
treatment of despair in works by Kyd, Ralegh, and others.

1524. Koller, Kathrine. "Spenser and Ralegh." *ELH: A Journal of
English Literary History* 1 (1934): 37–60. Discusses the
Ralegh-Spenser friendship, and summarizes critical opinion of
the treatment of Ralegh in *The Faerie Queene.*

1525. Krapp, George Philip. *The Rise of English Literary Prose,*
428–35. New York: Oxford University Press, 1915. 551 pp.
Reprint. 1963. Discusses Ralegh's *History of the World.*

1526. Kuhl, E. P. "Hercules in Spenser and Shakespeare." *Times
Literary Supplement,* 31 December 1954, 860. Says that both
poets' references to Hercules relate to the Earl of Essex and that
for Spenser, by the mid-1590s, Essex had superseded Ralegh as
the hope of imperial Britain.

1527. Kunitz, Stanley Jasspon, and Howard Haycraft, eds. *British
Authors Before 1800: A Biographical Dictionary,* 427–29.
New York: Wilson, 1952. 584 pp.

1528. Labelle, Jenijoy. "Theodore Roethke's Dancing Masters in
'Four for Sir John Davies.' " *Concerning Poetry* 8 (1975): 29–
35. Discusses the poetic influence of Ralegh, Davies, and Yeats
on Roethke.

1529. Langford, John Alfred. "Sir Walter Ralegh and his *History of
the World.*" In *Prison Books and their Authors,* 83–123.
London: William Tegg, 1861. 357 pp. Describes the prison
writings of Ralegh and eleven others.

1530. Latham, Agnes M. C. "Sir Walter Ralegh's Cynthia." *Review
of English Studies* 4 (1928): 129–34. Claims the numbers
"21th" and "22" in the Hatfield manuscript of *The Ocean to
Cynthia* should be "11th" and "12," a change Latham
incorporated in her later editions of Ralegh's poems.

1531. _____. "Sir Walter Ralegh's *Instructions to his Son.*" In
*Elizabethan and Jacobean Studies Presented to Frank Percy
Wilson in Honour of His Seventieth Birthday,* edited by
Herbert Davis and Helen Gardner, 199–218. Oxford:
Clarendon Press, 1959. 355 pp. Examines the publication
history of the essay, concludes that it was written during
Ralegh's imprisonment from 1603 to 1616, and classifies it as a
worldly-wise work.

1532. Le Comte, Edward. *Milton and Sex,* 45. New York: Columbia
University Press, 1978. 154 pp. Suggests that Ralegh's refusal to

condemn polygamy in his *History* influenced Milton in his *De Doctrina Christiana.*

1533. Lefranc, Pierre. *Sir Walter Ralegh écrivain: l'oeuvre et les idées.* Québec: Presses de l'Université Laval; Paris: Librairie Armand Colin, 1968. 733 pp. Discusses the nature and contents of the prose and poetry attributed to Ralegh, summarizes recent scholarly work on the Ralegh canon and excludes a number of works formerly attributed to him, and gives much attention to his thought and the intellectual world in which he moved.

1534. ———. "L'oeuvre écrite de Sir Walter Ralegh (1554–1618)." *L'Information Historique* 31 (1969): 131–34. Questions Ralegh's authorship of three philosophical works, "A Treatise of the Soule," "The Prince, or Maxims of State," and "The Scepticke," taking issue with Strathmann who used "The Scepticke" to interpret Ralegh as a skeptical-Christian fideist.

1535. ———. "Une Nouvelle version de la 'Petition to Queen Anne' de Sir Walter Ralegh." *Annales de la Faculté des Lettres et Sciences Humaines de Nice* 34 (1978): 57–67. Discusses a 78-line version of the poem beginning "My dayes delight, my spring tyme ioyes foredun."

1536. Legouis, Emile. "Sir Walter Raleigh d'après ses lettres." *Revue Anglo-Americaine* 4 (1926): 1–11.

1537. Lerner, Laurence. *An Introduction to English Poetry.* London: Arnold, 1975. 230 pp. Analyzes fifteen poems, including "The Lie" by Ralegh.

1538. Levin, Harry. *The Overreacher: A Study of Christopher Marlowe,* 4, 154–55. Cambridge, Mass.: Harvard University Press, 1952. 204 pp. Examines antecedents to Marlowe's "Passionate Shepherd" and Ralegh's "Nymph's Reply."

1539. Levy, F. J. *Tudor Historical Thought,* 286–94. San Marino, Calif.: Huntington Library, 1967. 305 pp. Sees Ralegh as epitomizing the achievements of the Tudor historian.

1540. Lewis, C. S. *English Literature in the Sixteenth Century Excluding Drama,* 519–20. Oxford: Clarendon Press, 1954. 696 pp. Notes that poetry was a small part of Ralegh's life and concludes that he "has no style of his own; he is an amateur blown this way and that (and sometimes lifted into real poetry) by his reading."

1541. Lewis, Joseph Woolf. "Unfinished Works of the Sixteenth Century: *The Faerie Queene, The New Arcadia,* and *The*

Ocean to Scinthia." Ph.D. diss., Temple University, 1982. 231 pp. Theorizes that the late sixteenth century may have prized an "aesthetic of incompletion," and explicates *The Ocean to Cynthia* accordingly.

1542. Lieb, Michael. *Poetics of the Holy: A Reading of Paradise Lost*, 209–10. Chapel Hill: University of North Carolina Press, 1981. 442 pp. Notes that Ralegh's discussion of created light in *The History of the World* may have influenced Milton's depiction of created light as *lumen*.

1543. Lockwood, William Jeremiah. "The Thought and Lyrics of Sir Walter Ralegh." Ph.D. diss., University of Pennsylvania, 1969. 282 pp. Traces Ralegh's philosophic idealism to Augustine and the Neoplatonists and assesses its relationship to his poems.

1544. Long, Percy W. "Spenser's *Minor Poems*. Edited by Ernest de Sélincourt." *Englische Studien* 44 (1912): 260–66. Claims that Spenser dated *Colin Clout's Come Home Again* from Kilcolman because Ralegh helped Spenser obtain title to the estate.

1545. Low, Anthony. "New Science and the Georgic Revolution in Seventeenth-Century English Literature." *English Literary Renaissance* 13 (1983): 231–59. Suggests that *Observations Touching Trade and Commerce with the Hollander*, [doubtfully] attributed to Ralegh, helped regenerate interest in the mode of Vergil's *Georgics*.

1546. Luciani, Vincent. "Ralegh's *Discourse of War* and Machiavelli's *Discorsi*." *Modern Philology* 46 (November 1948): 122–31. Says that Ralegh assimilated Machiavelli's writings and based his *Discourse* on Machiavelli's *Discorsi*.

1547. ———. "Ralegh's *Cabinet-Council* and Guicciardini's Aphorisms." *Studies in Philology* 46 (January 1949): 20–30. Traces to Guicciardini 24 reflections in Chapter 25 of Ralegh's *Cabinet-Council*.

1548. ———. "Ralegh's *Discourses on the Savoyan Matches* and Machiavelli's *Istorie fiorentine*." *Italica* 29 (1952): 103–7. Considers Machiavelli's influence on Ralegh profound and notes Ralegh's direct borrowing from the *Istorie fiorentine*.

1549. Lyons, Jessie M. "Spenser's *Muiopotmos* as an Allegory." *Publications of the Modern Language Association* 31 (1916): 90–113. Reads "Muiopotmos" as an allegory of Ralegh's problems at court and identifies Clarion as Ralegh.

1550. M [Talbert Matthews]. "Raleigh and the 'Columbiad.' " *Notes and Queries* 161 (1931): 390. Cites sixteen lines praising Ralegh in the poem "The Columbiad," reprinted in *The Beauties of Sidmouth Displayed* (1810), and asks their origin.

1551. M., J. H. "Raleigh's 'Silent Lover.' " *Notes and Queries* 11 (1855): 171–72. Discusses the poem.

1552. M., R. B. "Ralegh's *History of the World* as a Chained Book." *Devon and Cornwall Notes and Queries* 22 (1943): 192. Notes two instances in churches.

1553. No entry.

1554. McCollum, John I., Jr. "Ralegh's *The History of the World.*" *Carrell: Journal of the Friends of the University of Miami Library* 5 (1964): 1–6. Sees Ralegh's *History* as combining mythological, religious, philosophical, national, and personal elements.

1555. MacDonald, George. "Spenser and His Friends." In *England's Antiphon*, 71–76. London: Macmillan, 1868. 332 pp. Reprints. 1874, 1890. Expresses a preference for Ralegh's prose, but praises his "Pilgrimage" and attributes to him a hymn, "Rise, oh my soul with thy desires to heaven."

1556. McEwan, R. J. "Influence of Machiavelli on Christopher Marlowe through Ralegh." Master's thesis, Catholic University, 1934. 65 pp.

1557. McLean, John. "Sir Walter Ralegh: Inedited Letter." *Notes and Queries*, 3d ser. 4 (1863): 3. Reprints a letter of 28 December 1589 (?) from Ralegh to his kinsman Sir George Carew.

1558. McNeir, Waldo F. " 'Raymundus' Again." *Times Literary Supplement*, 30 May 1936, 460. Says that the reference in Joseph Hall's *Satires* to "the third furnace," which might yet fill all of Ralegh's pots and pans with gold meant the third Guiana expedition, prepared in 1598 under the command of Sir John Gilbert.

1559. _____. " 'Raymundus' and Ralegh." *Times Literary Supplement*, 4 December 1937, 928. Substantiates his opinion in the previous item with two references from the John Chamberlain letters.

1560. _____. "Hall's 'Fortunio' and 'Raymundus' Once More." *Notes and Queries*, n.s. 6 (1959): 255–57. Argues that Ralegh is Raymundus in Joseph Hall's *Virgidemiarum*.

1561. McPeek, James A. S. *Catullus in Strange and Distant Britain*,

110, 133. Cambridge, Mass.: Harvard University Press, 1939. 411 pp. Claims that Ralegh was the first to translate into English portions of Catullus's "Vivamus, mea Lesbia," and discusses an image from Catullus that Ralegh uses in his *Ocean to Cynthia*.

1562. Mann, Francis Oscar, ed. *The Works of Thomas Deloney*, 365, 378–79. Oxford: Clarendon Press, 1912. 600 pp. Attributes the poems "Walsingham" and "Farewell false Love" to Deloney, not Ralegh.

1563. Manwaring, G. E. "Sir Walter Ralegh and John Keymer." *Times Literary Supplement*, 16 July 1925, 480. Denies that Ralegh wrote *Observations touching Trade and Commerce with the Hollander and Other Nations*, and attributes it to John Keymer, based on T. W. Fulton's discovery of the original manuscript.

1564. Maxwell, Baldwin. *Studies in Beaumont, Fletcher and Massinger*. Chapel Hill: University of North Carolina Press, 1939. 238 pp. Reprint. New York: Octagon Books, 1966. Suggests that Ralegh's betrayal by Stukeley may be portrayed in *The False One*.

1565. May, Steven W., ed. "Notes and Commentary" In *The Poems of Edward De Vere, Seventeenth Earl of Oxford, and of Robert Devereux, Second Earl of Essex. Studies in Philology* Texts and Studies Series 78 (1980): 5, 84–88, 106–8. Speculates on the reason for Essex's attack on Ralegh in "Muses no more, but mazes be your names," and describes two responses, which Essex may have written, to Ralegh's poem "The Lie."

1566. _____. "Companion Poems in the Ralegh Canon." *English Literary Renaissance* 13 (1983): 260–73. Pairs Ralegh's "Sweet are the Thoughts" and "Farewell False Love" with poems by George Whetstone and Sir Thomas Heneage.

1567. Mellers, Wilfred. "La Mélancolie au début du XVII siècle et le madrigal anglais." *Colloques Internationaux du Centre National de la Recherche Scientifique: Sciences Humaines* 5 (1954): 153–68.

1568. Meyer, Russell J. " 'Fixt in heauens Light': Spenser, Astronomy, and the Date of the Cantos of Mutabilitie." *Spenser Studies: A Renaissance Poetry Annual* 4 (1984): 115–29. Notes that through his relationship with Ralegh, Spenser was probably able to meet the astronomers Digges, Dee, and Hariot.

1569. Meyer, Sam. *An Interpretation of Edmund Spenser's "Colin Clout,"* 142–71. Cork, Ireland: Cork University Press, 1969. 218 pp. Disputes the view that *Colin Clout's Come Home Again* contains a literal account of Ralegh's visit to Kilcolman in 1589 and suggests that Ralegh may have made several visits there in that year.

1570. Michel-Michot, Paulette. "Sir Walter Raleigh as a Source for the Character of Iago." *English Studies* 50 (1969): 85–89.

1571. Mills, Jerry Leath. "Prudence, History, and the Prince in *The Faerie Queene,* Book 2." *Huntington Library Quarterly* 41 (1978): 83–101. Notes similarities between Ralegh's depiction of providential justice in his *History* and Spenser's chronicling of early British history in *The Faerie Queene.*

1572. Mistichelli, William John. "Tragic Perspective and Style in Sir Walter Ralegh's *The History of the World.*" Ph.D. diss., Syracuse University, 1977. 217 pp. Calls Ralegh's view tragic because he sees history as a cycle devoid of moral progress, though occasionally illuminated by individual excellence and virtue; terms Ralegh's writing *The History* a moral triumph.

1573. Montrose, Louis Adrian. "Of Gentlemen and Shepherds: The Politics of Elizabethan Pastoral Form." *ELH: A Journal of English Literary History* 50 (1983): 415–59. Discusses pastoral conventions in "The Ocean to Cynthia."

1574. ———. " 'Shaping Fantasies': Figurations of Gender and Power in Elizabethan Culture." *Representations* 1 (Spring 1983): 61–94. Discusses Elizabethan "politics of the unconscious" as revealed in Shakespeare's *Midsummer Night's Dream* and notes that some of the same politics appear in Ralegh's *Discovery of Guiana.*

1575. Moore Smith, G. C. "Sir Walter Raleigh as Seen by Sir John Harington." *Times Literary Supplement,* 10 March 1927, 160. Identifies Paulus in Harington's epigrams as Ralegh, from whom Harington had become alienated.

1576. Morris, Harry. "In Articulo Mortis." *Tulane Studies in English* 11 (1961): 21–37. Considers "The Passionate Man's Pilgrimage" as representative of a genre of deathbed repentance poems.

1577. Morris, Helen. *Elizabethan Literature*, 75–78, 131–32. London: Oxford University Press, 1958. 239 pp.

1578. Mounts, Charles E. "The Ralegh-Essex Rivalry and *Mother Hubberd's Tale*." *Modern Language Notes* 65 (December 1950): 509–13. Claims that in lines 615–630 of *Mother Hubberd's Tale* Spenser is alluding to Elizabeth's giving Ralegh a golden chain and thereby angering Essex.

1579. Muir, Kenneth. *Introduction to Elizabethan Literature*, 91–97. New York: Random House, 1967. 207 pp.

1580. Neele, Henry. "Ralegh's Poetry." In *Lectures on English Poetry*, lecture 6. London: Thomas, 1839. 229 pp. Mentions Ralegh and prints one of his poems.

1581. Neilson, William Allen, and Ashley Horace Thorndike. "Sir Walter Raleigh." In *A History of English Literature*, 105–9. New York: Macmillan, 1920. 467 pp.

1582. Nelson, Louise A. "*Muiopotmos*." *Calcutta Review*, 3d ser. 37 (1930): 339–41. Considers Spenser's poem an allegory of the rivalry between Ralegh and Essex.

1583. Nicholl, Charles. *A Cup of News: The Life of Thomas Nashe*, 103–12. 206–11. London: Routledge and Kegan Paul, 1984. 342 pp. Says that Nashe's *Pierce Penilesse* satirizes Ralegh and the group at Durham House, but denies that Shakespeare satirized Ralegh in *Love's Labour's Lost*.

1584. Oakeshott, Walter Fraser. "An Unknown Ralegh MS." *The Times* (London), 29 Nov. 1952, p. 7. Describes an autograph notebook compiled while Ralegh was imprisoned in the Tower, containing maps and notes for his *History of the World*, a list of his library there, and the text of his poem "Now we have present made."

1585. _____. "*Imago Mundi*: Collector's Piece 1." *Book Collector* 15 (Spring 1966): 12–18. Discusses Ralegh's annotations in a copy of this 1483 book by Pierre d'Ailly.

1586. _____. "Carew Ralegh's Copy of Spenser." *Library*, 5th ser. 26 (March 1971): 1–21. Discusses a 1617 edition of Spenser's works owned by Ralegh's son Carew in which his mother's annotations show that certain characters refer to her and to Sir Walter.

1587. O'Connell, Michael William. *Mirror and Veil: The Historical Dimension of Spenser's Faerie Queene*, 99–124. Chapel Hill: University of North Carolina Press, 1977. 220 pp. Argues that the Timias-Belphoebe episode in *The Faerie Queene* allegorizes Ralegh's fall from the queen's favor because of his marriage to Elizabeth Throckmorton.

1588. Ōgoshi, Katsuzo. "Shinshō no Ronri: Walter Ralegh no Cynthia no Baai." In *Gengo to Buntai: Higashida Chioki Kyōju Kanreki Kinen Ronbunshū*, edited by Chioki Higashida, 43–49. Ōsaka: Ōsaka Kyōiku Tosho, 1975. Considers the logic of images in Ralegh's poems to Cynthia.

1589. Olson, William Bruce. "A Lost Poem by Queen Elizabeth I." *Times Literary Supplement*, 12 September 1968, 1032. Supports Abraham's claim that Ralegh's poem "Fortune hath taken away my love" was the forerunner of the ballad "Fortune My Foe."

1590. Oram, William A. "Elizabethan Fact and Spenserian Fiction." *Spenser Studies: A Renaissance Poetry Annual* 4 (1984): 33–47. Describes Spenser's technique of using elements of historical figures and events, citing Ralegh and the Timias-Belphoebe episode.

1591. Ostriker, Alicia. "The Lyric." In *English Poetry and Prose, 1540–1674*, edited by Christopher Ricks. London: Barnie & Jenkins, 1970. 442 pp. Terms Ralegh's poetry terse and brilliant and suggests that much was lost because he did not condescend to publish it.

1592. Otis, William Bradley. *A Survey-History of English Literature*, 141–43. New York: Barnes & Noble, 1938. 670 pp.

1593. Pafford, J. H. P. "Schoole of Night." *Notes and Queries*, n.s. 4 (April 1957): 143. Suggests that in *Love's Labour's Lost* the phrase should read not "Schoole of Night" but "Shield of Night" or "Seele" or "Screen."

1594. Palk, Robert. "The Puzzle of *The Sonnets*—A Solution." *Times Literary Supplement*, 20 April 1916, 189. Reprinted in *Devonian Yearbook* (1917). Claims that, because Shakespeare's sonnets mirror Ralegh's life and character, Ralegh is their author.

1595. ———. "Sir Walter Ralegh and Shakespeare." *Times Literary Supplement*, 24 October 1918, 512. Reasserts that Ralegh wrote Shakespeare's sonnets and claims that the Dark Lady is Penelope Devereux, sister of the Earl of Essex.

1596. ———. "Shakespeare, Essex, Richard II." *Times Literary Supplement*, 10 December 1931, 1006. Claims that Ralegh wrote *Richard II* to warn the Earl of Essex against attempting the overthrow of Elizabeth.

1597. Patrides, C. A. *The Phoenix and the Ladder: The Rise and Decline of the Christian View of History*, 46–47. Berkeley: University of California, 1964. 101 pp. Condenses the argument in the next item.

1598. _____. *The Grand Design of God: The Literary Form of the Christian View of History*. London: Routledge & Kegan Paul; Toronto: University of Toronto Press, 1972. 157 pp. Argues that Ralegh's *History of the World* is an orthodox presentation of the providential view of history and the best of seventeenth-century histories.

1599. Pemberton, Henry, Jr. *Shakspere [sic] and Sir Walter Ralegh, Including Also Several Essays Previously Published in the New Shakespearana Edition after the Author's Death by Susan Lovering Pemberton from an Unfinished Manuscript with Kindly Revision by Her Husband's Friend, Carroll Smyth*. Philadelphia and London: Lippincott, 1914. 242 pp. Reprint. New York: Haskell House, 1971. Claims that Ralegh wrote Shakespeare's works.

1600. Penniman, J. H., ed. *The Poetaster by Ben Jonson and Satiromastix by Thomas Dekker*, lii–lvi. Boston: Heath, 1913. 456 pp. Claims that Puntarvolo and Amorphus in these plays represent Ralegh.

1601. Pennington, Edgar Legare. "Raleigh's Narrative of Guiana." *South Atlantic Quarterly* 21 (1922): 352–59. Contrasts the buoyancy and vigor of Ralegh's prose about his 1595 voyage to Guiana with the despondency and mechanical effect of his account of the 1617 voyage.

1602. Peterson, Douglas L. *The English Lyric from Wyatt to Donne: A History of the Plain and Eloquent Styles*, 113. Princeton: Princeton University Press, 1967. 391 pp. Traces the development of the plain style of poetry from Wyatt to Ralegh.

1603. Petti, Anthony G. "The Fox, the Ape, the Humble-Bee and the Goose." *Neophilologus* 44 (1960): 208–15. Argues that in allusions in Shakespeare's *Love's Labour's Lost* and *Troilus and Cressida*, the fox represents Lord Burghley; the ape, Robert Cecil; the humble-bee, the Earl of Essex; and the goose, Ralegh.

1604. Pinto, V. de Sola. *The English Renaissance, 1510–1688*, 211, 239–40. London: Cresset Press, 1938. 380 pp.

1605. Popkin, Richard H. "A Manuscript of Ralegh's 'The Scepticke.' " *Philological Quarterly* 36 (April 1957): 253–59. Describes a manuscript in the library of Trinity College, Dublin, and its variants from other versions.

1606. Potez, Henri. "L'Oeuvre critique de Sir Walter Raleigh." *Revue Germanique* 10 (1914): 294–313.

1607. Potter, G. R. "Shakespeare's Will and Ralegh's *Instructions to His Son.*" *Notes and Queries* 158 (1930): 364–65. Says that Shakespeare's leaving his wife so little in his will and Ralegh's stating that most of a man's estate should go to his children, not to his widow, reflect attitudes of that era.

1608. Power, William. "*The Phoenix,* Raleigh, and King James." *Notes and Queries,* n.s. 5 (1958): 57–61. Notes that Ralegh was satirized as Proditor, a scheming courtier in Thomas Middleton's play *The Phoenix.*

1609. Pratt, S. M. "The Authorship of Four Poems in *The Garland of Good Will.*" *Notes and Queries,* n.s. 1 (1954): 327–28. Affirms that Ralegh wrote "A farewell to love."

1610. Praz, Mario. "Un machiavellico inglese: Sir Walter Ralegh." *La Cultura* 8 (1929): 16–27. Claims that Machiavelli deeply influenced Ralegh's conduct and writings.

1611. Prescott, Anne Lake. *French Poets and the English Renaissance: Studies in Fame and Transformation,* 154–55. New Haven and London: Yale University Press, 1978. 290 pp. Praises Ralegh's "Like to a Hermite poore" as the best English version of Desportes' "Diane."

1612. Prouty, C. T. *George Gascoigne: Elizabethan Courtier, Soldier, and Poet,* 241. New York: Columbia University Press, 1942. 351 pp. Notes that Ralegh's poem in commendation of Gascoigne's "Steel Glass" (1576) was Ralegh's first published poem.

1613. Puttenham, George [supposed author]. "Who in any age have bene the most commended writers in our English Poesie, and the Authors censure given vpon them." In *The Arte of English Poesie,* 73–77. Kent, Ohio: Kent State University Press, 1970. 320 pp. Facsimile reprint of 1906 ed. First published 1589. Commends Ralegh as an excellent but private poet.

1614. Quiller-Couch, Sir Arthur, and John Dover Wilson. "Introduction." In *Love's Labour's Lost,* by William Shakespeare, xxviii–xxxiv. Cambridge: Cambridge University

Press, 1923. 212 pp. Elaborates on the theory that Ralegh and his associates are satirized in the play.

1615. Racin, John, Jr. "An Analysis of Sir Walter Ralegh's *The History of the World*." Ph.D. diss., Ohio State University, 1961. 256 pp.

1616. _____. "The Early Editions of Sir Walter Ralegh's *The History of the World*." *Studies in Bibliography* 17 (1964): 199–209. Argues that there were three, not five, printings of the *History* between 1614 and 1621: namely, the Stansby 1614, 1617, and Jaggard 1621, and the last two were unrevised reprints of no textual authority.

1617. _____. *Sir Walter Ralegh as Historian: An Analysis of The History of The World*. Salzburg, Austria: Institut für Englische Sprache und Literatur, Universität Salzburg, 1974. 216 pp. Surveys the publishing history of Ralegh's *History* and analyzes his use of classical and providential interpretations of history.

1618. Reed, Newman Thomas. "The Philosophical Background of Sir Walter Raleigh's *History of the World*." Ph.D. diss., Northwestern University, 1934. Argues that Ralegh started to write his *History* in the medieval pattern of moral history, but as a Renaissance man was obliged to adopt Machiavellian amoral explanations of history.

1619. Rees, Ennis. *The Tragedies of George Chapman: Renaissance Ethics in Action*, 53. Cambridge, Mass.: Harvard University Press, 1954. 223 pp. Notes praise for Ralegh in Chapman's poem "De Guiana" (1596).

1620. Reese, Max Meredith. *The Cease of Majesty: A Study of Shakespeare's History Plays*, 16–18. London: Edward Arnold, 1961. 350 pp. Considers Ralegh's Renaissance combination of religious and secular approaches to history as evinced in *The History of the World*.

1621. Rivers, Isabel. *Classical and Christian Ideas in English Renaissance Poetry: A Student's Guide*, 11. London: George Allen and Unwin, 1979. 231 pp. Discusses Renaissance philosophical tenets expressed in *The History of the World*.

1622. Robbins, Frank Egleston. *The Hexaemeral Literature: A Study of the Greek and Latin Commentaries on Genesis*, 89–91. Chicago: University of Chicago Press, 1912. 104 pp. Calls the first chapters of the *History* representative hexamera of the Renaissance.

1623. Roberts, John C. de V. "Sir Walter Ralegh in Life and Letters." *Report and Transactions of the Devonshire Association for the Advancement of Science, Literature, and Art* 101 (1969): 115–24. Considers the treatment of Ralegh in biography and historiography to have been continually marred by inaccuracies and inconsistencies repeated from book to book.

1624. Rollins, Hyder Edward. *The Paradise of Dainty Devices*, lx–lxi, 183. Cambridge, Mass.: Harvard University Press, 1927. 298 pp. First published in 1576.

1625. ———. "Sir Walter Raleigh and *The Phoenix Nest*." *Times Literary Supplement*, 12 December 1929, 1058. Notes that Ralegh's "Like to a hermit" is a translation of a sonnet in Desportes' *Amours de Diane*.

1626. Rosati, Salvatore. "Il 'Pastore dell'Oceàno': Sir Walter Ralegh." *Nuova Antologia* 439 (1947): 306–14.

1627. Rosbaugh, Constance G. "Aspects of Renaissance Melancholy in the Works of Spenser, Raleigh and Donne." Master's thesis, Columbia University, 1943.

1628. Roston, Murray. "A Fallen Favorite." In *Sixteenth-Century English Literature*, 153–57. London: Macmillan; New York: Schocken Books, 1982. 235 pp. Discusses Ralegh's emphasis on mutability in his poetry and praises the prose of his *History*.

1629. Rowse, A. L. *Christopher Marlowe: A Biography*, 125–26. London: Macmillan, 1964. Discusses Ralegh's reply to Marlowe's "Passionate Shepherd."

1630. Rozwenc, Edwin C. "Captain John Smith's Image of America." *William and Mary Quarterly*, 3d ser. 16 (1959): 26–36. Suggests parallels between Smith's concept of history and literary imagination and Ralegh's.

1631. Rudick, Michael. "The 'Ralegh Group' in *The Phoenix Nest*." *Studies in Bibliography* 24 (1971): 131–37. Recounts the controversy over Ralegh's authorship of sixteen poems in *The Phoenix Nest*, and considers him the author of only "Calling to mind mine eye long went about" and "Like truthless dreams, so are my joys expired."

1632. Russell, Sandra Joanne. "Ralegh's Universe." Ph.D. diss., Columbia University, 1964. 276 pp. Maintains that Ralegh's world-view was orthodox.

1633. Sackton, Alexander. "The Rhetoric of Literary Praise in the Poetry of Raleigh and Chapman." *Texas Studies in Literature and Language* 18 (1976): 409–21. Contends that Ralegh's poem prefatory to Gascoigne's "Steel Glass" (1576) marks the introduction of critical evaluation into commendatory poetry.

1634. Saintsbury, George. *A History of English Prose Rhythm*, 158–61. London: Macmillan, 1912. 489 pp. Praises the rhythmic flow and solemn cadence of Ralegh's prose.

1635. Sakbani, Ayda Yegengil. "Sir Walter Raleigh: An Inquiry into the Nature of His Moral and Artistic Sensibilities and a Study of his Poetry." Ph.D. diss., New York University, 1970. 150 pp.

1636. Sampson, George. "Sir Walter Ralegh." In *The Concise Cambridge History of English Literature*, 181–82. Cambridge: Cambridge University Press, 1941. 1094 pp.

1637. Sandison, Helen Estabrook. "Arthur Gorges, Spenser's Alcyon and Ralegh's Friend." *Publications of the Modern Language Association* 43 (1928): 645–74. Discusses the close relationship between the minor poet, Arthur Gorges, and his cousin, Ralegh, and Ralegh's impact upon Gorges's written works.

1638. _____, ed. *The Poems of Sir Arthur Gorges*, 201, 209–12. Oxford: Clarendon Press, 1953. 254 pp. Claims that "Woolde I were changde into that golden showre" and "Her face—Her tongue—Her wytt" belong to the "Ralegh Group" in *The Phoenix Nest* and that their attribution to Ralegh by Agnes Latham is doubtful.

1639. Sargent, Ralph M. *At the Court of Queen Elizabeth: The Life and Lyrics of Sir Edward Dyer*, 92–93, 141–42, 146–47, passim. London and New York: Oxford University Press, 1935. 229 pp. Notes links between Ralegh and Dyer, and attributes "Alas my heart, mine eye hath wronged thee" to Dyer, rather than to Ralegh as Rollins did in editing *The Phoenix Nest*.

1640. Saunders, J. W. "The Stigma of Print: A Note on the Social Bases of Tudor Poetry." *Essays in Criticism* 1 (April 1951): 139–64. Discusses the purposes of Tudor poetry and the seemingly casual attitudes of Tudor poets such as Ralegh to their poetry.

1641. Schelling, Felix E. *English Literature During the Lifetime of Shakespeare*. New York: Henry Holt, 1910, 1927. 492 pp. Refers to Ralegh passim.

1642. Schmidt, Michael. "Sir Walter Raleigh." In *A Reader's Guide to Fifty British Poets, 1300–1900*, 92–97. London: Heinemann; Totowa, N.J.: Barnes and Noble, 1980. 430 pp.

Classifies Ralegh's poems as either aphoristic or elaborated, criticizes his occasional mixing of styles, and praises his imagination and personalizing of conventions.

1643. Schrickx, W. "Shakespeare and the School of Night: An Estimate and Further Interpretations." *Neophilologus* 34 (1950): 35–44. Believes that the main target of the satire in *Love's Labour's Lost* is Chapman and his adherents rather than Ralegh.

1644. _____. "The School of Night." In *Shakespeare's Early Contemporaries: The Background of the Nashe-Harvey Polemic and "Love's Labour's Lost,"* 26–37. Antwerp: De Nederlandsche Boekhandel, 1956. 291 pp. Elaborates on the theory in the preceding item.

1645. Seymour-Smith, Martin. *Poets Through Their Letters*, 21–27. London: Constable, 1969. 464 pp. Maintains that *The Ocean to Cynthia* reflects Ralegh's dismay over the Queen's slighting of him as a political advisor.

1646. Shapiro, Deborah. "Sir Walter Raleigh's 'The Ocean's Love to Cynthia.'" Master's thesis, University of North Carolina, 1968. 49 pp. Discusses the place of the poem in the Ralegh canon, and finds in the poem traces of the "stream-of-consciousness" and "imagist" techniques.

1646[a]. Sharma, Durga. "Time and Mutability in Late Elizabethan Poetry, with special reference to Sir Walter Ralegh." Master's thesis, Lakehead University, 1979. 174 pp.

1647. "Sidney and Raleigh." *Atlantic Monthly* 22 (1868): 304–13. Finds Ralegh and Sidney to have been quite different in character.

1648. Sirugo, Marilyn S. "The Site of 'Love Among the Ruins' Revisited." *Studies in Browning and His Circle* 4 (1976): 41–48. Says that Browning's poem draws upon Ralegh's *History of the World*.

1649. "Sir Walter Ralegh's Prose." *Times Literary Supplement*, 31 January 1935, 53–54. Notes that Ralegh's *Discovery* was a bestseller and considers his influence on Shakespeare and Milton.

1650. Smith, M. van Wyk. "John Donne's 'Metempsychosis.'" *Review of English Studies*, n.s. 24 (February and May 1973): 17–25, 141–52. Argues that Donne's satirical poem is directed against Robert Cecil, whose betrayal of Ralegh angered Donne.

1651. Southern, H. "Sir Walter Raleigh's *Remains.*" *Retrospective Review* 2 (1820): 329–40. Describes the collection of prose works and quotes extensively from "Advice to His Son," "Advice of a Loving Son to His Aged Father," and "The Sceptick."

1652. Sprague, C. J. "The Lie." *Atlantic Monthly* 20 (1867): 598–602. Discusses whether Ralegh wrote the poem and cites two versions, one by Sylvester.

1653. Sprott, S. E. "Ralegh's 'Sceptic' and the Elizabethan Translation of Sextus Empiricus." *Philological Quarterly* 42 (April 1963): 166–75. Compares four manuscripts of the work and finds the evidence for Ralegh's authorship inconclusive.

1654. Starkey, Lawrence G., and Philip Ropp. "The Printing of *A Declaration of the Demeanor and Cariage of Sir Walter Raleigh*, 1618." *Library*, 5th ser. 3 (1948–49): 124–34. Contends that the traditional sequence of the two impressions should be reversed.

1655. Starrett, Vincent. "With Sword and Pen." In *Books Alive*, 99–120. New York: Random House, 1940. 360 pp. Discusses Ralegh as soldier-writer and terms tobacco his greatest legacy.

1656. Staton, Walter F., Jr. "Ralegh and the Amyas-Aemylia Episode." *Studies in English Literature 1500–1900* 5 (Winter 1965): 105–14. Contends that in Cantos 8 and 9 of Book 4 of *The Faerie Queene*, Spenser meant to administer a mild corrective to Ralegh by showing that love is unsuitable where social rank differs greatly.

1657. Sternfeld, Frederick W. " 'Come Live with Me and Be My Love.' " In *The Hidden Harmony: Essays in Honor of Philip Wheelwright*, edited by Oliver Johnson et al., 173–95. New York: Odyssey, 1966. 195 pp. Discusses Ralegh's reply to Marlowe's poem.

1658. Stibbs, John H. "A Detailed Study of the Shorter Prose Works of Sir Walter Raleigh." Ph.D. diss., University of Michigan, 1942. 255 pp.

1659. ———. "Sir Walter Raleigh's *Discourse of Tenures.*" *Tulane Law Review* 22 (1947): 273–83. Cites the *Discourse* as the first work in England to show that tenures existed before the Norman Conquest and that civil law is much less useful than common law.

1660. ———. "Ralegh and Holinshed." *Modern Language Review* 44 (1949): 543–44. Contends that Holinshed's *Chronicles* (1587) is the source for Ralegh's *Prerogative of Parliaments*.

1661. ———. "Raleigh's Account of Grenville's Fight at the Azores in 1591." *North Carolina Historical Review* 27 (1950): 20–31. Maintains that Ralegh's account of the battle, while containing some inaccuracies attributable to patriotism, is the most complete account of it.

1662. ———. "The Concept of Natural Law in the Prose Writings of Sir Walter Raleigh." *Tulane Law Review* 26 (1952): 194–201. Finds that Ralegh held the traditional view of natural law as the law of God, given to men and known through reason, implying equality for all men, with some exceptions, and of human law as based upon natural law but made by the reason of those in authority.

1663. Strathmann, Ernest A. "An Epitaph Attributed to Ralegh." *Modern Language Notes* 60 (1945): 111–14. Points out that a satirical epitaph on the Earl of Leicester was attributed to Ralegh only once in his era.

1664. ———. "The Textual Evidence for the 'School of Night.'" *Modern Language Notes* 56 (1941): 176–86. Opposes the view of Bradbrook and Yates that Ralegh and his group are satirized in *Love's Labour's Lost*.

1665. ———. "A Note on the Ralegh Canon." *Times Literary Supplement*, 13 April 1956, 228. Observes that the treatise entitled *The Cabinet-Council* attributed to Ralegh and published by John Milton in 1658 appeared earlier in nine manuscripts as *Observations Political and Civil* attributed to other authors, never to Ralegh.

1666. ———. "Ralegh's *Discourse of Tenures* and Sir Roger Owen." *Huntington Library Quarterly* 20 (1957): 219–32. Finds no evidence for Ralegh's authorship of the *Discourse*, which in fact consists of parts of chapter 18 of a manuscript by Owen (1573–1617), which was widely but anonymously circulated in that era.

1667. Sullivan, Ernest W., II. "John Donne's Probleme, 'Why was Sir Walter Raleigh thought ye fittest Man, to write ye Historie of these Times?'" *Papers of the Bibliographical Society of America* 74 (1980): 63–67. Describes the four printed versions and transcribes the version in Tanner Manuscript 299, fol. 32, in the Bodleian Library.

1668. Sutherland, James. *On English Prose*, 43. Toronto: University of Toronto Press, 1957. 123 pp. Considers Ralegh's prose to be oratorical.

1669. Tannenbaum, Samuel Aaron. "Unfamiliar Versions of Some Elizabethan Poems." *Publications of the Modern Language Association* 45 (1930): 809–21. Reports a copy of "The Lie" found in a seventeenth-century commonplace book.

1670. Tapley-Soper, H. "Raleigh and the 'Columbiad.'" *Notes and Queries* 161 (1931): 463. Answers the query by M. that the *Columbiad* was by Joel Barlow of Connecticut and was published in 1807 in Philadelphia and in London in 1809.

1671. Taylor, Henry Osborn. "Raleigh, Sidney, Spenser." In *Thought and Expression in the Sixteenth Century*. 2 vols. 2:207–37. New York: Macmillan, 1920. 2d ed. 1930. Calls Ralegh a complete and wonderful Elizabethan genius and notes the strains of cynicism and melancholy in most of his poetry.

1672. Tennenhouse, Leonard. "Sir Walter Ralegh and the Literature of Clientage." In *Patronage in the Renaissance*, edited by Guy Fitch Lytle and Stephen Orgel, 235–58. Princeton: Princeton University Press, 1981. 389 pp. Notes the importance of clientage in almost all of Ralegh's literary works and discusses the relationship of Ralegh and the queen reflected in his poetry.

1673. Thorpe, W. A. "'Even Such is Time.'" *Times Literary Supplement*, 12 October 1951, 645. Notes use of Ralegh's stanza in seventeenth-century epitaphs.

1674. Thurston, Marjorie H. "The Literary Form of Sir Walter Raleigh's *History of the World*." Ph.D. diss., University of Minnesota, 1941. 425 pp.

1675. Tipple, Alexandra Louise. "Biblical Allusion as a Structural Element in Two Poems by Sir Walter Ralegh." Master's thesis, University of North Carolina, 1984. 78 pp. Sees parallels between The Song of Songs in the Bible and "Walsingham" and *The Ocean to Cynthia*.

1676. Trimpi, Wesley. *Ben Jonson's Poems: A Study of the Plain Style*, 114. Stanford: Stanford University Press, 1962. 292 pp. Classifies Ralegh as a poet in the plain school of Gascoigne, but notes some similarities to Jonson in attitude.

1677. Tucker, Martin, ed. *Moulton's Library of Literary Criticism of*

English and American Authors Through the Beginning of the Twentieth Century. 4 vols. 1:277–84. New York: Frederick Ungar, [1966]. Provides a sketch of Ralegh and various comments about him.

1678. Tuve, Rosemond. *Elizabethan and Metaphysical Imagery: Renaissance Poetic and Twentieth-Century Critics*, 217, 306–8. Chicago: University of Chicago Press, 1947. 442 pp. Cites Ralegh as a precursor of the metaphysical poets.

1679. ———. *Allegorical Imagery: Some Medieval Books and Their Posterity*, 164–65. Princeton: Princeton University Press, 1966. 461 pp. Compares the imagery in "The Passionate Man's Pilgrimage" with imagery in medieval devotional treatises.

1680. Unger, Leonard and William Van O'Connor, eds. "Sir Walter Ralegh." In *Poems for Study: A Critical and Historical Introduction*, 97–100. New York: Rinehart. 743 pp. Considers "The Lie."

1681. Ure, Peter. "Two Elizabethan Poets: Samuel Daniel and Sir Walter Raleigh." In *The Age of Shakespeare*, edited by Boris Ford, 131–46. Harmondsworth and New York: Penguin Books, 1955. 479 pp. Reprint. 1982. Examines Ralegh in the light of Sidney's definition of poet as philosopher, using "The Passionate Man's Pilgrimage," "A Poesie to Prove Affection is not Love," and *The Ocean to Cynthia*.

1682. ———. "The Poetry of Sir Walter Ralegh." *Review of English Literature*, 1 (1960): 19–29. Reprinted in *Elizabethan and Jacobean Drama; Critical Essays*, edited by J. C. Maxwell. New York: Barnes and Noble; Liverpool: Liverpool University Press, 1974. Praises Ralegh as a minor poet who incorporated personal feeling into his works, ranks "Methought I saw the grave where Laura lay" as one of the best sonnets of the period and "The Passionate Man's Pilgrimage," if by Ralegh, as his best poem.

1683. Ustick, W. Lee. "Advice to a Son: A Type of Seventeenth-Century Conduct Book." *Studies in Philology* 29 (July 1932): 409–41. Terms the book an epitome of worldy wisdom rather than a work of idealism, and compares it with Burghley's *Precepts*.

1684. Vear, John. "The Man Behind the Verse." *Bolt* 1 (1970): 23–27. Describes the treatments of "Come live with me and be my love" by Marlowe, Donne, Ralegh, and C. Day Lewis.

1685. Ward, A. C. *Illustrated History of English Literature.* 3 vols. 1:133–36. London and New York: Longmans, Green, 1953.

1686. Ward, C. A. "Raleigh and Milton." *Notes and Queries,* 5th ser. 3 (1875): 302. Notes that in 1658 Milton published Ralegh's *Cabinet Council* and praises the practical statesmanship of Ralegh, Bacon, and Machiavelli.

1687. Warton, Thomas. *History of English Poetry.* 3 vols. 3:438. London: Dodsley, 1774–81. Includes Warton's note that in *Englands Helicon* (1600) "Ignoto" below the "Reply" to Marlowe's "Passionate Shepherd" signifies Ralegh. This claim was dropped by W. Carew Hazlitt, editor of Warton's *History* in 1871.

1688. Wedgwood, C. V. *Seventeenth-Century English Literature,* 19–21. London: Oxford University Press, 1950. 186 pp. Says that Ralegh's influence on later writers has been underestimated and notes the popularity of his *History* among Puritans.

1689. Weidhorn, Manfred. "Satan's Persian Expedition." *Notes and Queries,* n.s. 5 (1958): 389–92. Compares Milton's Satan to Xerxes in Herodotus and in Ralegh's *History of the World.*

1690. Wendell, Barrett. *The Temper of the Seventeenth-Century in English Literature,* 184–92. New York: Scribner; London: Macmillan, 1904. 360 pp.

1691. West, Michael. "Raleigh's Disputed Authorship of 'A Description of Love.'" *English Language Notes* 10 (1972): 92–99. Argues on the basis of style that Ralegh wrote the poem.

1692. Whipple, E. P. "Sir Walter Raleigh and Sir Philip Sidney." *Atlantic Monthly* 22 (1868): 304–13. Reprinted in his *Literature of the Age of Elizabeth.* Boston: Houghton, Mifflin, 1891.

1693. Whiting, George W. "Sicily in Ortelius and in Raleigh." *Times Literary Supplement,* 11 July 1936, 580. Quotes parallel passages to show that a description of Sicily in "Of the First Punick War" in *The History of the World* was borrowed almost verbatim from Abraham Ortelius's *Theatrum Orbis Terrarum* (1606).

1694. ———. *Milton's Literary Milieu,* 15–93. Chapel Hill: University of North Carolina Press, 1939. 401 pp. Reprint. New York: Russell and Russell, 1964. Argues that Ralegh's *History of the World* profoundly influenced Milton's *Paradise Lost.*

1695. Wiley, Margaret L. *The Subtle Knot: Creative Skepticism in Seventeenth-Century England*, 31–59. Cambridge, Mass.: Harvard University Press; London: Allen & Unwin, 1952. 303 pp. Sees Ralegh, like Montaigne, advocating Greek skepticism as a defense against authoritarianism.

1696. Wilkes, G. A. "The Authorship of 'The Passionate Man's Pilgrimage.'" *Notes and Queries*, n.s. 4 (1957): 335–36. Provides further evidence that Ralegh wrote the poem.

1697. Williams, Arnold L. "The Influence of the Genesis Commentary on the Genesis Material of Sir Walter Ralegh and Sir Thomas Browne." Ph.D. diss., University of North Carolina, 1935. 183 pp. Argues that the Genesis material in the first four chapters of Ralegh's *History of the World* draws heavily on the commentaries on Genesis.

1698. ———. "Commentaries on Genesis as a Basis for Hexaemeral Material in the Literature of the Late Renaissance." *Studies in Philology* 34 (1937): 191–208. Condenses the preceding item.

1699. ———. *The Common Expositor: An Account of the Commentaries on Genesis, 1527–1633*. Chapel Hill: University of North Carolina Press, 1948. 297 pp. Incorporates Williams's previous work on Ralegh.

1700. Williams, Edith Whitehurst. "The Anglo-Saxon Theme of Exile in Renaissance Lyrics: A Perspective on Two Sonnets of Sir Walter Ralegh." *ELH: A Journal of English Literary History* 42 (1975): 171–88. Compares Ralegh's treatment of the exile in "Like truthless dreams" and "Like to a poor hermit" with the Old English lyrics "The Wanderer" and "Deor."

1701. Williams, O. C. "Raleigh's *Walsingham*." *Explicator* 9 (1951): item 27. Sees the mistress in the poem as the personification of ideal love.

1702. Williamson, George. "Mutability, Decay and Jacobean Melancholy." In *Seventeenth-Century Contexts*, 9–41. London: Faber and Faber, 1960. 291 pp. Rev. ed. Chicago: University of Chicago Press, 1969. Compares Ralegh's arguments for the decay of the world in his *History* with Godfrey Goodman's in his *Fall of Man*.

1703. Williamson, James A. "The Propagandists of the Tudor Period." In *The Ocean in English History*, 56–85. Oxford: Clarendon Press, 1941. Asserts that although Tudor propaganda was not very effective, it illustrates what advanced minds were then thinking, and calls Ralegh the last of the Tudor propagandists.

1704. Wilson, Frank P. *Elizabethan and Jacobean,* 58–60. Oxford: Clarendon Press, 1945. 144 pp. Considers that Ralegh developed as a poet from talented imitation to passionate originality.

1705. Wilson, George P. "You All." *Georgia Review* 14 (1960); 38–54. Notes occurrences of the phrase in Ralegh.

1706. Wilson, Jean. *Entertainments for Elizabeth I,* 21–22. Woodbridge, England: Brewer; Totowa, N.J.: Rowman and Littlefield, 1980. 179 pp. Classifies Ralegh's poem "Walsingham" as part of the "cult of Elizabeth."

1707. Wilson, John Dover, ed. *Love's Labour's Lost,* by William Shakespeare, 2d ed. Cambridge: Cambridge University Press, 1962. 1st ed. 1923. Reviews the extensive scholarship about the "school of night" in the play as the "school of atheism" known for its astronomical speculations and headed by Ralegh.

1708. Winters, Yvor. "The Sixteenth-Century Lyric in England: A Critical and Historical Reinterpretation." *Poetry* 53 (1939): 258–72, 320–35; 54 (1940): 35–51. Reprinted in *Elizabethan Poetry: Modern Essays in Criticism,* edited by Paul J. Alpers. New York: Oxford University Press, 1967. Classifies Ralegh with the plain style poets such as Gascoigne, whom Winters considers superior to the Petrarchan poets such as Spenser and Drayton.

1709. ———. "Aspects of the Short Poem in the English Renaissance." In *Forms of Discovery: Critical and Historical Essays on the Forms of the Short Poem in England,* 1–120. Chicago: Alan Swallow, 1967. 337 pp. Incorporates the preceding item.

1710. Wood, H. Harvey. "A Seventeenth-Century Manuscript of Poems by Donne and Others." *Essays and Studies* 16 (1931): 179–90. Discusses six of the eight poems attributed to Ralegh in the manuscript.

1711. Woods, Frances Susanne. " 'The Passionate Sheepheard' and 'The Nimphs Reply': A Study of Transmission." *Huntington Library Quarterly* 34 (1970): 25–33. Suggests that these poems were transmitted as popular songs.

1712. ———. "The Poetry of Sir Walter Ralegh." Ph.D. diss.,

Columbia University, 1970. 192 pp. Discusses problems of the Ralegh canon, Ralegh's poetic voice, and "Cynthia 21."

1713. _____. " 'The Passionate Man's Pilgrimage': Ralegh Is Still in the Running." *Modern Language Studies* 8 (1978): 12–19. Contends that the early seventeenth-century manuscript tradition assigning the poem to Ralegh should not be lightly disregarded and neither the content nor the style of the poem eliminates him as its author.

1714. Wright, W. H. "Sir Walter Raleigh (1552–1618)." In *West-County Poets: Their Lives and Works*, 389–94. London: Elliot Stock, 1896. 488 pp. Concludes this account of Ralegh's poems by remarking that they contain nothing traceable to Devon.

1715. Wurtsbaugh, Jewel. *Two Centuries of Spenserian Scholarship (1609–1805)*, 83–84. Baltimore: Johns Hopkins, 1936. 174 pp. Discusses Spenser's "Letter to Ralegh."

1716. Yarborough, Mary Jane. "The Autobiographical Element in the Poetry of Sir Walter Ralegh." Master's thesis, University of North Carolina, 1968. 43 pp.

1717. Yates, Frances A. *A Study of Love's Labour's Lost*. Cambridge: Cambridge University Press, 1936. 224 pp. Maintains that Shakespeare intended to satirize Chapman, Northumberland, and Florio, rather than Ralegh.

1718. _____. *Astraea: The Imperial Theme in the Sixteenth Century*, 29–111. London and Boston: Routledge and Kegan Paul, 1975. 233 pp. Describes the "cult of Elizabeth" and surveys Ralegh's political attitudes and poetry in that context.

1719. Yerger, O. M. "Sir Walter Raleigh's Last Poem." *Tyler's Quarterly Historical and Genealogical Magazine* 18 (1937): 129–32. Praises "Even Such is Time" and "The Passionate Man's Pilgrimage," and recounts some of Ralegh's troubles with James I.

1720. Zacher, Christian K. *Curiosity and Pilgrimage: The Literature of Discovery in Fourteenth-Century England*, 153–54. Baltimore: Johns Hopkins University Press, 1976. 196 pp. Says that Mandeville's *Travels* influenced Ralegh's *Discovery of Guiana*.

Chapter 6.

RALEGH IN LITERATURE,

MUSIC, THE VISUAL ARTS,

AND BOOKS FOR CHILDREN

1721. A. "Walter Raleigh's Portrait." *Wiltshire Notes and Queries* 6 (1908): 88.

1722. Allen, F. M. [Edmund Downey]. "Raleigh in Munster." In *Through Green Glasses*, 198–236. New York: Appleton, 1887. 236 pp. London: Ward and Downey, 1888. New York: Lupton, 1899. A burlesque.

1723. Anderson, Maxwell. *Elizabeth the Queen: A Play in Three Acts.* London and New York: Longmans, 1930. 168 pp. Includes Ralegh in this drama about Elizabeth and Essex.

1724. "Answer to the Lie." In *Courtly Poets, from Raleigh to Montrose,* edited by John Hannah, xxvii–viii. London: Bell and Daldey, 1870. 33, 261 pp. A hostile reply to Ralegh's poem.

1725. Arner, R. D. "Romance of Roanoke: Virginia Dare and the Lost Colony in American Literature." *Southern Literary Journal* 10 (1978): 5–45. Examines the literary history of the story of the Lost Colony.

1726. _____. *The Lost Colony in Literature.* Raleigh, N.C.: America's Four Hundredth Anniversary Committee, North Carolina Department of Cultural Resources, 1985. 55 pp.

1727. Baker, Nina Brown. *Sir Walter Raleigh.* New York: Harcourt, Brace, 1950. 191 pp. Fictionalized biography for young readers.

1728. *The Ballad of Sir Walter Rauleigh his Lamentation: who was beheaded in the old Pallace at Westminster the 29 of October, 1618. To the tune of Welladay.* London: Printed for Philip Birch, n.d. 8 pp. Facsimile ed., edited by C. H. Firth. London: Oxford University Press, 1919.

1729. Banks, John. *The Unhappy Favourite; or, the Earl of Essex. A tragedy acted at the Theatre-Royal by their Majesty's servants,*

Prologue and Epilogue by Mr. Dryden. London: Printed for R. Wellington and E. Rumball, 1704. 64 pp. Altered by James Ralph, and published as *The Fall of the Earl of Essex* (1731).

1730. "The Baptism of Virginia Dare." *North Carolina Teacher* 6 (1930): 272–73. Discusses and reproduces the painting "The Baptism of Virginia Dare" by William Steene which was commissioned by the North Carolina Society of Colonial Dames and given to the State Literary and Historical Association.

1731. Barlow, Joel. ["Raleigh"]. In *The Columbiad: A Poem*, Book 4, lines 250–80. Philadelphia: Conrad, 1807. 454 pp. Praises Ralegh as hero, scholar, and wise chief, who established colonies near "wild Hatteras."

1732. Barrington, E. [Mrs. Lily M. A. Beck]. "Her Majesty's Godson." In *The Gallants, following according to their wont the ladies!* Boston: Atlantic Monthly Press, 1924. 308 pp. Boston: Little, Brown, 1927. A love story, featuring Sidney, Ralegh, and others.

1733. Bayes, Ronald H., ed. *North Carolina's 400 Years: Signs Along the Way*. Durham, N.C.: Acorn Press, 1986. 83 pp. Anthology dedicated to the Lost Colonists, containing poems by 61 North Carolina poets and twelve pictures by Lumbee Indians.

1734. Bellis, Hannah. "Walter Raleigh." *They Made History*, 4 vols. 2:26–39. London: Cassell, 1962. For young readers.

1735. Borden, Lucille Papin. *King's Highway*. New York: Macmillan, 1941. 485 pp. A novel about the Starforths, who leave England and seek religious freedom in the New World.

1736. Bothwell, Jean. *Lost Colony: The Mystery of Roanoke Island*. Philadelphia: John C. Winston, 1953. 182 pp. Fiction for children.

1737. ———. *Lady of Roanoke*. New York: Holt, Rinehart and Winston, 1965. 254 pp. A novel for children, about the Roanoke colonists moving to the mainland to live with friendly Coree Indians.

1738. Boykin, Edward Nathaniel. "Sir Walter Raleigh." *North Carolina Teacher* 7 (1890): 397. A poem.

1739. Brushfield, T. N. "Harrow Song." *Western Antiquary* 8 (1889): 180. Prints a song from Harrow school, entitled "When Ralegh Rose," written by E. E. B., in three eight-line stanzas with a four-line chorus.

1740. ———. "The Boyhood of Ralegh." *Devon Notes and Queries*
1 (1900): 97–101. Discusses Millais's painting that hangs in the
Tate Gallery.

1741. ———. "Rare Engraved Portrait of Sir W. Ralegh." *Devon
Notes and Queries* 2 (1902): 177–78.

1742. Buch, Carl von. *Sir Walter Raleigh: A Poem*. Oxford: n.p.,
1880. 18 pp.

1743. Buchan, John. *Sir Walter Raleigh*. London: Nelson; New York:
Holt, 1911. 236 pp. Reprints. 1923, 1927, 1929. A life of
Ralegh in eleven episodes, intended for boys.

1744. ———. "The Hidden City." In *The Path of the King*. London:
Hodder & Stoughton, 1921. 310 pp. New York: Doran, 1921.
London: Nelson, 1925.

1745. Buckmaster, Henrietta [Henrietta Henkle]. *Walter Raleigh:
Man of Two Worlds*. New York: Random House, 1964. 181 pp.
Another ed., *All About Sir Walter Raleigh*. London: Allen,
1965. Biography for children ages 11–12.

1746. Burnham, Smith. *Hero Tales From History*, 113–18. Chicago:
John C. Winston, 1930. 393 pp.

1747. C., R. W. "The Raleigh Window in St. Margaret's Church,
Westminister." *Western Antiquary* 2 (1882): 54–55. The
window depicts Ralegh landing in Virginia, though in fact he
never landed there.

1748. Cameron, Verney Lovett. *The History of Arthur Penreath,
sometime Gentleman of Sir Walter Ralegh, from his own
writings*. London: Griffith, Farran, Okeden and Welsh, 1888.
309 pp. A novel about a Cornishman who follows Ralegh into
many adventures, especially in Guiana.

1749. Campbell, Elizabeth A. *The Carving on a Tree*. Boston and
Toronto: Little, Brown, 1968. 88 pp. Account of the Lost
Colony, with illustrations by William Bock, for young people.

1750. Campbell, Helen Jones. *The Story of the Lost Colony of
Roanoke*. Williamsburg: Usry, 1952. 24 pp. Coloring book
with text.

1751. Capern, Edward. "A Recently Discovered Portrait of Sir Walter
Raleigh." *Western Antiquary* 1 (1881): 126. Reports a half-
figure portrait of Ralegh, painted life-size and signed "I. O.,"
possibly Isaac Oliver, pupil of Frederigo Zucchero.

1752. Capes, Bernard. *Where England Sets Her Feet*. London: W.
Collins, 1918. 358 pp.

1753. Carr, Julian S. "Monument to Sir Walter Raleigh." In *Literary and Historical Activities in North Carolina 1900–1905*, 249–50. Raleigh: North Carolina Historical Commission, 1907. 623 pp. Reports a movement to erect a statue of Ralegh with money collected from the state's school children.

1754. Clapp, Henry. *With Walter Raleigh to British Guiana*. London: Frederick Muller, 1965. 142 pp. For children.

1755. Clemens, Samuel Langhorne [Mark Twain]. *[Date 1601] Conversation, as it was by the Social Fireside, in the Time of the Tudors*. West Point, N.Y.: Academie Press, 1882. 11 pp. Often reprinted. An imaginary and bawdy conversation between Queen Elizabeth, Ben Jonson, Beaumont, Ralegh, the Duchess of Bilgewater, and others.

1756. Cock, Morris F. "Sir Walter Ralegh." In *Devonian Year Book*, 1929, 48. A poem.

1757. Cooke, E. V. "Raleigh, a Poem." *Chautauquan* 31 (1900): 364.

1758. Cotten, Sallie Southall. *The White Doe: The Fate of Virginia Dare*. Philadelphia: Lippincott, 1901. 89 pp. Reprint. Roanoke Island Historical Association, 1937.

1759. Crake, E. E. *In Mortal Peril: A Tale of the Great Armada*. London: Religious Tract Society, 1908. 213 pp. A novel for children, featuring Elizabeth, Ralegh, Essex, and Drake.

1760. Cresswell, Beatrix F. "The Vision of Sir Walter Raleigh." In *Devonian Year Book*, 1919, 55. A poem.

1761. Croft, R. C. *Raleigh's Queer Dream: Or the Pipe, the Potato, the Pixie*. London: n.p., [c. 1873]. 24 pp. A musical play in rhyme, performed at the Royal Polytechnic Institution under the direction of Dr. Croft.

1762. Cruso, Henry Alfred Anthony. *Sir Walter Ralegh, A Drama in Five Acts*. London: Fisher Unwin, 1907. 178 pp.

1763. Cust, Lionel. "The Portraits of Sir Walter Raleigh." *Publications of the Walpole Society* 8 (1919): 1–15.

1764. D., F. S. *Queen Elizabeth: A Dramatic Poem in Five Acts*. London: Mozley, 1862. 207 pp. Dramatizes Ralegh's feuds with Burleigh and Essex.

1765. Davidson, Gladys. *Story of Sir Walter Raleigh Retold*. London: Blackie, 1931. 48 pp. For children.

1766. De Leeuw, Adele Louise. *A World Explorer: Sir Walter Raleigh*. Champaign, Ill.: Garrard, 1964. 96 pp. London: Muller, 1967. Biography for children, illustrated by Adolph LeMoult.

1767. Devereux, William, and Stephen Lovell. *Raleigh: A Romance of Elizabeth's Court*. Philadelphia: Lippincott, 1909. 320 pp. London: Greening, 1910. A novel.

1768. Dixon, William John. *Sir Walter Ralegh. A Tragedy in Five Acts*. London: Chiswick Press, 1897. 90 pp.

1769. Douglass, John Jordan. "Raleigh and Roanoke." *Proceedings of the State Literary and Historical Association of North Carolina* 28 (1922): 112–18. A poem.

1770. Drake, Lawrence. "Life of Sir Walter Raleigh." In *The Heroes of England: Stories of the Lives of the Most Celebrated British Soldiers and Sailors*, 65–95. London: Joseph Cundall, 1843. 312 pp. Biography for children.

1771. Duncan, Robert. "A Seventeenth-Century Suite in Homage to the Metaphysical Genius in English Poetry (1590–1690): Being Imitations, Derivations & Variations upon Certain Conceits and Findings made among Strong Lines." In *Groundwork: Before the War*, 70–93. New York: New Directions, 1984. 175 pp. Includes a poem titled "from Sir Walter Ralegh's What is Our Life?"

1772. Edgar, John G. "Sir Walter Raleigh." In *Sea Kings and Naval Heroes: A Book for Boys*, 119–45. London: Bell and Daldy, 1861. 336 pp.

1773. ———. "Sir Walter Raleigh." In *Heroes of England*, 97–120. London: Dent; New York: Dutton, 1910. 299 pp. Biography for young people.

1774. Elias, Edith L. "Sir Walter Raleigh." In *In Tudor Times*, 194–202. London: Harrap, 1910. 256 pp. New York: Crowell, 1911.

1775. Emden, Cecil Stuart. "A New Portrait of Sir Walter Raleigh." *Oriel Record* 7 (1953): 10–11. Maintains that the portrait identified as that of Henry Howard, Earl of Northampton, is seen to be of Ralegh when it is compared with the known Ralegh portrait in Vienna.

1776. Fecher, Constance. *Queen's Delight*. London: Hale, 1966. 287 pp. A novel.

1777. ———. *The Last Elizabethan: A Portrait of Sir Walter Ralegh*. New York: Farrar, Straus, and Giroux, [1972]. 241 pp. For children.

1778. Fell, William J., and Charles B. Lower. *History into Drama; A*

Source Book on Symphonic Dramas, Including the Complete Text of Paul Green's "The Lost Colony." New York: Odyssey Press, c. 1963. 243 pp.

1779. [Ferguson, Robert]. "The Vision of Raleigh" and "Affection with Simplicity." In *The Social Pipe; or Gentlemen's Recreation: A Poem*, 25–29. London: Thomas Gosden, 1826. 31 pp.

1780. Field, Walter T. *Finding the New World*, 208–309. Boston: Ginn, 1935. 428 pp.

1781. Finger, Charles J. *Heroes from Hakluyt*. New York: Henry Holt, c. 1928. 331 pp. For young people.

1782. Fiske, Maude. *This Heritage, a Play Concerning Eleanor Dare and Those English Colonists Who Went with Her From Roanoke*. Gainesville, Ga.: Brenau College, 1940. 58 pp.

1783. Fletcher, Inglis Clark. *Raleigh's Eden*. Indianapolis: Bobbs-Merrill, 1940. 662 pp. Reprints. New York: Bantam, 1970; Hillsdale, N.J.: Queens House, 1976. A novel.

1784. ———. *Roanoke Hundred*. Indianapolis: Bobbs-Merrill, 1948. 492 pp. Reprints. New York: Bantam, 1972; Larchmont, N.Y.: Queens House, 1978. A novel.

1785. Foote, Dorothy Norris. *The Constant Star*. New York: Scribner, 1959. 340 pp. A novel about Frances Walsingham, wife of Sir Philip Sidney, in which Ralegh appears.

1786. Fryer, Eugenie M. "Raleigh." In *A Book of Boyhoods*, 42–50. New York: Dutton, 1920. 302 pp.

1787. Garrett, George P. *Death of the Fox*. Garden City, N.Y.: Doubleday, 1971. 739 pp. A novel involving Ralegh's conflicts with King James.

1788. ———. *The Succession: A Novel of Elizabeth and James*. Garden City, N.Y.: Doubleday, 1983. 538 pp.

1789. Gilliat, Edward. *Heroes of the Elizabethan Age*, 255–300. London: Seeley; Philadelphia: Lippincott, 1911. 336 pp. An account for teenagers, of Ralegh as colonizer, prisoner, writer, and victim.

1790. Gilman, Arthur. "Tales of the Pathfinders, 3: How a colony was lost." In *Wide Awake*, 1883, 45–49. Reprinted in *Tales of the Pathfinders*. Boston: Lothrop, 1884.

1791. "Go, Eccho of the minde; A careless troth protest; make answere yt rude Rawly No stomack can Digest." In *Poems by Sir Henry Wotton, Sir Walter Raleigh, and Others*, edited by

John Hannah, 93–94. London: Pickering, 1845. 76, 136 pp. Reprinted in *The Courtly Poets, from Raleigh to Montrose* (1870). Apparently an answer to "The Lie" by Ralegh.

1792. Gordy, W. F. *American Leaders and Heroes*, 31–41. New York: Scribner, 1901. 329 pp.

1793. _____. *Stories of American Explorers*, 124–41. New York: Scribner, 1906. 206 pp.

1794. Goring, George Ingram. "Raleigh Had a Daughter." In *Chronicle Christmas Annual*, 1952, 9. A short story.

1795. Graham, Winston. *The Grove of Eagles*. Garden City, N.Y.: Doubleday, 1964. 498 pp. A novel about the adventures of a boy serving under Ralegh.

1796. Green, Paul. *The Lost Colony: An Outdoor Play in Two Acts.* Chapel Hill: University of North Carolina Press, 1937. 138 pp. Reprints. 1938, 1939.

1797. _____, composer. *The Lost Colony Song-book.* New York: Carl Fischer, 1938. 39 pp.

1798. _____. *The Lost Colony, A Symphonic Drama in Two Acts.* Chapel Hill: University of North Carolina Press, 1946. 202 pp. Second edition, called "Memorial Edition."

1799. _____. "Lost Colony; Story Behind It." *Theatre Arts* 36 (1952): 72–73.

1800. _____. *The Lost Colony, A Symphonic Drama of American History.* Chapel Hill: University of North Carolina Press, 1954. 70 pp. Third edition, called "Roanoke Island Edition."

1801. _____. *The Lost Colony, A Symphonic Drama of Man's Faith and Work.* Durham, N.C.: privately printed, 1980. 142 pp. Fourth edition, called "Four Hundredth Anniversary Edition."

1802. Greenwood, L. B. *Sherlock Holmes and the Case of the Raleigh Legacy.* New York: Atheneum, 1986. 184 pp. A novel.

1803. Grindrod, Charles F. "King James I" In *Plays from English History*, 353–454. London: Kegan, Paul, Trench, 1883. 454 pp.

1804. H., J. "On my Venture in Sir Walter Rawleigh's Voiage" and "Censures on the Voyage to Guyana." In *The Hovse of Correction: or, Certayne Satyricall Epigrams*, 31–32, 34. London: Printed by Bernard Alsop for Richard Redmer, 1619. 41 pp. Satirizes Ralegh's last voyage to Guiana.

1805. H., J. J. "The Portraits of Sir Walter Raleigh (Query by A.; Answer by J. J. H.)." *Wiltshire Notes and Queries* 6 (1908): 88,

97–98.

1806. Harden, John W. "The Lost Colony." In *The Devil's Tramping Ground and Other North Carolina Mystery Stories*, 79–87. Chapel Hill: University of North Carolina Press, 1949. 178 pp.

1807. Hatton, Joseph. *The White King of Manoa. An Anglo-Spanish Romance; being the Life, Loves, and Adventures of David Yarcombe, Protégé and Fellow Voyager of Sir Walter Raleigh, Knight.* London: Hutchinson, 1899. 338 pp. A novel involving Ralegh's Guiana ventures, in which Yarcombe discovers the Golden City of Manoa and becomes its White King.

1808. Hayward, A. M. "Gallant Sir Walter Raleigh: A Poem." *St. Nicholas* 46 (1919): 776.

1809. Haywood, Marshall DeLancey. "Roanoke Island or the Landing of Captain Ralph Lane, with Sir Walter Raleigh's Colonists, on the Coast of Carolina in 1585." *North Carolina Booklet* 13 (1913): 45–46. A poem.

1810. Henderson, Walter Brooks Drayton. *The new Argonautica, an heroic poem in eight cantos, of the voyage among the stars of the immortal spirits of Sir Walter Raleigh, Sir Francis Drake, Ponce de Leon and Nunez da Vaca.* New York: Macmillan, 1927; London: Cape, 1928. 352 pp.

1811. Henty, G. A. *By England's Aid; or The Freeing of the Netherlands.* London: Blackie; New York: Scribner, 1890. 384 pp. A novel for young readers, which includes an account of Ralegh's attack on Cadiz in 1596.

1812. Hinkson, Katherine Tynan. *The Great Captain, an Historical Tale of Sir Walter Raleigh.* New York: Benziger, 1902. 122 pp.

1813. Holland, Rupert Sargent. "Walter Raleigh, the Boy of Devon." In *Historic Boyhoods*, 35–47. Philadelphia: G. W. Jacobs, 1909. 272 pp.

Housman, A. E. *See* White.

1814. Hubbard, Elbert. *The Silver Arrow.* East Aurora, N.Y.: Roycrafters, 1923. 38 pp. A tale in which Virginia Dare, represented both as an illegitimate daughter of Ralegh and as a woman banished to Virginia, is raised by Indians who call her White Doe.

1815. Johnson, Lionel. "Sir Walter Raleigh in the Tower." In *The Queen's Gold Medal English Verse.* Chester: Phillipson & Golder, 1885. 12 pp. A poem in blank verse.

1816. Johnston, Mary. *Croatan*. Boston: Little, Brown, 1923. 298 pp. A novel about the Roanoke colonies.

1817. Jones, Henry. *The Earl of Essex. A Tragedy. As It Is Acted at the Theatre Royal in Covent-Garden*. London: Printed for R. Dodsley, 1753. 62 pp. Reprinted in *The British Theater*, v. 22 (1817?); in *London Stage* (1824–27); and in *British Drama* (1826).

1818. Kelly, Margaret Duncan. *The Story of Sir Walter Raleigh*. London: Jack; New York: Dutton, [1906]. 120 pp. London: Jack, 1924. Translated into Portuguese as *História de Sir Walter Raleigh*. Lisbon: Edições Europe, n.d. A biography for children.

1819. Kelly, Robert. *Ralegh*. Los Angeles: Black Sparrow Press, 1972. 7 pp. A poem.

1820. Kent, William Charles Mark. "Walter Raleigh—the Adventurer." In *Footprints on the Road*, 99–122. London: Chapman and Hill, 1864. 420 pp.

1821. Kimball, Gwen. *The Puzzle of Roanoke, The Lost Colony*. New York: Duell, Sloan and Pearce, 1964. 136 pp. Fiction for children.

1822. King, Henry. "An Elegy Upon Sir Walter Ralegh." In *Poems of Henry King*, edited by Margaret Crum, 66. Oxford: Clarendon Press, 1965. 264 pp.

1823. Kingsley, Charles. *Westward Ho! or the Voyages and Adventures of Sir Amyas Leigh, Knight, of Burrough, in the Country of Devon, in the Reign of Her Most Glorious Majesty Queen Elizabeth*. Cambridge: Macmillan; Boston: Ticknor and Fields, 1855. 588 pp. Includes Ralegh among the minor characters.

1824. Kjelgaard, James A. "Croatan." In *Buckskin Brigade*, 33–62. New York: Holiday House, 1947. 310 pp. A collection of frontier adventure stories for young readers.

1825. Koch, Frederick Henry. *Raleigh, the Shepherd of the Ocean; a Pageant-drama, Designed to Commemorate the Tercentenary of the Execution of Sir Walter Raleigh*, with a foreward by Edwin Greenlaw. Raleigh, N.C.: Edwards and Broughton, 1920. 95 pp.

1826. Lacy, Dan Mabry. *The Lost Colony*. London and New York: Franklin Watts, 1972. 87 pp. An account for young readers.

1827. Lefranc, Pierre. "Ralegh and Cynthia." *Times Literary Supplement*, 17 March 1966, 223. Discusses Ralegh's portrait in the National Portrait Gallery.

1828. Leighton, Robert. *The Golden Galleon: being a narrative of the adventures of Master Gilbert Oglander, and of how, in the year 1591, he fought under the gallant Sir Richard Grenville in the great seafight off Flores, on board Her Majesty's ship The Revenge.* London: Blackie; New York: Scribner; New York: Burt, 1897. 352 pp. An adventure story for young readers, in which Ralegh appears.

1829. Lessius, Leonardus. *Sir Walter Rawleigh's Ghost: or, His apparition to an intimate friend, willing him to translate into English, this learned book of L. Lessius intituled, (De providentia numinis, & animi immortalitate.) Written against the atheists and politicians of these days . . . .* London: Printed by T. Newcomb for J. Holden, 1651. 384 pp.

1830. Levitin, Sonia. *Roanoke: A Novel of the Lost Colony.* New York: Atheneum, 1975. 213 pp. Features a boy's adventures with Indians.

1831. Lewis, Nell Battle. "Lay of the Lost Colony." *Uplift* 29 (1941): 16–17.

1831ª. _____. *The Life of Sir Walter Raleigh.* London: Knevett, Arliss and Baker, 1811. 72 pp. Biography for children.

1832. Little, Alla Pearl. *Roanoke Suite.* Hickory, N.C.: n.p., 1950. 7 pp. A musical composition.

1833. Lobdell, Helen. *The King's Snare.* Boston: Houghton, Mifflin, 1955. 218 pp. An adventure story for teenagers, in which Ralegh's young secretary goes along on the Orinoco expedition.

1834. Lofts, Norah R. *Here Was a Man: A Romantic History of Sir Walter Raleigh, His Voyages, His Discoveries, and His Queen.* New York: Knopf, 1936. 304 pp. Reprint. London and Sydney: Invincible Press, 1947.

1835. Lok, Henry. "To the valorous Knight, Sir Walter Rawleigh." In *Ecclesiastes, otherwise called The Preacher.* London: Richard Field, 1597. Approx. 300 pp. Reprinted, by A. B. Grosart, in *Miscellanies of the Fuller Worthies Library* (1871). A sonnet praising Ralegh as a knight "sworne to Mars and Pallas."

1836. "The Lost Colony." *True Comics* 16 (1942): 9–15.

1837. Lowell, Robert. "Lady Ralegh's Lament." In *For the Union Dead,* 28. New York: Noonday Press, 1969. 72 pp. A poem.

1838. M., Mrs. M. "The White Doe Chase, A Legend of Olden

Times." *Our Living and Our Dead* 3 (1875): 753–71. Tells how Virginia Dare was changed to a White Doe by Great Medicine and doomed to be hunted until the red man is driven out of the land.

1839. M., R. B. "Raleigh in Verse." *Devon and Cornwall Notes and Queries* 20 (1939): 279–80. Prints an unpublished poem about Ralegh, signed J. D. in a seventeenth-century commonplace book; the style is not that of John Donne.

1840. McChesney, Dora G. *The Wounds of a Friend*. London: Smith & Elder, 1908. 306 pp. A romantic novel describing Ralegh's part in colonizing the New World.

1841. MacNeice, Louis. "Suite for Recorders." In *Ten Burnt Offerings*, 13–18. London: Faber and Faber, 1952. 96 pp. Reprinted in *The Collected Poems of Louis MacNeice*, edited by E. R. Dodds. London: Faber and Faber, 1966; New York: Oxford University Press, 1967. Mentions Ralegh in this poem about the political and intellectual atmosphere in England around 1600.

1842. Madden, Eva Anne. "Great America Maker." *St. Nicholas* 46 (1919): 771–76.

1843. Manwaring, George E. "Contemporary Verses on the Death of Ralegh." *Times Literary Supplement*, 22 December 1921, 860. Reprints a manuscript poem of two stanzas on Ralegh's death, found on the flyleaf of a copy of *A Declaration of the Demeanor and Carriage of . . . Raleigh* (1618) at Eaton Hall. Aubrey and Wood quote the second stanza.

1844. Marks, Edward N. "Sir Walter Raleigh, the Ambitious Courtier." In *Men of Deeds and Daring*, 1–32. [i.e., 219–50] London: Dean, 1861. [274] pp. A book for boys.

1845. Marshall, Beatrice. *The Queen's Knight Errant: A Story of the Days of Sir Walter Raleigh*. New York: Dutton; London: Seeley, 1905. 322 pp.

1846. _____. *Sir Walter Raleigh*. New York: Stokes; London: Harrap, 1914. 191 pp. For young readers.

1847. Marshall, Edison. *The Lost Colony*. Garden City, N.Y.: Doubleday, 1964. 438 pp. Reprint. New York: Popular Library, 1965.

1848. Martin, A. Patchett. "The Execution of Sir Walter Raleigh (A Historical Ballad)." In *Fernshawe: Sketches in Prose and Verse*, 119–22. London: Griffith, Farran, Okeden and Welsh, [1885].

216 pp. Imagines that Oliver Cromwell witnessed Ralegh's execution and thus learned to treat with scorn the divine right of kings.

1849. Marvell, Andrew. "Britannia and Rawleigh." In *The Poems and Letters of Andrew Marvell*, 3d ed., edited by H. M. Margoliouth et al. 2 vols. 1:194–99. Oxford: Clarendon Press, 1971. Political satire, first published in *State Poems* (1689), in which the ghost of Ralegh responds briefly to Britannia's account of the woes of contemporary England.

1850. Mason, A. E. W. *Fire Over England*. London: Hodder & Stoughton, 1936. 316 pp. A novel about the Elizabethans' conflicts with Spain.

1851. Mason, Francis van Wyck. *Golden Admiral*. Garden City, N.Y.: Doubleday, 1953. 345 pp. A novel about Drake, the Spanish Armada, and Ralegh's role in that crisis.

1852. Mathis, Alexander. *The Lost Citadel*. New York: Pageant, 1954. 273 pp. A novel about Ralegh's Roanoke enterprise.

1853. Meeker, Ann. *The Queen's Rings: The True Romance of Elizabeth, Queen of England*. Chicago: Ryerson, 1936. 278 pp. A novel involving Bacon, Essex, and Ralegh.

1854. Merrill, Anthony F. "Miracle at Manteo." *Carolina Play-Book* 12 (1939): 47–48. Describes the impact on Manteo of staging Paul Green's drama *The Lost Colony*.

1855. Milner, James D. "Portraits of Walter Raleigh and Francis Drake." *Burlington Magazine* 33 (1918): 157–58.

1856. Moore, William H. *Virginia Dare: A Story of Colonial Days*. Raleigh, N.C.: Edwards & Broughton, 1904. 67 pp. A narrative poem.

1857. Morris, Charles. *Heroes of Discovery in America*, 2d ed., 166–75. Philadelphia: Lippincott, 1919. 365 pp. 1st ed. 1906.

1858. Morris, Mowbray Walker. "El Dorado." In *Tales of the Spanish Main*, 170–220. London: Macmillan, 1901. 357 pp.

1859. Nelmes, Thomas E. *Kilcolman: or Raleigh's Visit to Spenser, and other compositions in verse*. New York: Printed for S. Nelmes, Hamilton, Bermuda, 1875. 216 pp. Includes "Kilcolman," a poem of fourteen stanzas on pages 7–69, followed by "Thanks," pages 70–72, a poem addressed to Ralegh for introducing tobacco.

1860. Nida, W. L., and Stella H. Nida. *Pilots and Pathfinders*, 120–26. New York: Macmillan, 1928. 411 pp.

1861. Norman, Charles. *The Shepherd of the Ocean: Sir Walter Raleigh*. New York: David McKay, 1952. 179 pp. Biography for young people.

1862. Noyes, Alfred. "Raleigh." In *Tales of the Mermaid Tavern*, 205–34. New York: Stokes, 1913. 234 pp. A poem in which Ben Jonson discusses Ralegh's final years.

1863. Nye, Robert. *The Voyage of the Destiny*. New York: Putnam, 1982. 387 pp. A novel.

1864. O'Conor, Joseph. *Lion Trap*. London: Hutchinson, 1969. 272 pp. A novel.

1865. "Of all the birdes that flyeth with wynge The Robin hath no pere." In *Ancient Biographical Poems, on the Duke of Norfolk, Viscount Hereford, the Earls of Essex, and Queen Elizabeth*, edited by J. P. Collier. London: Camden Society, 1855. 26 pp. In his *Life of Spenser* (1862), Collier says that the robin signifies Essex and the nightingale Ralegh, to whom the poem, in twelve-line stanzas, is hostile.

1866. *Of Legacy-Hunting. The Fifth Satire of the Second Book of Horace imitated. A Dialogue between Sir Walter Raleigh and Merlin the Prophet*. London: Printed for J. Brindley, 1737. 22 pp.

1867. Overby, Mack. *The Story of Sir Walter Raleigh*. Raleigh, N.C.: Bynum, 1970. 60 pp. A play.

1868. Palgrave, Francis T. "El Dorado." In *The Visions of England*, 142–53. London: Macmillan, 1881. 353 pp. A poem in quatrains about Ralegh's fatal obsession.

1869. Payson, William Farquhar. *John Vytal: A Tale of the Lost Colony*. New York: Harper, 1901. 318 pp.

1870. Peach, L. du Garde. *Sir Walter Raleigh*. Loughborough: Wills & Hepworth, 1957. 50 pp. For children up to age eleven.

1871. Pelham, Randolph. *Raleigh's Rival*. London: Hale, 1972. 221 pp. A novel in which Randulph Carew sails with the fleet against Spain.

1872. Piatt, Sallie M. B. "A Call on Sir Walter Raleigh at Youghall, Ireland." *Atlantic Monthly* 51 (1883): 758–59. A poem in quatrains, depicting Ralegh and Spenser in Ireland.

1873. Pollard, Eliza F. *The Old Moat Farm: A Story of Queen Elizabeth's Days*. London: Blackie, 1905. 238 pp. Adventure story about two children, in which Ralegh appears.

1874. "The Portraits of Sir Walter and Lady Raleigh." *Apollo* 28 (1938): 212–13. Describes two portraits presented to Williamsburg, Virginia.

1875. Power, Rhoda D. *Great People of the Past*, 194–202. Cambridge: Cambridge University Press, 1932. 326 pp.

1876. Prideaux, W. F. "Ballads and Poems Connected with Sir Walter Ralegh." *Western Antiquary* 6 (1887): 248–49. Describes the Heber copy of "Sir Walter Raleigh Sailing in the Low-Lands," and notes three satires in J. O. Halliwell's *Poetical Miscellanies*.

1877. Prideaux, W. F., and Thomas Nadauld Brushfield. "Ballad of 'Sir Walter Raleigh Sailing in the Lowlands.'" *Western Antiquary* 7 (1887): 20–22. Reprints a copy probably from the 1680s of the ballad on which the song "The Golden Vanity" was based.

1878. "Prosopoeia: Or, Sir Walter Raleigh's Ghost." In *Phoenix Britannicus: Being a collection of scarce and curious tracts . . . which are no where to be found but in the Closets of the Curious*, edited by J. Morgan, no. 4, 310–24. London: Printed for the compiler and T. Edlin, 1732. 584 pp. Reproduced from a manuscript of 1622.

1879. *Raleigh Wrote Shakespeare or, The Grate Crab-Tree-Cram*. Glasgow: David Robertson, 1888. 20 pp. A satire on Ignatius Donnelly, who claimed that Bacon wrote Shakespeare's works.

1880. *Rawleigh his Ghost: Or, A Feigned Apparition of Syr Walter Rawleigh, to a friend of his, for the translating into English the Booke of Leonard Lessius (that most learned man), entituled, De prouidentia Numinis, & Animi immortalitate: written against Atheists and Politicians of these dayes*, translated by A. B., [Douay?]: n.p., 1631. 447 pp.

1881. "Rawleighs Caueat to Secure Courtiers." In *Ballads from Manuscripts*. 2 vols. 2:262–68. London: Ballad Society, 1868. Includes "The dispairinge complainte of wretched Rawleigh for his treacheries wrought against the worthy Essex. Whereunto is added his caueat to secure Courtiers, 'To whome shall cursed I my case complaine,'" a poem in thirty-nine seven-line stanzas, and "I speake to such if any such there bee."

1882. Raymont, F. W. I. *Sir Walter Raleigh*. London: Chambers, 1938. 48 pp. For children.

1883. Rice, W. "First American Sailors: Poem." In *Verse for Patriots, to Encourage Good Citizenship*, compiled by Jean Broadhurst and Clara Lawton Rhodes, 85–88. Philadelphia: Lippincott, 1919. 367 pp.

1884. Richings, Emily. *Sir Walter's Wife: A Story of Two Reigns.* London: Henry J. Drane, 1900. 201 pp. Gives an account of Ralegh's life and of his marriage.

1885. Rodd, Rennell. *Newdigate Prize Poem: Raleigh.* Oxford: T. Shrimpton, 1880. 18 pp. Recited in the Sheldonian Theatre, 9 June 1880, by Rennell Rodd of Balliol College.

1886. Rodd, Rennell, and Julian Corbett. "The Story of Sir Walter Raleigh (1552–1618.)" In *Drake and Raleigh.* London: Macmillan, [1913]. 96 pp. For children.

1887. Rollins, Hyder E. "An Analytical Index to the Ballad-entries in the Registers of the Company of Stationers of London." *Studies in Philology* 21 (1924): 1–324. Mentions Ralegh in the following items: 650, Dulcina, beginning "The golden god Hyperion"; 1595, "If all the world and love were young"; 2419, "As at noon Dulcina rested"; 2680 and 2682, "The Traitours Arrayned at Winchester."

1888. Rolt-Wheeler, Francis. "The Tragedy of Roanoke." In *The Coming of the Peoples*, 25–40. New York: Doran, [1922]. 267 pp. An account for children.

1889. Rose, Mark. *Golding's Tale.* New York: Walker, 1972. 188 pp. A novel involving Ralegh.

1890. Ross, George. "A Scene in Hades, Between Shakespeare, Raleigh, and Jonson." In *Studies: Biographical and Literary*, 1–6. London: Simpkin, Marshall, 1867. 168 pp.

1891. Rossetti, Dante Gabriel. "Raleigh's Cell in the Tower." In *The Poetical Works of Dante Gabriel Rossetti*, edited by William M. Rossetti, 341. London: Ellis and Elvey, 1903. 380 pp. A sonnet contrasting the narrowness of Ralegh's cell with the range of his mind.

1892. Russell, Harry K. "Mark Bennett on Roanoke: Poem." *Poet Lore* 48 (Spring 1942): 3–46.

1893. Sabatini, Rafael. "Sir Judas: The Betrayal of Sir Walter Ralegh." In *The Historical Nights' Entertainment*, 156–80. Boston and New York: Houghton Mifflin, 1919. 404 pp. Relates Ralegh's betrayal by Sir Lewis Stukeley.

1894. Sadler, John. *Loyalty, Attended with Great News from Drake's and Raleigh's Ghosts.* London: Printed for the Author, 1705.

16 pp. Reprinted in *Harleian Miscellany* (1810). Heroic poem addressed to Queen Anne.

1895. Schoonover, Lawrence L. *To Love a Queen: Walter Raleigh and Elizabeth R.* Boston: Little, Brown, 1973. 383 pp. New York: Ballantine Books, 1974. A novel.

1896. [Scott, Thomas]. *A tongue-combat, lately happening between two English souldiers in the tilt-boat of Gravesend, the one going to serve the King of Spaine, the other to serve the States Generall of the United Provinces, wherein the cause, course, and continuance to those warres is debated, and declared.* London: n.p., 1623. 104 pp. Contains references to Drake and Ralegh.

1897. _____. *Sir Walter Rawleigh's Ghost, or England's Forewarner. Discouering a secret Consultation, newly holden in the Court of Spaine. Together with his tormenting of Count de Gondomar; and his strange affrightment, confession and publique recantation: laying open many treacheries intended for the subuersion of England.* Utrecht: Printed by John Schellem, 1626. 41 pp. Reprint. Norwood, N.J.: Walter J. Johnson, 1974. Scott, an English minister at Utrecht, was assassinated in 1626.

1898. Scott, Sir Walter. *Kenilworth: A Romance.* 3 vols. Edinburgh: Constable, Ballantyne, Hurst, Robinson, 1821. Misrepresents Ralegh as actually landing in Virginia.

1899. Selden, Samuel. " 'The Lost Colony' and the Greeks." *Carolina Play-Book* 12 (June 1939): 49–50. Maintains that although some critics see elements of Greek tragedy in Paul Green's play because it is given in a large roofless theater and uses a chorus, the play is essentially American.

1900. Sewell, George. *The Tragedy of Sir Walter Raleigh. As it is Acted at the Theatre-Royal in Lincolns-Inn-Fields.* London: Printed for John Pemberton and John Watts, 1719. 63 pp. Often performed and reprinted in the 18th century.

1901. Seymour, Arthur James. *Guiana Book.* British Guiana: Argosy, 1948. 44 pp. Poems by a Guiana poet, including "Raleigh Comes to Guiana" and "El Dorado."

1902. _____. "From Ralegh to Carew. The Books of Guiana." *Kyk-over-al* (British Guiana Writers' Association) 27 (1960): 74. Reprints a P.E.N. Presidential Address of April 1960.

1903. Shackelford, E. A. B. *Virginia Dare: A Romance of the*

Sixteenth Century. New York: Thomas Whittaker, 1892. 270 pp.

1904. Shakespeare, William. *Love's Labour's Lost.* A play in which Ralegh and his circle may be satirised as "The School of Night."

1905. Shostakovich, Dimitri. *Six Romances for Bass and Pianoforte to Words by Burns, Shakespeare, and Walter Raleigh*, Opus 62 (1942). Ontario: Leeds Music, 1951. First published by Music Fund of U.S.S.R, 1943. Orchestrated as Opus 140 (1971).

1906. "Sir Walter Raleigh: The Thoughts and Feelings which led him to propose his scheme concerning El Dorado." *Dublin University Magazine* 31 (1848): 404–5. One hundred lines of blank verse.

1907. *Sir Walter Raleigh Sailing in the Low-lands, shewing how that famous Ship called the Sweet Trinity was taken by a false Gally and how it was again restored by the craft of a little Sea-boy, who sunk the Gally, as the following Song will declare. To the tune of The Sailing in the Low-Lands.* London: Printed for J. Conyers, [1685?]. Reprinted in J. O. Halliwell-Phillipps, *Catalogue of Broadside Ballads* (1856) and in *Hazlitt's Early English Literature* (1867).

1908. Sitwell, Dame Edith. *The Queens and the Hive.* Boston: Little, Brown, [1962]. 542 pp. An account of Queen Elizabeth's life, with occasional references to Ralegh.

1909. Slaughter, Frank Gill [C. V. Terry]. *The Golden Ones: A Novel.* Garden City, N.Y.: Hanover House, 1957. 285 pp.

1910. Slous, Angiolo Robson. *True to the Core: A Story of the Armada.* London: Tinsley, 1866. 61 pp. A four-act play in prose which won the T. P. Cooke Drama Prize in 1866.

1911. South, Robert. *Sir Walter Ralegh: a Drama.* London: John Long, 1904. 122 pp.

1912. Southworth, Gertrude V. D. *Builders of Our Country.* 2 vols. 1:64–72. New York: Appleton, 1906.

1913. Spenser, Edmund. *The Faerie Queene.* London: William Ponsonbie, 1590. 606 pp. An epic poem, the allegory of which Spenser discusses in a letter to Ralegh at the end of Book 3. Ralegh and his wife are often considered to be represented as Timias and Amoret in Book 4.

1914. ———. *Muiopotmos, Or the Fate of the Butterflie.* London:

William Ponsonbie, 1590. 9 pp. A poem about the battle
between the butterfly and the spider, often interpreted as an
allegory of the feud between Ralegh and Essex.

1915. _____. *Prosopopoia, Or Mother Hubberds Tale*. London:
William Ponsonbie, 1591. 64 pp. A satire on court affairs
which may contain allusions to Ralegh.

1916. _____. *Colin Clouts Come Home Againe*. London: William
Ponsonbie, 1595. 79 pp. A pastoral poem, dedicated to Ralegh
in its introductory letter, and featuring him as "the shepheard
of the Ocean."

1917. Stevenson, Augusta. *Virginia Dare, Mystery Girl*. Indianapolis:
Bobbs-Merrill, 1957. 192 pp.

1918. Stimpson, Mary S. *The Child's Book of English Biography*,
13–21. Boston: Little, Brown, 1916. 226 pp.

1919. Stockard, Henry Jerome. "Sir Walter Raleigh." In *Literary and
Historical Activities in North Carolina, 1900–1905*, 239–40.
Raleigh, N.C.: North Carolina Historical Commission, 1907.
623 pp. A poem.

1920. Strang, Herbert [George Herbert Ely and C. J. L'Estrange]. *A
Gentleman-at-Arms: being passages in the life of Sir
Christopher Rudd, knight, as related by himself in the year
1641*. London: Henry Frowde and Hodder & Stoughton, 1914.
387 pp. An adventure story for young readers, with Ralegh
among the characters.

1921. Strong, Jay. *Of Courage and Valor*, 69–71. New York: Hart,
1955. 318 pp.

1922. Strong, Roy C. *Tudor & Jacobean Portraits*. 2 vols. London:
Her Majesty's Stationery Office, 1969. Discusses each of his
five known portraits (1:254–59) and reproduces them (2:503–
7).

1923. Sutcliff, Rosemary. *Lady in Waiting: A Novel*. New York:
Coward-McCann, 1957. 253 pp. Features Elizabeth
Throckmorton, who married Ralegh while serving as Queen
Elizabeth's lady-in-waiting.

1924. Syme, Ronald. *Walter Raleigh*. New York: William Morrow,
1962. 96 pp.

1925. Synge, M. B. "Sir Walter Raleigh Searches for El Dorado." In
A Book of Discovery, 285–89. London: Thomas Nelson,
[1912]. 554 pp.

1926. Tannenbaum, Samuel Aaron. *The Knight and the Crystal Sphere*. New York: The author, 1946. 70 pp. A dramatic fantasy about Ralegh and Queen Elizabeth.

1927. Taylor, George Coffin. "The Statue of Sir Walter Raleigh Presented to the University by Colonel Owen Kenan." *Alumni Review* [University of North Carolina] 19 (May 1931): 205–6. Describes the lifesize statue carved from a solid pine log and evidently of the school of Grinling Gibbons.

Terry, C. V. *See* Slaughter.

1928. Thompson, Edward John. *Last Voyage*. London: Macmillan, 1934. 125 pp. A play dealing with Ralegh's 1617 voyage to Guiana and death.

1929. Towle, George Makepeace. *Sir Walter Ralegh, his Exploits and Voyages*. Boston: Lee & Shepard, 1881. 273 pp. Boston: Lee & Shepard; New York: C. T. Dillingham, 1882. Biography for children.

1930. Tracy, Don. *Roanoke Renegade*. New York: Dial, 1954. 367 pp. A novel about Fernando, Roanoke pilot, and the suppression of the Indians.

1931. Trease, Geoffrey. *Fortune, My Foe; The Story of Sir Walter Raleigh*. London: Methuen, 1949. 179 pp.

1932. ———. *Sir Walter Raleigh, Captain and Adventurer*. New York: Vanguard, 1950. 248 pp. For teenagers.

1933. ———. "Sir Walter Raleigh: The Last Elizabethan." In *Children's Book of Famous Lives*, edited by Eric Duthie, 336–46. London: Odhams, 1960. 415 pp.

1934. *The True History of a Now Historical Cloak*. Budleigh Salterton: n.p., 1896. 8 pp. A burlesque account about Ralegh's laying down his cloak for Queen Elizabeth and introducing the potato and tobacco into England.

1935. Tupper, Martin F. *Raleigh: His Life and His Death: A Historical Play in Five Acts*. London: Mitchell, Lacy, 1866. 81 pp.

1936. Turner, Judy. *Raleigh's Fair Bess*. New York: St. Martin's, 1974. 192 pp. A novel about Ralegh's wife, Elizabeth Throckmorton.

1937. Tuthill, Cornelia L. "Virginia Dare; or, the Colony of Roanoke." *Southern Literary Messenger* 6 (September 1840): 585–95. A short story about Virginia Dare's life among the Indians, who called her the "White Angel of Mercy."

1938. Unstead, Robert John. *People in History.* 4 vols. 3:281–89. London: Black, 1955.

1938ᵃ. W., W. H. K. "Walter Raleigh: Poem." *Western Antiquary* 5 (1886): 182.

1939. Wall, Mary Virginia. *The Daughter of Virginia Dare.* New York: Neale Publishing, 1908. 194 pp.

1940. Walter, Lavinia Edna. *Walter Raleigh.* London: Newner Educational Publishing, 1953. 47 pp.

1941. "Water thy plaints with grace divine." In *Poetical Miscellanies from a Manuscript Collection of the Time of James I*, edited by James Orchard Halliwell, 14–15. London: Percy Society, 1845. 47 pp. Reprinted in *Works of Ralegh* (1829). A lampoon in five quatrains, condemning Ralegh for his ambitiousness..

1942. "Watt, I wot thy overweeninge witt, Lead by ambitious humours, wrought thy fall." In *Poetical Miscellanies from a Manuscript Collection of the Time of James I*, edited by James Orchard Halliwell, 15–18. London: Percy Society, 1845. 47 pp. A lampoon in sixteen sestets, favoring Essex and King James and attacking Ralegh.

1943. Welch, Helena. *When They Were Children*, 84–86. Nashville, Tenn.: Southern Publishing Association, 1965. 136 pp.

1944. Wendell, Barrett. "Ralegh in Guiana." *Scribner's Magazine* 21 (1897): 776–84. Reprinted in *Ralegh in Guiana, Rosamond and a Christmas Masque.* New York: Scribner, 1902. Reprint. Great Neck, N.Y.: Core Collection, 1979. A one-act play, mainly in blank verse, about Ralegh's final expedition and his son Walter's death.

1945. Whedbee, Charles H. "The Ghost Deer of Roanoke." In *Legends of the Outer Banks*, 7–25. Winston-Salem, N.C.: Blair, 1966. 165 pp.

1946. White, W. "Un Poème Inédit de A. E. Housman: Sir Walter Raleigh." *Etudes Anglaises* 6 (1953): 346–49. Reproduces a poem praising Ralegh and denouncing James I which Housman wrote at age fourteen.

1947. Whitman, Grace I. *The Shepherd of the Ocean and Other Tales of Valour.* London: Gardner, Darton, 1914. 444 pp. New York: Stokes, 1915.

1948. Williams, Robert Folkeston. *Shakespeare and his Friends.* New York: Burgess, Stringer, 1848. 315 pp. Fictionalized account of some of Ralegh's adventures.

1949. Williams, Thomas A., and Joe A. Paget, Sr. *A Tarheel Masterpiece: The Sir Walter Raleigh Wood Sculpture.* Greenville, N.C.: Era Press, 1975. 22 pp. Tells how sculptor Robert K. Horniman carved a statue of Ralegh from a five-hundred-year-old cypress into the world's largest free-standing wood carving, 24 feet high and weighing 15,000 pounds.

1950. Williams, William Carlos. "Sir Walter Raleigh." In *In the American Grain*, 59–62. Norfolk, Conn.: New Directions, 1925. 235 pp. A rhapsodical prose evocation of Ralegh's character and his influence upon America.

1951. Willis, Carrie Hunter, and Lucy S. Saunders. "Walter Raleigh, A Favorite Knight." In *Those Who Dared: Stories of Early Days in Our Country*, 24–35. Chapel Hill: University of North Carolina Press, c. 1935. 314 pp. A children's book.

1952. *Willobie his Avisa, 1594: with an essay on Willobie his Avisa*, edited by G. B. Harrison. London: John Lane; New York: Dutton, 1926. 271 pp. Facsimile reprint. Edinburgh: Edinburgh University Press, 1966. Reprints the anonymous work, and argues that it was written by Ralegh's friend Matthew Roydon, against Essex and Southampton for sponsoring Shakespeare's *Rape of Lucrece* in which, according to Harrison, Tarquin the ravisher represents Ralegh the seducer.

1953. "Wilye Watt, wilie Wat." In *Poetical Miscellanies from a Manuscript Collection of tne Time of James I*, edited by James Orchard Halliwell, 13–14. London: Percy Society, 1845. 47 pp. A lampoon in six quatrains, condemning Ralegh and favoring Essex, and ending "Damnable fiend of hell, Mischevous Matchivell."

1954. Wood, Eric. "Gilbert's and Raleigh's American Settlements," and "Raleigh in Search of El Dorado." In *Famous Voyages of the Great Discoverers*, 210–19, 257–63. London: Harrap, 1910. 270 pp. For young readers.

1955. Woodburn, J. A., and T. F. Moran. *Finders and Founders of the New World*, 84–88. New York: Longmans, Green, 1925. 265 pp.

Chapter 7.

1956. Brushfield, T. N. "The Bibliography of the *History of the World*, and of the *Remains* of Sir Walter Ralegh." *Library Chronicle* 3 (1886): 8–15. Reprints. London: Dryden Press, 1886; Folcroft, Pa.: Folcroft Library Editions, 1972.

1957. _____. *The Bibliography of Sir Walter Ralegh, with notes.* Plymouth: Luke; Exeter: Commin, 1886. 36 pp. Incorporates four lists by Brushfield published in *Western Antiquary*, January–April 1886.

1958. _____. "*The History of the World*, by Sir Walter Ralegh, a Bibliographical Study." *Report and Transactions of the Devonshire Association for the Advancement of Science, Literature and Art* 36 (1904): 181–218.

1959. _____. *A Bibliography of Sir Walter Ralegh Knt. Second edition with notes revised and enlarged with Portraits and Facsimiles.* Exeter: Commin, 1908. 181 pp. Reprint. New York: Burt Franklin, 1968.

1960. Capps, Nancy E. "A Bibliography of Sir Walter Raleigh: Works by or Relating to Raleigh, Published 1905–1965, In the Raleigh Collection of the Library of the University of North Carolina." Chapel Hill, 1965. 27 pp. Mimeographed typescript.

1961. Eames, Wilberforce. *A Bibliography of Sir Walter Raleigh.* New York: Roy, 1886. 35 pp. Reprints the section on Ralegh in Joseph Sabin's *Dictionary of Books Relating to America*, 16:250–82 (1886), and provides complete titles and collations for many of Ralegh's works, including early translations.

1962. Humber, John Leslie. "Raleigh & Roanoke Bibliography." Chapel Hill, 1961. 25 pp. Mimeographed typescript.

1963. Mills, Jerry Leath. "Recent Studies in Ralegh." *English Literary Renaissance* 15 (1985): 225–44. Reviews scholarship about Ralegh since the 1930s.

1964. _____. *Sir Walter Ralegh: A Reference Guide.* Boston: Hall, 1986. 116 pp. Lists writings about Ralegh from 1901 to 1984, arranged by year of publication, and provides detailed annotations.

1965. Sorenson, Frederick. "A Bibliography of Sir Walter Raleigh." Master's thesis, Stanford University, 1934. 253 pp.

1966. Tonkin, Humphrey. *Sir Walter Ralegh: 1900–1968,* Elizabethan Bibliographies Supplements, 17. London: Nether Press, 1971. 79 pp. Lists 869 items, a few with brief annotations.

1967. Wright, W. H. K. "Bibliography of Sir Walter Raleigh." *Western Antiquary* 2 (1883): 178–79.

INDEX OF AUTHORS AND

SELECTED TOPICS

Note: Many of these topics are
treated in the biographies about
Ralegh as well as in the items noted
below.